نهاية الأقدام في علم الكلام

NIHĀYAT AL-IQDĀM FĪ ʿILM AL-KALĀM

The Summa Philosophiae of Al-Shahrastānī

Muhammad Ibn Abd al-Karim Shahrastani

Translated into English By
Alfred Guillaume

Qadeem Press

Qadeem Press

Qadeem Press Edition
Breathing Life into Forgotten Pages
www.qadeempress.com

Originally Published by OUP in 1934
Reprinted by Qadeem Press in 2025

Find our titles on your favourite online bookstore using the keyword 'Qadeem Press'

PREFACE

IT has been my endeavour to translate what my author wrote in such a way as to make him intelligible to the reader, while preserving the idiom which he employed. The danger of this method is obvious: if the style and arrangement of the Arabic is followed too closely the meaning in English will inevitably be somewhat obscure. (Those who have used Haarbrücker's translation of the *Milal* will readily admit that the German is sometimes unintelligible by itself.) On the other hand, to paraphrase a work of this kind and to force its terminology into the mould of contemporary or medieval philosophy is a greater danger. It is common knowledge that a great many ideas of the Ash'arites passed over to Christian scholasticism, but they suffered a sea change. I have endeavoured to leave them as they are. I hope, I do not claim, that I have done my author justice. Where I have failed I enjoy distinguished company. Shahrastānī writes with one eye on Avicenna. Now Algazel, who attacked Avicenna as the man responsible for the system he hated, and Averroës who attacked him as the man responsible for the incoherence of philosophy, agree on one thing, namely the obscurity of Avicenna's diction, which sometimes defeated their attempts to grasp his meaning.

Chapter I, which forms the basis of the writer's view of God and the universe, I have translated very fully. Chapter VI, too, which deals with Nominalism, I have reproduced fairly fully; it is a good example of acute reasoning and dialectic. The rest of the book I have treated less generously, but without, I hope, omitting anything of real importance.

It had been my intention (as I announced when Part I was published in 1930) to write an excursus on the philosophical background of the Muslim creeds. But in 1932 Professor Wensinck published his masterly treatise on *The Muslim Creed, its Genesis and Historical Development*, which relieves me of that duty. It had also been my intention to contribute some notes on the relation of Shahrastānī's position to that of his predecessors and successors. This, with great regret, I have had to postpone indefinitely owing to the pressure of administrative duties which have frequently compelled me to lay aside my books for months at a time just when the solution of a problem seemed in sight. To study the metaphysical niceties in which Shahrastānī delighted, and to compare them with conflicting theories in works which are only accessible in a few libraries, in my present circumstances is an impossible task. Nevertheless, I hope that this, the first work of its kind on Arabic scholasticism to be published in this country, will not be without value to scholars who, to quote the words of Cureton's preface to his *Milal*, 'being able to estimate the difficulty of my undertaking and the labour which I have bestowed upon it, will be ready upon every occasion to accord me the fullest indulgence'.

I have pleasure in recording my deep gratitude to the Council of the British Academy who made a handsome grant towards the heavy cost of printing this work, and to the University of Oxford who by vote of Convocation authorized the James Mew Scholarship Fund to make a substantial contribution to the same. Without this aid the publication of the book would not have been possible.

I also thank the Librarians of the Bodleian and the Bibliothèque Nationale for allowing me to have photographs of the manuscripts in their possession. Especially I desire to thank the Librarian of the Preussische Staatsbibliothek in Berlin for his kindness in placing the manuscript at my disposal, thus saving me considerable expense and the uncertainty which constantly resides in a photograph of an altered reading or a decayed page.

My thanks are also due to the Imprimerie Catholique at Beyrouth for the careful reading of the rotographs. Some of the rather numerous mistakes could have been avoided had I been able to see a final proof before the sheets were printed off, but to send final proofs from Syria to England and back would have caused intolerable delay.

I cannot adequately thank my friend Professor Nicholson who, amid his innumerable activities, has found time to read the whole of the Arabic text of this book in proof, and has made numerous corrections which I have almost always adopted. I am also indebted to Mr. Reade, sub-Warden of Keble College, for allowing me to consult him on some of the problems of the subject-matter; and most especially to the Rev. Father Walker, S.J., who very kindly read my translation of the first two chapters and made many helpful criticisms and suggestions. Lastly I would thank Professor Margoliouth, at whose suggestion I undertook this work, for his advice and help in the difficulties which I encountered at the beginning of the enterprise, and for his ready elucidation of some of the obscurities in Chapter I.

ALFRED GUILLAUME

Culham, Oxon.
March, 1934.

CONTENTS

INTRODUCTION ix

ADDENDA TO TRANSLATION xvi

TRANSLATION

I. Proof that the World had a Beginning and a Demonstration of the Impossibility of Anything without a Beginning and of the Existence of Bodies Infinite . 1

II. That all things that exist had a beginning through God's Origination. Herein is a refutation of the Doctrines of the Mu'tazila, Dualists, and Natural Philosophers, and a proof of *kasb*, and the difference between *kasb* and *ījād* and *khalq* 25

III. The Divine Unity 39

IV. The Refutation of Anthropomorphism 43

V. The Refutation of those who deny the Divine Attributes 50

VI. States (or Conditions of Things) 52

VII. Is the Non-existent a Thing? Of Matter and a Refutation of the Theory that Matter exists without Form 60

VIII. Proof that the Propositions connected with the Divine Attributes can be known . 66

IX. Proof that the Eternal Attributes can be known 69

X. Concerning the Eternal Knowledge in Particular; that it is Eternally One, embracing all that is Knowable, both Universals and Particulars 78

XI. Of the Divine Will 84

XII. That the Creator speaks with an Eternal Speech 91

XIII. That God's Speech is One 97

XIV. On the Reality of Human Speech and Psychic Utterance 105

XV. Concerning our Knowledge that the Creator is Hearing, Seeing 112

XVI. That the Vision of God is an Intellectual Possibility and a Dogma of Revelation 115

XVII. Concerning what is to be considered Honourable and what Base, showing that Reason makes nothing incumbent on God, and that nothing was incumbent on Men before the coming of the Sacred Law . 119

XVIII. A Refutation of the Assertion (*a*) that the Acts of God have a Purpose or a Cause; (*b*) of Utility in God's Acts (*ṣalāḥ*), and that He must do what is best (*aṣlaḥ*) and bestow Sufficient Grace (*luṭf*) upon His Creatures. The Meaning of the terms *taufīq*, Efficient Grace; *khidhlān*, Abandoning; *sharḥ*, Opening, and *khatm*, Shutting of the mind; *ṭab'*, Sealing; *ni'ma*, Favour; *shukr*, Kindness; *ajal*, Fixed Term; and *rizq*, Sustenance 126

XIX. The Proof of Prophecy, of the Reality of Miracles, and that the Prophets must needs be Impeccable . 133

INTRODUCTION

SINCE William Cureton, in 1846, published in two volumes the text of *Kitābu-l-Milal wal-Niḥal*, al-Shahrastānī[1] has justly been held in high regard by all students of the history of religions. For the greater part of a century the *Milal* has been used as a mine from which to extract information about the religion and philosophy of the Near East. Though the publication of similar works such as *al-Farq bain al-Firaq* and Ibn Ḥazm's *Milal* have robbed Shahrastānī's work of the unique importance it achieved in Europe after the publication, in 1850, of Theodor Haarbrücker's translation under the title *asch-Schahrastânî's Religionspartheien und Philosophen-Schulen*, its careful summary of the points of difference which divide the multitudinous sects, and its succinct account of their general characteristics make it for all time indispensable.

The *Nihāyatu-l-Iqdām fī ʿIlmi-l-Kalām* was clearly designed by al-Shahrastānī as a complementary sequel to his *Milal*. In it he frequently cites the latter. He was conscious, no doubt, that he lay open to the charge of excessive objectivity in his treatment of the tenets of the sects—a charge which has justly been preferred against him more than once.[2] In this volume he clears himself so far as, and only so far as, the principal Muslim sects are concerned. His object is to indicate the farthest point reached by the philosophical thinkers of his day and to show how far their tenets are reasonable and reconcilable with orthodoxy, and in what respects they are wrong or defective.[3]

As would be expected, Shahrastānī's chief difficulties lay in combating the speculations and arguments of the Muʿtazila who were much more strongly entrenched in a somewhat defective, but on the whole defensible, system of philosophy.

Shahrastānī himself gave a general, but by no means blind, allegiance to the Ashʿarite school.

While the present book was being printed Dr. H. Ritter published in Stambul al-Ashʿarī's *Maqālātu-l-Islāmiyyīn*.[4] This latter work,

[1] According to al-Samʿānī, his full name was Abū-l-Fatḥ Muḥammad ibn Abū-l-Qāsim ʿAbd al-Karīm ibn Abū Bakr Aḥmad al Shahrastānī. He was born in 479/1086 and died in 548/1153. (Other dates of his birth are given as 467 and 469.) He was a native of Shahrastān in the province of Khurāsān.

[2] E.g. by D. S. Margoliouth in *Encyclopaedia of Religion and Ethics*, article *Kalam*. See also *Encyclopaedia of Islam*, article *Shahrastānī*, p. 263.

[3] E.g. his attack on Avicenna's theory of God's relation to the world in Ch. I.

[4] Part I in 1929; Part II in 1930. The suggestion in Dr. Ritter's Introduction (Arabic, p. 21) that Shahrastānī himself was the scribe of the MS. of the *Maqālāt*,

despite its comparative lack of criticism and discussion, is extremely important in the light it throws on the subjects discussed by Muslims in Ashʿarī's day. He was the founder of the school of theological thought which has dominated the minds of the majority of Muslims down to the present time.

I venture to think that the long overdue publication of Shahrastānī's *Nihāya*, which might be rendered *The Present Position of Speculative and Dogmatic Theology*, will enhance the importance of the *Maqālāt*, as its own importance will be increased by the latter. These two works are separated by more than two centuries of bitter controversy in theological and philosophical circles, and the stream of thought has left indelible marks upon the later work. Islam as al-Ashʿarī left it had to be adapted and reinterpreted to meet the needs of the growing intellectualism: Shahrastānī's work indicates the nature and extent of that growth during the two centuries.

This particular Summa has a very real importance of its own. Shahrastānī (1086–1153) survived by some forty years or more the Imām al-Ghazālī who dealt philosophical studies among Muslims a heavy blow in his *Tahāfutu-l-Falāsifa*. I do not think that any clear trace of the *Tahāfut* will be found in these pages, from which it may be right to infer that, while Baghdad remained the intellectual centre of Islam, the more negative propositions of Ghazālī failed to carry the support of Islamic scholars.[1] Shahrastānī is the last great philosopher of Islam before Averroës. He has some claim to be regarded as an original thinker. The fact that he did not retain in the eyes of his co-religionists that eminence as a theologian to which his ability entitled him may be attributable to a number of causes. First, his sturdy intellectual independence made him appear somewhat of a dangerous modernist in an age which threatened to go to pieces. (See al-Ghazālī on this subject.) Secondly, he had not that command of Arabic which would commend him to a later generation, though, of course, it is possible to exaggerate the effect of this shortcoming; and thirdly, the growing reaction against *kalām* which followed the publication of al-Ghazālī's attack on philosophy as a whole tended to force all such books into the background where they were studied only by the learned, and ceased to form a normal part of the teaching of philosophy and theology.[2]

owing to the lines *laqad ṭuftu*, &c., mentioned by Ibn Khallikān being on the Haidarabad copy, is interesting. See p. 3 of the Arabic text of the *Nihāya*.

[1] This is a subject to which I hope to return in the future.

[2] However, Yāqūt, iii. 63, 13 says that al-Ḥasan b. al-Ẓi'r (d. 598), who was a distinguished Cairene scholar, made it his practice to commit to memory one authoritative manual on each of the sciences, and he chose our author's *Nihāya* as his manual of Kalām. I owe this reference to Prof. Margoliouth. I find a further, and much later,

The principal facts of Shahrastānī's life have already been given by Cureton in his Preface to the *Milal*. They go back to Ibn Khallikān. The only addition of any importance which I have been able to find comes from Subkī's *Ṭabaqātu-l-Kubrā*[1] (727/1327–771/1370). Subkī says that it is stated in Dhahabī's (673/1274–748/1348) History that Ibn al-Samʿānī says that Shahrastānī was suspected of Ismāʿīlī leanings; and that in Ibn al-Samʿānī's *Taḥbīr* Shahrastānī is said to have been suspected of heresy and undue fondness for the Shīʿas. Subkī goes on to say that he cannot think where Ibn al-Samʿānī got his information, as his *Dhail* says nothing about these heretical tendencies of Shahrastānī, and all Shahrastānī's writings give the lie to such a belief. In his view, Ibn al-Samʿānī never made the statement at all, but the libel is probably due to the author of the *Kāfī*,[2] who wrote that Shahrastānī would have been the Imām, had he not dealt with matters of faith in an uncertain spirit and inclined towards heresy and controversy. Further, it was felt that Shahrastānī went too far in supporting and defending the tenets of the philosophers whenever conferences and discussions were held—at least so said al-Khwārizmī.

Shahrastānī was a deeply religious man. The intensity of his devotion to the faith of Islam cannot be doubted by any one who reads this work, which in itself is a sufficient refutation of the calumnies of his detractors. It would not be germane to this presentation of the author's book to discuss the gulf between the learned and the uneducated Muslim which may well account for the suspicion which gathered round his memory. His deep distress at the ungodliness and wickedness of his age finds noble expression[3] in his discussion of the problem of evil; and his faith in an all-wise and beneficent providence rises spontaneously to the surface of an argument with a rival school.

If he is more patient with the sects than his fellow schoolmen it is because he sees more deeply into the causes of the differences. His summing up at the end of the chapters is generally mediating in tendency, unless the point of issue is fundamental and admits of no

reference to the *Nihāya* in Jurjānī's commentary on Ījī's *Mawāqif*, p. 11. Jurjānī died in A.H. 816, i.e. A.D. 1413.

[1] iv. 78.

[2] I can only hazard a guess as to the author of this book. By eliminating the works quoted by Brockelmann, ii. 658, which were written before Shahrastānī's day and after Dhahabī, the most probable offender would seem to be Muwaffaq al-Dīn al-Maqdisī 541/1146–620/1223. Brockelmann gives the full title of the work as al-Kāfī fī-l Furūʿ, and the only copy known to him is the Paris MS. 1104. This man was only a child of seven when Shahrastānī died, but he studied in Baghdad, and, as a Hanbalite, he would hardly be likely to sympathize with Shahrastānī's liberal attitude towards the problems of philosophy and theology which the Hanbalites refused even to discuss.

[3] p. 266.

compromise. When he can he accepts his adversaries' arguments and tries to show that they demand or admit of another conclusion. Only when he comes to the eschatological beliefs of Islam does he falter. His rapid passage over the 'bridge', the 'balance', and the 'basin', marks a reluctance to commit himself. In any case, such matters are dogmas of faith, not of reason.

His quotations from al-Ashʿarī are interesting in view of the meagre remnants that have been published of this outstanding personality whose literary activity and religious influence were so potent in Islam. In common with many Arabic writers he does not always mark the end of his quotations and the limit must be inferred.[1] Nor does he deign to mention the name of the work which he is quoting.

Perhaps the characteristic most to be admired in Shahrastānī is his intellectual honesty. Where reason fails, and where he feels that the rationalists have good ground for their objections, as in the *Visio Dei*, he says frankly that it is a revealed rather than an intellectual truth. And where he feels it impossible to hold the prevailing opinion of the orthodox Ashʿarite school, as on p. 411, he has the courage to say so.

The titles of his known works indicate that his interest was always primarily in speculative theology. Besides the present work and the *Milal* he wrote:

Muṣāraʿatu-l-Falāsifa.
Ta'rīkhu-l-Ḥukamā.
Al-Manāhij wal-Bayānat.
Talkhīṣu-l-Aqsām li Madhāhib al-Anām.

The Manuscripts

According to Brockelmann, there are extant four manuscripts of the *Nihāyatu-l-Iqdām*. Three of these, MS. Marsh 356 in the Bodleian Library, Oxford; MS. Petermann II. 579 in the Preussische Staatsbibliothek, Berlin; and MS. arabe 1246, in the Bibliothèque Nationale, Paris, I have collated throughout. The fourth, in the Jeni Library, was inaccessible to me when this work was begun; and I could not at a later stage contemplate a further addition to the large sum I had already spent on photographs of two of the three manuscripts which I have consulted. Nor, in view of the tolerably accurate condition of the text, and the antiquity of the three documents on which the printed text rests, do I consider it essential to invoke the aid of the Constantinople MS., though possibly it would help to clear up more than one of the obscurities which are unavoidable in a work of

[1] The quotation from Avicenna's *Shifā'* on p. 222 is a case in point.

this kind. Metaphysics and speculative theology are apt to prove abstruse in any language, and our author wrote at a time when an exact philosophical terminology had not been fixed with any rigidity.[1] Moreover, he was not an Arab, and his Arabic style leaves a good deal to be desired.

The Bodleian MS. (O. = ا) was the only complete text at my disposal, and therefore I made it the basis of my text, though it is certainly inferior to the more ancient part of the Paris MS. Part I was finished on Friday the 19th of Shawwal, 590: Part II on the 10th of Rabīʿu-l-awwal, three years later, only forty years or so after the author's death; so that it may well have been copied from manuscripts bearing the imprimatur of al-Shahrastānī himself. It consists of 304 folios beautifully written in the *naskhī* character and freely vocalized (not always correctly). As in many manuscripts of this period, the vowels are written where they are least needed, as for instance with the conjunction or with an alif; they are often omitted where the sense is vitally affected as in *mūjib* and *mūjab*. The scribe was a certain ʿUthmān ibn Yūsuf ibn ʿAbd Allāh, the mudarris in Qalyūb. This manuscript was bequeathed to the Bodleian Library by Archbishop Marsh in 1713. Marsh obtained some of his Oriental MSS. from Huntingdon, who was at one time chaplain to the English merchants at Aleppo; others he acquired from the sale of Golius's library at Leyden in 1696. No. 356 bears the motto *πανταχῇ τὴν ἀλήθειαν* which is conjectured to have been that of Golius. At any rate, many hooks in this collection bear that motto.

The Berlin MS. (B. = ب) contains 172 folios described in the catalogue as 19½×15; 13½×10 cm. It is but little junior to O. being written by a certain Ismāʿīl ibn Murhaq(?) ibn Muḥammad ibn Fāris al-Ḥassanī on the 10th of Ṣafar 607. Ten folios are missing after folio 9. They correspond to 16 v.–33 in O. and only affect the first chapter. On 176 v. the author announces his intention of composing another book of twenty chapters like the present *fī bayān nihāyat auhām al ḥukamā al ilāhiyyīn*. This is, perhaps, the *Manāhij wal-bayānat* (*v.s.*). Folios 1 v.–4 v. have been inked over somewhat carelessly by a later scribe who has omitted the diacritical points. This *Ausbesserung* or *Verbesserung* goes on sporadically through the volume, and it is often for the worse. Characteristic examples of this man's work are سلكم for سَلكم on 15 v. of B. = O. 43 v., line 10

[1] Here I should like to pay a tribute to the help afforded by Dr. Max Horten's *Verzeichnis philosophischer Termini im Arabischen* (Leipzig, 1912), published in an *Anhang* to his *Die spekulative und positive Theologie des Islam*. This has been of great value to me. The task of tracing the technical significance of metaphysical terms through the numerous Arabic lexicons is daunting. Much of the otherwise unavoidable labour has been done for future workers in this field by Dr. Horten.

(p. ١٥, l. ٢). He has failed to see that the preceding اخترعتم cannot refer to the disputants but to the Creator, and consequently he has had to alter the whole meaning of the author, بعثهم على سبيل محبته being changed to نفيتم عن and قدمهم to قدمتم and so on. The notes on 106 v. are fair examples of the corruptions of this manuscript. I have passed over in silence some of the more unintelligent emendations of the reviser of B. Nor have I thought it advisable to add to the heavy cost of printing by introducing minutiae into the footnotes. Many slight deviations from O. have also been passed over in silence: thus B. very frequently writes تعالى for سبحانه, a fact of little consequence. The syntax of B., though on the whole sound, is not unexceptionable. The indicative is sometimes written for the subjunctive, cf. fol. 96 v., and the accusatives are often wrong, as indeed they sometimes are in all three manuscripts.

The Paris MS. (P. = ب) contains 211 folios said in the catalogue to be 24 × 16 cm.[1] It was written by a certain Isḥāq Muḥammad b. ʿUmar b. Muḥammad al Sharwānī, and was finished at the end of Jumādā-l-'Ûlā in the year 580. It is thus the oldest of the three; but unfortunately not quite half of it is in the original writer's hand. Folios 8–57 have been written by a series of copyists, at least three, and probably four. The Paris catalogue which speaks of 'un copiste du xviie siècle' is probably right as to date, though I should have liked to guess the eighteenth century; but as I have only seen a photograph of the original it is hardly fair to cavil at the date in the catalogue. Of the presence of more than one writer there can be no doubt whatever. This later portion contains seventeen lines of closely written Arabic in a crabbed hand, while the ancient part has only thirteen lines per page in a bold free *naskhī*. Consequently, as the modern writer ceased his work at O. 104 v., l. 14 (page 161) and the ancient writer's work is only extant from O. 175 v., l. 11 (page 275), the Paris MS. is of practically no independent value in the first half of the book. Had P. been extant in its entirety I should have made it the basis of my text. It will be obvious that the later partial restoration could not be allowed to stand as the basis of the printed text; so I have felt justified in maintaining O. throughout. The critical apparatus will allow scholars to form their own opinions. O. certainly enjoys the advantage of being itself a collated text, as the collator's remarks in the margin testify; and it has also been carefully checked by a corrector. On the other hand, its scribe has been guilty of some serious omissions and several blunders.

[1] At the end of the volume there is a history in Persian of the Blessed Virgin and her Son in Egypt. This has nothing to do with Shahrastānī's work, and its presence here must be due to some accident of possession.

I have sometimes allowed a reading which is obviously poor Arabic to stand, because I think it is what the author wrote. He was not an Arab, but a native of Khurāsān. Here I am in good company, for my predecessor in editing Shahrastānī's better-known work did the same. As my views coincide with his I quote his words:[1]

'My object has been in every instance to endeavour, upon the evidence before me, to ascertain to the best of my judgment what the author himself wrote, and to make that my text. I conceive it to be the duty of an editor to represent faithfully even all the manifest errors of his author, and to make his own corrections or observations thereon in notes or other wise;[2] nor ought he, upon his own authority, to make any change of expression, or even to alter a single word, for the sake of improving the style or of giving it greater perspicuity. I mention this, because I believe I have discovered some errors as to facts in parts of this book; and further, because the style of the author, being a native of Khurasan, is frequently not in perfect accordance with the precepts of the best Arabic grammarians: and I have therefore often passed over a reading in one MS. which appeared to me in itself to be the most preferable, when the authority of the rest of the copies has preponderated in favour of another. It appears much more probable that phrases not strictly grammatical or logical should have been corrected in one MS. by a scribe of taste and intelligence, than that different scribes should have made exactly the same solecism in four or five other copies, both of greater and less antiquity.'

A good illustration of the working of this latter principle occurs on O. 53 v., l. 9 (page ٧٩, ١۴), which I am convinced is what the author wrote. O. has بين حركة الضرورة والاختيارية. B. has corrected this into بين حركتي الضرورة والاختيار. P. in turn perceived the inelegance, but his emendation is rather clumsy though it is grammatically unexceptionable. He gives us بين للحركة الضرورية وللحركة الاختيارية. Another good example will be found on O. 87 v., l. 9.

However, I fear I may not have been consistent in applying this principle. Every one who has dealt with ancient manuscripts will know that the dictum that the harder reading is the more likely to be original leads an editor sadly astray unless allowance be made for a tired eye and a waning attention. Therefore I have felt myself at liberty to correct the text in a few instances rather than to perpetuate errors which seem to be due to the scribes rather than to the author; but these instances are duly indicated in the footnotes.

The larger numbers in the margin indicate the pages of O. They do not correspond, because the Bismillah in O. is at the top of folio 3 v. The following note may be useful: on page ۲ of the text the figure ۲

[1] *Book of Religious and Philosophical Sects*, by Muhammad al-Shahrastani . . . edited . . . by William Cureton, London, 1846, p. vii.

[2] Unhappily, he never published his notes.

in the margin at the right of line ٣ corresponds with fol. 4 r. of the Bodleian MS., the figure ٥ agreeing with fol. 4 v. and so on. Consequently to find the Bodleian MS. from the marginal numbers after folio 4 the scheme is $\frac{\text{marginal number}-4}{2} = \text{O}$. For 'adds' I have used the letter ز and for 'omits' س. The letter ن means that I owe the note to Professor Nicholson.

ADDENDA TO TRANSLATION

[WHILE this book was in the press a valuable study of Avicenna's *Ḥudūd* was published in Paris, by Mlle A.-M. Goichon. Shahrastānī's thought and language owe much to Avicenna, as readers of his *Milal* are aware. Mlle Goichon's work traces the exact significance of the terms used by Avicenna. No student of *Kalām* can afford to neglect it.]

p. 7, note 2. But see now Goichon, *Introduction à Avicenne. Son Épître des Définitions*, p. 69.

p. 27, line 3. The text continues: The difference in every object is to be referred to the receivers (*sc.* of form). The unpointed consonants of B imply *qawābil.* The reading of O, *fawāṣil,* means 'the specific differences'. Avicenna (Ishārāt, 15) says that *faṣl* answers the question 'What is it?'.

p. 36, line 22. Here I have taken *maqdūraini* as the equivalent of *qudrataini* (Wright, i. 132 CD); but it may be that the ordinary passive meaning is intended.

p. 48, para. 1. Cf. Avicenna, *Najāt,* pp. 356 and 363-4: 'The active participle presents an object as something beginning to exist; the passive presents it as something which has received a temporal existence.'

p. 68. The speakers in the second paragraph are probably the opponents, while the author himself would seem to be speaking in the next paragraph.

p. 83, line 35, after 'emanating' add: 'so that matter is disposed to receive form'.

p. 85, note 2. See now Goichon, p. 151, for an explanation of subjective entities in their relation to 'place'.

p. 104, last para. Shahrastānī's statement is roundly denied by Ibn Taimiyya, iii, p. 105, Būlāq, 1322. Prof. Margoliouth has kindly told me of this reference to the *Nihāyatu'l-Iqdām.* Another reference to Shahrastānī, though the *Nihāya* is not mentioned by name, occurs in i. 251.

p. 118, para. 2. Al-Ash'arī's words will be found in his *Ibāna*, p. 13 f. Shahrastānī's discussion is interesting in showing the objections which later thinkers raised to al-Ash'arī's arguments, apart from the answers with which he meets them.

p. 123, last para. The point is that the disputants have no standing because they have engaged in a controversy without orders from God.

CHAPTER I

Proof that the World had a Beginning and a Demonstration of the Impossibility of Anything without a Beginning and of the Existence of Bodies Infinite.

All men of true religion hold that the world had an origin as the object of God's[1] creation. 'God was and there was naught with Him.' The ancient philosophers Thales, Anaxagoras, Anaximenes, Pythagoras, Empedocles, Socrates, and Plato, all agree in this. We have discussed their various opinions about the origin of things in our book *Al-Milal wal-Niḥal.*

The school of Aristotle and his followers, such as Proclus, Alexander of Aphrodisias, and Themistius, to whom moderns like al-Fārābī and Ibn Sīnā among Islamic philosophers pay allegiance, assert that the 6
world was made and brought into being by One who is in His essence the necessarily existent One, the world being in its essence capable of existence (yet) necessarily existent through the necessarily existent One, (and) not originated in time with an origin preceded by non-existence.[2] The meaning of its origin (*ḥudūth*) is its necessary existence through God, its proceeding from Him, and its need of Him. It exists eternally through Him.

The Creator caused through His essence (*aujaba*) an intelligence which was a non-material self-subsistent substance. By means of this He caused another intelligence, and a soul and a heavenly body. Through these two intelligences the elements and the compounds came into being. From the One only one thing can proceed; and the meaning of 'procession from' (*ṣudūr ʿan*) is necessity through Him. A necessitator without a necessitated is inconceivable, so the world is eternal (*sarmadī*) and so are the movements of the spheres; they had no beginning and every movement is preceded by another movement, so that they are infinite as to number and time.

These men also agreed that the existence of an infinite (sequence of) cause and effect was impossible, and that actually infinite bodies were impossible. The governing principle of their school in regard to the finite and infinite is that the units of every number can be con-

[1] I have avoided the use of the name Allāh, because much of the language of this author belongs to the philosophy of theism, and might have been written by a member of any of the theistic religions.

[2] The point is fundamental. Avicenna held that the world was both 'possible' and 'necessary': possible, because it could not exist by itself; necessary, because it exists eternally with God. Thus God's relation with the world is one of necessity. The Mutakallimūn asserted that the relation was a relation of existence.

ceived as existing simultaneously, it having a conventional order[1] (*tartīb waḍ'ī*); or its units can be conceived as existing in sequence, it having a natural order. Hence the existence of the infinite is impossible. An example of the first kind is a body of infinite dimension, and an example of the second kind is an infinite (sequence) of cause and effect. There is, however, an exception. The units of every totality and number can be conceived simultaneously or in sequence without a conventional or natural order. And so the existence of that without an end is not in this case impossible.

7 Examples of the first kind are infinite human souls, they being simultaneous in existence after separation from the body.[2] Examples of the second kind are circular movements which exist in sequence.

The question really turns on the difference between bringing into existence and causation, and priority and posteriority. Everything comprised by being is finite without distinction between the parts, and the infinite is inconceivable except by the imagination apart from perception and intellect.

In popular terminology *priority* can be in time, as father to son; in place, as the leader to the led, (though this is sometimes said to be priority of rank); in merit, as the learned to the ignorant; in essence (*dhāt*), as the cause to the effect. But it is not right to weaken the meaning of essential so that it is the mere equivalent of causal. They ought to say priority resides in the causal, so the final cause precedes the effect in the mind and thought of the agent, not in existence: it is posterior in existence, prior in mind, unlike the efficient cause and
8 the formal cause, for these are not conjoined in existence. Examples are cited from the rays of the sun with the sun itself and the movements of the sleeve with the movement of the hand. These movements, though conjoined in time, yet, if regarded as cause and effect respectively, cannot be conjoined in existence, because the existence of the one is derived (*mustafād*) from the existence of the other, and the existence of the origin cannot be conjoined with that which is derived from it. But if the existence of both is taken as derived from the giver of forms then they are conjoined in existence, for then one is not cause nor the other effect.

Some add a fifth form of priority which they call natural, e.g. the priority of one to two. Why should there not be a sixth form, say priority in existence regardless of essential necessity (*al ījāb bil-dhāt*) and of time and place? The priority of one to two is apposite here,

[1] This is explained better by Avicenna himself, cf. *Najāt*, section *Tabī'iyyāt*.

[2] This argument (abbreviated to a bald statement by Shahrastānī) was combated by al-Ghazālī (*Tahāfut*, ed. Bouyges, p. 34). Even if an 'infinite' series of immortal souls had been born in the past, there would at any given moment be an actual finite number of them, which on Avicenna's principles would be impossible.

for one is not a cause requiring the existence of two necessarily; for we can imagine two things, one of which exists in its essence while the other's existence is derived from another source.

Further, it must be determined by inquiry whether derivative being comes by choice, by nature, or by essence. Then the priority of the existence of the origin over the derivative must be assumed only *qua* existence without considering whether the origin is essentially its cause or is its producer by means of a quality (*biṣifatin*).
Next, is the derived existence a necessary existence through it (the 9
origin) because it (the origin) is its cause, or is its existence not necessary through it (the origin) because necessity through another adheres to it? For it would be right to say 'This came into being from it and so was necessary through it', but it is impossible to say 'It was necessary through it and so came into being from it'.

Every sense of priority and posteriority implies concomitance in rank; but here they belong to another order. Concomitance cannot be predicated of the Creator and the world. We do not admit the existence of temporal priority as applied to the Creator. He was neither prior to nor with the world in time. As we deny temporal priority so we deny temporal concomitance. That which is not of time and whose being is not temporal can have nothing to do with limitations and order of time any more than with limitations of space.

When our opponents say the world was eternally existent with the Creator they use ambiguous language of time, for it may be said that of two things one may be prior in essence while both are concomitant in time, for priority in essence does not exclude concomitance in time (cf. the examples given above). But how can the word concomitance
be used of that which is not susceptible of time? 10

We do not deny that fancy can toy with the idea of time before the world as with space above the world, but that is pure phantasy. There is no space and no 'separation' as al-Karrāmī[1] supposes. If a world above this were conjectured that would not justify the assumption that there were worlds, i.e. bodies of infinite extent, as the impossibility of infinite distance in the plenum and vacuum has been demonstrated: similarly with infinite time and numbers.

Even if there were a body of infinite extent it would not follow that it was 'with' the Creator in space, nor would movements infinite in time require that they should be 'with' the Creator in time, because He is not susceptible of time or place; 'God was and naught was with Him'. To call God *Mūjid* (He who brings into existence) does not imply that the *mūjad* is 'with' Him in existence. Concomitance in any shape or form in reference to God is to be denied.

[1] See *al-Milal*, p. 80.

11 We will begin with the methods of the *Mutakallimūn* and then deal with the points at issue. The *Mutakallimūn* have two methods, (*a*) Positive, which establishes the doctrine that the world was produced; (*b*) Negative, which refutes the doctrine of its eternity.

As to (*a*) they assert (1) the existence of accidents, (2) that they had a temporal origin, (3) that no substance is free from them, (4) the impossibility of temporal objects without a beginning. From these premisses it follows that something that temporal things do not precede is itself temporal.[1]

Al-Ashʿarī said: If we assume the pre-existence of atoms they must either have been grouped together or separate, or neither grouped nor separate; and as their relation one to another has changed and they do not change of their own essence because essence is unchangeable there must have been one who joined and separated them. So that it follows that something that temporal things do not precede is itself temporal.

12 Abū Isḥāq al-Isfarā'inī adopted this view, though he expressed it differently. Al-Ashʿarī maintained that man was formed of mingled seed into the various species of mankind. It is not to be doubted that the diversities in man were due to an eternal, omnipotent, and omniscient maker rather than to man himself, his parents, or nature. Said he: What laws can be applied to the individual can be applied to all, because all share the property of corporeality.

The Imāmu-l-Ḥaramain (Abū-l-Maʿālī ʿAbdu-l-Malik al-Juwainī),[2] taking another path, said: According to our opponents the earth is surrounded by (successive circles of) water, air, fire, and planets which are spatial bodies. We know that the supposition that these bodies might move from their place or alter in size is not an impossible one. Now anything that has a specific nature of any possible kind, when any other nature would have been possible, must necessarily have needed one to give it that specific nature. It will be seen in what follows that the world's existence is essentially contingent whether it be conceived as essentially infinite or finite as to place and time. Our opponents ascribe contingency to the world, although it is (according to them) essentially infinite as to time while finite as to place. We will divide the questions into local and temporal finitude, taking the need of a determining principle[3] as accepted, or necessary, or practically necessary.

Objection. What is the proof that the principle of contingence

[1] If we imagine temporal things as points on a line, each will be preceded by its fellow until we reach the first. Nothing temporal preceded it, yet it is itself of time.

[2] Of his two important works (*al-Burhān fī Uṣūli-l-Fiqh* and *al Waraqāt fī Uṣūli-l-Fiqh*) the first is lost and the second has not been printed. He was obscure even to those who admired his works.

[3] *al-mukhaṣṣiṣ*.

applies to all the universe? We answer that reason ascribes contin- 13
gence to all parts of it, and as the whole is composed of the parts contingence must attach to the whole.

Objection. What is the proof that bodies are essentially finite? We answer that a supposed body or distance of infinite extent must be infinite either from all points of view or from one only. Whichever way we look at it we can imagine a finite point in it to which an infinite line is joined. Moreover, we can imagine another point on a line smaller than the first by a cubit and bring the points together in such a way that the smaller line coincides with the longer. If both lines extend to infinity then the less is equal to the greater which is absurd. If the shorter fails to equal the longer in finitude then the former is finite and so is the latter, seeing that the shorter has fallen short of it in finitude and the longer has exceeded it in finitude and what exceeds something in finitude is itself finite. In any case if one were greater than the other the infinite would contain greater and smaller, more and less, which is absurd also. Hence to assert the existence of infinite body or distance in plenum or vacuum is absurd.

This demonstrative proof can be applied to infinite numbers and individuals. If we assert that a body is finite and might be greater or smaller than it is and if one of these possibilities has already been determined it needed a determinant.[1] . . .

This determinant must either be an essential cause, necessitating 14
by nature, or one who produces by will and choice. The first is folly, because the essential cause does not distinguish like from like, seeing that so far as it is concerned spatial bodies, direction, size, shape, and all the attributes are one. We can assert the existence of a creator only by those operations in which there are indications of a choice which determined characteristics that could have been other than they are. Therefore we know of a certainty that the creator is not an essential cause, but one who produces by will and knowledge.

This is an admirable position to take up, save that it requires us to verify premisses by which we can come to know that the world originated in time and needed a creator. Such are: the assertion (*a*) that bodies are finite in essence and dimension, (*b*) that there is a vacuum beyond the world in which the supposition of deviation to right or left (of the planets) is possible, (*c*) the denial of phenomena without beginning. (Our opponents admit that the world's existence is essentially contingent and that it needed a determinant to tip the scale of being[2] against non-being, yet they say that the world

[1] *al-mukhaṣṣiṣ*.

[2] The figure has become a technical term for the action of the *mukhaṣṣiṣ*.

eternally existed with the determinant.) (*d*) The confining of phenomena to bodies and that which subsists in bodies. (Our opponents have asserted the existence of objects outside these two categories which exist eternally through another, essentially not temporarily, substantially not locally, without shape or dimension.) (*e*) The assertion that the essential cause is like the natural necessity. (Our opponents do not admit this, but distinguish between the two.)

15 We divide intelligibles into three: the necessary, the possible, and the impossible. The necessary is that which must exist, inasmuch as its non-existence would be an impossibility: the impossible is that which must be non-existent because its existence would be an impossibility: while the possible need neither exist nor not-exist. The world and its intellectual substances and bodies with senses and the accidents which subsist therein we assume to be finite [and infinite].[1] Similarly, if we assume that it is an individual or many individuals either it must necessarily exist or necessarily not-exist. But that is impossible because its parts change in condition before our eyes and the necessarily existent never changes.

Our position is that everything that alters or increases has a contingent existence in relation to its essence and so its existence is through the production of another. The world alters, and therefore it owes its being to the creative activity of another. If the units composing a whole are contingent then the whole must necessarily be contingent. That which tips the scale of being cannot be such in essence and in respect of his existence only, because existence is
16 common to both the necessary and the possible, so that if it (the tipper) gave the thing an existence[2] in respect of himself being existence or an essence, neither object would have a better claim to be brought into existence than the other. Hence it is clear that it (the world) is produced owing to its being an existence (merely) by way of an attribute or an essence by way of an attribute.

Again, essential cause does not distinguish like from like: its relation to both is the same. Therefore where existence has been determined as against non-existence there must necessarily be a determinant in addition to its being an essence, so essential causation is vain. Again, the essential cause, having no relation whatever to the thing caused, does not produce it. If we imagine two essences or things with no connexion between them but each of them has its own real peculiarity the one cannot have proceeded from the other. The necessary existent one *per se* is an essence holy and far removed from all relations and connexions, unique in his reality. It is the necessity

[1] I suspect that the words *waghaira mutanāhin* are wrongly added by the copyist.
[2] Professor Margoliouth suggests that *aujada* should be read.

of his existence and not an attribute additional to his necessary essence. It is not necessary that anything should come into existence from him by way of essence, so that essential cause is unintelligible when relations and connexions have been ruled out.

You say that as the cause (*mūjib*) was one it was impossible that 17
two things should proceed from it at the same time; and since it was pure intellect, i.e. non-material, it caused an active (*bil-fiʿl*) intelligence which was also non-material; and since causation involves mutual relation, and relation involves mutual resemblance so that the one can stand in the place of the other, there may be posited of the necessarily existent and of that which stands in its place in causation one and the same thing. But essential causation is false and so it is clear that selective creation alone stands.[1]

Objection. Agreed that the world is contingent and needed a necessarily existent One, but why should its existence through another require its temporal origin from non-being? If a thing exists through something else it does not exclude the possibility of its having existed through it eternally. The matter will only become clear if we settle the question 'If He gave the world a beginning from non-existence, was the precedence of non-existence a condition in the originating itself?'[2] We say that it cannot be a condition, for the originated is only related to the originator by way of existence; and non-existence has no influence in bringing into existence, so it is possible that the world eternally existed through something else.

Answer. The use of the term 'non-existence' in the sense of a thing of which time before and time after, or source of origin can be predicated is fantastic ambiguity. We cannot imagine primacy (*al-auwaliyyah*) in a phenomenon (*ḥādith*) unless it is supported upon the notion of time and space; just as finitude in the world rests on the
notion of the vacuum and just as we cannot suppose a void between 18
the existence of the Creator and the world, so we cannot suppose that there was time between the existence of the Creator and the world. But neither concomitance in time nor in place follow from this. This distinction should be carefully observed.

Let it be supposed that the existence (variant 'origin') of a thing which does not arise from another thing is the meaning of its origin from non-existence. We mean by origin (*ḥudūth*) having a beginning. 'It was not and it became' is the meaning of 'preceded by non-existence'.

Again, if the world is contingently existent in relation to its essence

[1] See footnote to p. 1.

[2] *fī taḥaqquq al-iḥdāth*; I follow Lāhījī, who defines *taḥaqquq* as *wujūd* (*Verzeichnis*, p. 152).

if it came into existence it was only in relation to that which gave it existence. Were it not for the latter it would 'deserve' non-existence. The necessarily existent preceded it in essence and existence. Were it not for the latter it would not have existed. Its existence could not be concomitant with the necessarily existent in essence and existence because *before* and *together with* in essence and existence are not found in one thing. It could not be *with* the necessarily existent in time
19 because that would require that the latter should be temporal. *With* is a correlative which yokes both parties together. Nor could it be with the necessarily existent in rank and dignity . . . so that the saying 'God was and there was naught with Him' is right.

What do you mean by saying that that which is possible (i.e. the world) continually exists in or with the necessary? Can it be that you suppose that the continual existence (*dawām*) of the creator is temporal, made up of infinite moments as you suppose the existence of the world to be? A wretched confusion of terms! The continual existence of the Creator means that He is necessary *per se* and in His essence: He is the first without a beginning preceding and the last without a later following; His beginning is His end and His end is His beginning. As to the world, it had a beginning and its continuance (*dawām*) is temporal, subject to increase and decrease. . . . If *dawām* could be applied to both in the same sense the Creator's existence would be temporal, or the world's existence would be essential;[1] both false assertions. The folly of this will become plain when we have established the impossibility of phenomena without a beginning, and of the existence of anything infinite.

As to your assertion[2] that a phenomenon is only related to its producer by its existence, and non-existence does not affect it, we
20 answer that if this were so everything that is brought into existence would be so related and that would entail an infinite chain. It is not related to the necessarily existent because it exists, but only because it is 'possible'. Possible existence precedes existence. We say that the world came into existence because it was potentially existent, not that it was potentially existent because it came into existence. The possibility of its existence is essential to it; its existence is accidental, and the essential precedes the accidental. Thus the possible is essentially non-existent apart from the author of its existence and is preceded by non-existence and the said author.

Objection. What is the difference between the world's being the necessary result of God's causation and its existence being given by Him? For if the world was essentially contingent and came into being through another then it was necessary through Him. This is

[1] It has been maintained that it is *'alā ṣifatin.*

[2] *V.s.*, p. 7.

the law of every cause and effect: effect is always rendered necessary by the cause and is contingent in relation to its essence, necessary in relation to its cause. Cause precedes effect in essence though they are concomitant in existence. You say 'My hand moved and so the key in my sleeve moved'. You cannot say 'The key moved in my sleeve and so my hand moved', even though the two movements are simultaneous in being.

21 *Answer.* A thing's existence through the author of its existence (*mūjid*) making it exist is correct in word and meaning as opposed to a thing's necessity through the necessary cause making it necessary. Contingent means that a thing may exist or may not exist. Not that it may be necessary or may not be necessary. Its existence, not its necessity, is derived from the determinant.[1] You may say: When it came into existence necessity with reference to the cause befell it (*ʿaraḍa lahu*) because the cause conferred necessity upon it so that it could be said it became necessary through the cause making it necessary.[2] Nay rather (the cause) conferred existence upon it so that it would be right to say it came into existence by (the cause) conferring existence upon it, and necessity befell it as an accident, and thus its existence was related to necessity because it had been (previously) potentially (*mumkin*) existent, not potentially necessary. This is a nice point which must always be kept in mind.

Potential is midway between the necessary and the non-necessary. . . . Existence and non-existence are mutual opposites with no intermediate term. The potential owes its existence or non-existence to the giver of existence. Therefore necessity can only be attached to the world as an accident and an accidental thing is not to be referred back to the giver of existence. If you say, 'Its existence is necessary through His causation,' you seize upon the accidental. When we say, 'It came into existence by His production,' we seize upon the essential reality of that which is derived from another. It may be said that if the potential came into existence at an appointed time or in a definite form its existence then and thus must be necessary because the Creator knew and willed it so and because what is contrary to His foreknowledge cannot possibly happen. But its necessity was only in the 22
causation of knowledge and will; and if it is established that existence, not necessity, is that which is derived in things of time, essential causation, which they adduce as an argument for the world being contemporary with the Creator, is false. This leads to ridiculous statements, for sometimes they will not admit that the movement of the hand is the cause of the movement of the sleeve and the key, and they will not accept the doctrine of necessary consequence (*tawallud*:

[1] *al-murajjiḥ*.

[2] The next four words should be omitted.

see *Milal*, p. 44), refusing to admit the causal force of the particle *fa* in *fataḥarraka al-miftāḥ* 'and so the key moved'. With them matter is the cause of the existence of form, so that it would be correct to say that form without matter could not have existed and they are concomitant in existence. Form does not exist because matter makes it exist but because of the action of the giver of forms. If that be conceded, cause can precede effect in essence and be contemporaneous with it. The impossible is the co-existence of that which had a beginning with that which has no beginning, as has already been explained. . . . The only relation subsisting between the Creator and the world is that of activity and object.

If it be asked whether the world could have been created before it actually was, it should be replied that its beginning and end is a
23 necessary intellectual concept (*taṣawwur*). Anything that goes beyond that is mere supposition which is called 'intellectual possibility'. Such suppositions and possibilities are endless. . . .

Objection. Granted that an infinite body cannot actually exist, demonstrate to us that infinite movements in sequence and continuous phenomena cannot possibly exist. With us finitude and infinity are referred to four divisions. Two of them cannot exist infinitely as to essence, viz. that which has a definite position (*tartīb waḍ'ī*)[1] like a body, or a natural order like a cause. A body infinite as to essence cannot exist, nor can causes and effects infinite in number.
24 A body has a definite position and parts;[2] and each part is related to another part so that a body cannot be infinite at any one time. Causes have a natural order; the effect depends on the cause and they are both related. Infinite causes are not possible. Two classes are infinite in essence, viz. phenomena and movements which have no necessary relation to each other but follow each other in an infinite temporal sequence—an intellectual possibility. Also human souls, for they do not follow one another but exist together without a position like bodies or a nature like causes, and can exist *ad infinitum*.

Answer. Whatever existence comprises is finite, and the existence of the infinite is inconceivable whether in a definite or a natural order or not. Any plurality which is infinite must either be so from one aspect or from every aspect. Now we can mark off mentally a part of the plurality and take the plurality with that part as one entity or we can take the plurality by itself as an entity. In that case the plurality with the addition must be equal to the plurality without it in number or extent, which would mean that the less was equal to
25 the greater, or not equal to it, and that would mean that there would be two infinite pluralities, one greater and the other less. These sup-

[1] Cf. *Metaphysica Δ*, Book V, ch. xix, and Ibn Ṭumlūs, ٦٢.
[2] Or, atoms.

positions are absurd. (There follows a similar argument drawn from Avicenna's *Najāt.*)[1]

Avicenna said: 'There is a difference here.

A point can be singled out in a body which has a definite position, and then it is possible to conceive a body of similar size and its extension to infinity.[2] But movements which are consecutive have no definite position, for they do not exist together and you cannot single out one movement and apply the principle of a corresponding 26
something capable of extension, because that which has no order in position or nature is not susceptible of *inṭibāq*.'

It was said to him: Your answer about this difference falls into two sections. In one you suppose a point in a spatial body which you project to an imaginary infinity and you assume a corresponding body. Assume then that past movements still exist in sequence and that past moments of time are still present in sequence like an imaginary line of infinite extent composed of consecutive points. The dividing points (*ḥudūd*) in the movements and the (atomic) moments in the times are like the points in the lines, and the sequence of the one is as the consecution of the other.[3]

The cause which makes infinity impossible and necessitates finitude is that which leads to the less being like the more, and this is present in both places. The Mutakallim applies this argument to time, making to-day the starting-point forwards and backwards, and comes to the same conclusion, viz. that infinite time is an impossible concept.

Secondly, if movements and individuals have no definite position they have a natural order like causes and effects, and thus must be finite. Every effect is contingently existent in essence, and its exis- 27
tence is only necessary through its cause, so that its existence depends on the existence of its cause and you are driven back to a first cause which is not contingent. The relation of father and son is similar: the son's existence depends on the father's, and the father's on his father's. Why do you not say they depend on an ultimate first father? According to you individuals are infinite. Then, for every individual human being a rational soul is to be enumerated,[4] and it remains united in existence (with that being). But if individuals are infinite,

[1] Shahrastānī has made a few changes in Avicenna's terminology, cf. *Najāt*, Cairo, 1331, p. 202.

[2] The argument is that anything which is subject to *inṭibāq* (the placing of a corresponding cover) cannot be infinite. The finite is 'covered' by the hypothetical infinite which overlaps it and by so doing shows that it is capable of division and is *ipso facto* not infinite.

[3] The argument as to the finitude of space is the same as that used by al-Ghazālī of number; see note to p. 2.

[4] Emend the text.

and their existence is possible, because they follow one another not united together in existence, what have you to say about souls? For they are united and infinite.

Avicenna maintained that souls have no natural or fixed order. It was said: If individuals are ranged as begetter and begotten, so are souls also, because one of the accidents which especially accompany souls is that they are such that out of their individuals other individuals proceed. The relation persists with them, and therefore they have an order.

Another proof that infinite phenomena and movements have no real existence. Suppose we discuss the age in which we live: without doubt the past is finished, and a thing that is finished is finite. If we isolate the past from the present it is clear that past movements are
28 finite, seeing that they have come to an end. For every movement that is created or annihilated movements have passed away before it without number. A finite number of movements is always in existence which is after the past and before the number that lies in the future. Every movement and every revolution has beginning and end. If it is finite at one end it is finite at the other. So all movements are essentially finite as to beginning and end. They are numbered in time and it is time that numbers them; hence that which is numbered and that which numbers are finite as to beginning and end.

Can it be said that movements are infinite in number? We say that every existing number can be increased or decreased and is therefore finite. This judgement applies to numbers whether they are of things existing together like human souls, or in sequence like individual human beings. But according to them souls are infinite in number while subject to increase or decrease, and so are individual human beings. Therefore, if the individuals are compared with the souls they must correspond. But if the individuals fall short of the number and the remainder is made to correspond with the number of the souls, if both are infinite the less is like the greater; and if they are finite our
29 object is achieved. An argument used against the Dahriyya (atheists; cf. *Milal*, p. 444) is that the movements of Saturn in the seventh sphere are like those of the moon in the first, inasmuch as neither have an end. But it is notorious that Saturn's movements are greater than the moon's. Yet they are the same as, and greater than, the moon's movements—a monstrous absurdity![1]

If it is said that their movements are equal because the moon moves more slowly in completing its smaller orbit we reply that their movements are those of circumference and axis. They are in infinity,

[1] Cf. al-Ghazālī, op. cit., pp. 31, 32. Ibn Ḥazm (Cairo, A.H. 1347, p. 20) uses similar arguments.

yet the movement of Saturn is twice that of the moon. The point is unanswerable.

Objection. You posit irregularity (*tafāwut*) in God's cognitions and decrees. With you knowledge is connected with the necessary, the possible and the impossible, while Power (*qudra*)[1] is only connected with the possible. Therefore, what God knows is more than what He decrees. Less and more point to two species both of which are infinite.

Answer. We do not say that God's cognitions and decrees form an infinite number. They are indeed infinite, but knowledge is a quality by which what is rightly knowable is known, and Power is a quality by which what can rightly come into existence is decreed; so both are infinite and there is no question of one being less than 30
another. Indeed, with us it is the existence of infinite numbers which is impossible. The infinite is a mere conception of the mind: it does not exist. Obviously you can go on doubling and redoubling a number, and as the mind can conceive of intelligibles and determinables infinite it may be said that the divine knowledge and will (*qudra*), are infinite. But knowledge and will are not a simple thing which exercises itself on infinite objects (lit. going in infinite directions) nor are intelligibles and determinables infinite pluralities. It should be understood that the meaning of our doctrine that the essence of the Creator is infinite is that He is one, and indivisible, and limitless.

The *Dahriyya.* You say that the world originated in time after it was not. In that case its existence was after the Creator's. Therefore:

Either it was later in time *or* not in time.

If not in time, then it was contemporaneous with the existence of the Creator. If later in time, then

Either it was later in finite time *or* in infinite time.

If the former the existence of the Creator must be finite: if the latter we must suppose that infinite objects exist in that infinite 31
time.

If infinite time is not impossible, neither is infinite number.

Answer. Your position is utterly untenable. You say that if the world were originated in time its existence would be 'after'. If by that you mean after God's existence in time it is inadmissible because we have demonstrated that the words *before*, *after*, and *contemporary with* cannot be used of God.[2]

[1] The Divine attribute *qudra* embraces both Power (*quwwa*) and Will or Volition (*irāda*). Elsewhere their proper activities are carefully defined. See ch. ix.

[2] It will be observed that controversialists in *Kalam* seldom attain common ground. Each difficulty is referred back to an earlier dogmatic assertion which the opponent has not accepted.

Moreover, the dichotomy 'The world is after in time or not-in-time' is false. You speak as though we admitted that the world was related to the Deity in time, and when we say that that is impossible you pretend that we are committed to its existence side by side with God, which is hypocrisy. The only sense in which 'after' can be used is that the Creator is He who gives existence, and the created is that which derives existence from Him. The one's existence has a beginning: the other's has not. But you cannot speak of 'after in time or not-in-time'.

Objections. There must be some sort of relation between Creator and created (*mūjid* and *mūjad*); and if relation is established, it must be either in finite or infinite time.

32 *Answer.* Such a relation must be denied. If it were established, God's existence would be temporal subject to change and movement. If any one were to ask what was the world's relation to God in that it existed and had a limit? Did it touch Him or not? If not was it in the void or in a finite or infinite distance?—the question would be absurd. So here.

Returning to the dichotomy, does 'time' mean something existent or the idea of something existent, or a pure non-entity? If it is existent then it is of the world and not before it, for the existent subsists either in itself or in another; in either case it cannot be supposed that it was before the world. If it has merely a hypothetical existence, it must be remembered that the suppositions of the mind are not always possible in actual existence. The mind can imagine an infinite number of other worlds, and infinite numbers themselves, and infinite spaces of time. If it means pure non-entity, there can be no finitude and no infinity in a non-entity.

33 Again. Why do you say that if time were finite the Creator's existence would be finite? The finitude of time is like the finitude of the world in place, and that is assuming the point at issue. The fact that the world is finite does not require that the Creator's essence should be finite, because place has no relation to Him. So also with time. Why, too, do you say that if time were not finite in our thought (infinite) objects might actually exist therein?[1]

Avicenna, following Aristotle, said that everything that comes into being from non-existence is necessarily preceded by the possibility of existence; and this is not pure non-existence, but is something capable of existence and non-existence, and that can only be conceived in matter, so that everything temporal is preceded by matter. Hence this antecedent matter can only be conceived in time, because 'before' and 'with' have only real existence in time. The non-exis-

[1] This is not precisely what the Dahriyya said, *v.s.*, p. 13.

tent 'before' is the non-existent 'with'[1] and is not the precedent possibility which accompanies existence, for in that case it (the non-existent) would have a temporal precedence. If the world were a phenomenon (*ḥādith*) arising from non-existence, the possibility of existence in matter would have preceded it in time. So either there would be an infinite chain, which is false, or (the possibility) would stop at a point where neither possibility nor non-existence preceded it, and so its necessity would be through another. This is our view. The Muʿtazila adopted this error in the belief that the non-existent was a thing. . . .

Answer. We have already explained that 'originated from non- 34
existence' means the thing (*al-maujūd*) which has a beginning. Antecedent possibility is not an essence—a thing needing matter—but it is a supposition, because of what cannot exist real existence (*thubūt*) cannot be predicated. . . . We regard the origin of the world in the same way as they regard the origin of the human soul—it has a beginning but not out of something else; so that it can be said that it was preceded by non-existence, i.e. it was not and then it became; and it is in its essence contingently existent, but this contingency does not require that it should be preceded by matter, for that would imply that its existence was material. Possibility as such does not require matter, and its precedence of an object is merely subjective, which you call 'essential precedence': and that precedence is not a temporal precedence. Similarly the first thing caused and all the souls; for their existence is essentially possible, and the possibility of their existence preceded their existence. Similarly the first body which is the sphere of the spheres. We hold that every phenomenon of a temporal origin or, as you would say, of essential origin, is preceded by the possibility of existence. The temporal object vacillates between existence and non-existence, and this vacillation between existence and non-existence, precedence, and possibility are all subjective suppositions, for the thing in its essence is in one attribute of existence, whereas existence so far as its essence is concerned is divided into (*a*) that whose existence pertains to an existence which it has *per se*, i.e. it is not derived from another so that it can be said
existence becomes it rather than non-existence, and is primary;[2] and 35
(*b*) that whose existence pertains to an existence which it has from another, so that it can be said existence does not become it and is not primary. This existence can only be asserted when something has a beginning preceded by the existence of something without a beginning and has in its essence the possibility of existence, i.e. preceded

[1] Var. 'after'.

[2] Or, perhaps, 'simple'. *Awwal* is sometimes used as a synonym of *basīṭ*.

by the possibility of existence. You cannot say that it is *existence* preceded by the possibility of existence. Rather the existence is essentially a possible existence. Here are two kinds of antecedents: the antecedent existence of the object, and the antecedent possibility of existence. All we know of the latter is that derived existence can only mean that it is possible in its essence. It vacillated between existence and non-existence and needed some one to tip the scale. Without Him it could not have real existence. If every temporal thing 'needs' precedent possibility, which in turn needs matter, which needs time, there is an infinite chain so that it can be said that that matter and time need other matter and other time; and no temporal thing would actually have existed! The foundation of their theory is vain. But there must have been a starting-point, viz. the first thing created (*mubdaʿ*) out of nothing, possible in its essence, but its possibility not requiring time and matter. Thus we must think of the precedence of possibility and of non-existence and of Him who brings into existence. The latter precedes in His existence *qua* existence, and consequently he precedes the non-existence and the possibility (latent) in the object by a logical precedence. Hence is established the difference between essential and existential precedence—a point which should be carefully noted.

Avicenna said: I admit that the world with its substances and accidents is *per se* possibly existent, but the question is: Is it necessarily existent through another, while existing eternally with him?
36 With regard to that which could not or could exist, and if it were designated by existence would need one to tip the scale of existence, it must either be said that what can come into existence from the determinant must necessarily come into existence, or must not necessarily come into existence. Then it comes into existence after it had not existed. But logical thought demands that if the one essence[1] was one in all respects and remains as it was—and nothing has been brought into existence from it in the past (though it could have been) and it is still in the same state, then nothing has been brought into existence from it. And if something had been brought into existence then indubitably something has originated from intention, will, nature, power, exercise of force, purpose, or cause. Therefore either that cause must have originated a quality in its essence, or originated something distinct from itself. The discussion about that originated something, whatever it may be, is the same as that about the world. In that case (forsooth)[2] it is impossible that anything should originate,

[1] From which all else proceeded.

[2] Possibly we should read: 'If it is impossible that anything should originate and if it was impossible then . . .'

and if it is impossible then there is no difference between the state of doing and not doing, yet action has occurred—which is absurd.

We have turned the adversaries' arguments against them by the hypothesis of a substance void of action which is false. The contrary position is the true one.

Answer: You are trying to establish three premisses: (1) the possibility of the world's existence from eternity; (2) that what could exist must exist; (3) that a temporal cause underlies a temporal thing.

(1) We have demonstrated the impossibility of the eternal coexistence of the possible *per se* with the necessary *per se*.[1] That which has a beginning cannot be coupled with that which has
no beginning. Wherever possibility and potentiality are the nature 37
of a thing eternity must be denied it. When you say that the world is possibly existent and all possible things must exist in eternity you have joined irreconcilable propositions and given your case away. If you ask why the world could not have existed in eternity, we reply that we have already demonstrated the impossibility of infinite originated things.

(2) Here we have contradiction in (*a*) word, and (*b*) meaning. (*a*) 38
Possibility and necessity are opposites except that it can be said of that which may possibly exist that its existence is necessary through another. Some even refuse to grant as much as this on the ground that this necessity is through another's causation and the possible only needs the necessary in its existence, not in its necessity, as has already been explained.[2] (*b*) If everything that could exist were necessarily to exist we should have an infinity of things at a stroke! If order is a condition in substances so that they come into existence in order up to a determined number, so it is a condition in the actual existence of things. The order in substances, prior and post, is like the order in existing objects first and last—a noteworthy point.

(3) This is a most pernicious cause of error. Our master and imām Abū-l-Qāsim Sulaimān ibn Nāṣir al-Anṣārī used to say that the mode of the Creator's activity was beyond the comprehension of men's minds. He said that the possibility of the world's existence is established by reason and its emergence in time is established by
deduction. It has a relation to the necessarily existent One and con- 39
troversy is only concerned with the nature of that relation. The relation of the temporal thing to him before, at the time of, and after, creation and when nothing at all had emerged, is all one. Why, then, did it come into existence, and why did He create, and what is the

[1] Nevertheless the assertions are repeated. I have omitted them.

[2] See p. 9.

meaning of creation and origination (*ibdāʿ*)? If you say He knew and willed its existence at that time it is replied that knowledge and will (*irāda*) are of universal application, so the relation of its existence to the universal will at that time in that form is the same as the relation of its existence at another time in another form.[1] Similarly with power (*qudra*). The divine attributes have no special application[2] so how can a special (divine) act be accounted for? It is here that some of the Mutakallimūn go wrong. The Karrāmiyya assert that temporal things such as volition and speech are in the divine essence,[3] and these designate the world by existence instead of non-existence. According to them the eternal will (*mashīʾa*) has a universal relation, and volition (*irāda*) a particular relation. They distinguish between production in time and the thing produced in time, and creation and the created. The Muʿtazila posit volitions in time which do not subsist in a substrate and which designate the world by existence, but they do not make the distinctions as to creation and created, &c. We will expose the futility of our adversaries' arguments and then indicate the plain meaning of bringing into being (*ījād*).

We say: It is agreed that the world is possible *per se*, needing one to tip the scale of existence against non-existence. Therefore, He who tips the scale of being must either do so inasmuch as He is an essence
40 (*dhāt*) or inasmuch as He is existence. Therefore, it could be argued (1) every essence and every existence could tip the scale of being, and (2) an infinite number of possible existents could originate, for everything is related to essence and existence in the same way: two absurdities. Either He tips the scale *qua* essence or existence by way of an attribute or by a modal relation (*ʿalā iʿtibār wa-wajh*). If He tips *qua* existence by way of an attribute the position is surrendered, and essential causation falls to the ground. If *qua* existence modally (*ʿalā wajh*) as our opponents say that He is necessarily existent *per se* and he only caused existence because He is necessary *per se*, He being a modal existence, that too is false, because necessarily existent *per se* is a negative term meaning 'His being is not derived from another' and we need not assume that that which is not derived from another confers existence on another. Similarly he who thinks, as our opponents do, that He (the maker of this world) is a knower, or an intelligence, or intelligent, need not think that He confers being on others because according to them 'intelligent' is a negative term meaning 'free from matter'; but it does not follow that His freedom from matter confers existence on something else, so essential causation fails from all sides, and it is clear that He (God) brought (the world) into being

[1] I.e. the theory that God willed it at a particular time implies ignorance of the nature of the divine will. [2] *khuṣūṣ*. [3] See *Al-Milal*, p. 81.

by way of an attribute. This attribute in respect of its essence is capable of conferring special characteristics and bringing into being universally. It is that which has made things as they are and not otherwise. Its relation to them and everything else is the same. Also it has a special mode (*wajh*) in relation to what happened as opposed to what did not.

We say that inasmuch as the Creator knew the existence of the world at the time it came into existence He willed its existence at that time. God's knowledge is universal in the sense that it is an 41
attribute by which He knows all that can be known. Intelligibles are infinite in the sense that God knows the world's existence, and the possibility of its existence before and after in every mode of logical possibility. God's will (*irāda*) is universal in the sense that it is an attribute which specifies everything that can be specified. Volitions (*murādāt*) are infinite in the sense that different ways of specifying are infinite; they are particular in that they[1] specify the object of God's knowledge with existence. God's power (*qudra*) is also universal because it is an attribute capable of bringing into existence without restriction, i.e. the production of everything that can possibly exist. It is also particular in that it produces what He knows and wishes to exist, for what is contrary to His knowledge cannot possibly exist or happen. So all the divine attributes are (*a*) universal in respect of the capacity of their existence and essence in relation to the infinite things that depend on them; (*b*) particular in their relation one to another. These attributes act in unison in conferring existence and cause no change in the Creator (*mūjid*). We cannot grasp this conception because we cannot create, and our attributes are not universal. Our knowledge, will, and power, are concerned with one object, and that not creatively. Our attributes cannot endure because they are accidents. Our minds and our senses demand a new cause for the production of a new thing. But could we embrace knowledge, will, and power, of universal and infinite relation, when 42
a specified time came for the production of a thing it would befall without alteration of our essence or a new thing or cause arising.

Our opponent urges this of the Active Intellect and its emanation, saying that its emanation is universal; it is the giver of forms, not dividing them nor specifying (in what object they shall reside). Then he postulates a kind of particularization in relation to the receivers and conditions which are generated, so that a 'preparation'[2] is brought about in the receivers. So the emanation is particularized by a particular receiver in a particular measure. The fact that an

[1] The reading of P., emending *bi'l-wujūd* for *bi'l-maujūd*, must be followed.
[2] See my article in *The Legacy of Islam*, p. 259.

emanation receives a special receptacle by way of a cause external to the emanator does not affect the universal character of the emanation so far as concerns its essence, despite the fact that essential causation according to our opponents is an essential emanation, a universal existence without particularization. From it only one emanates. From that one comes Intelligence, Soul, and Sphere; and from that Intelligence and Soul an Intelligence and Soul until the last Intelligence is reached, from which emanate the forms (which descend) upon the lower objects and end with the human soul.

We ask, Why confine objects in these essences if there is no particularization in emanation? The finitude of objects in number and place is the same as their finitude in beginning and time. If you say, Particularization with us means the receptivity of the bearers (of form) and the emanation gets its dimensions from them, we reply that
43 we are concerned with the origin of these bearers. Why are the heavens confined to seven or nine? Why four elements and so on? Why are these objects finite in number? Why should not these heavens be infinite as to place as their movements are as to time?

If you say, Logical demonstration forbids the assertion that the world is infinite as to place, We reply that that is precisely our position. Everything that you have said concerning the Divine Providence[1] which caused the order of existent things in the most perfect arrangement we predicate of the Eternal Will which decreed the particularization of things in order according to the knowledge of the Omniscient.[2] You have been driven from abstract existence to a particular necessity, and from necessity to a particular intellection (*taʿaqqul*) and thence to a particular providence. Then you say that these are relative or negative attributes which do not necessitate plurality or alteration in (God's) essence. What you call intellection we call eternal knowledge, and what you call providence we call eternal will. As with you providence results from knowledge, with us will is connected with the thing willed with the concurrence of knowledge. The only difference between the two schools is that they refer the Ideas of the Attributes to essence while the Mutakallimūn do not.

The opponents say that the order of procession from the Creator was thus: The first thing to proceed from the Creator was the First Intelligence. This caused another Intelligence and a soul and a body
44 which is the sphere of the spheres, and by means of each intelligence a successive intelligence and soul and sphere until the last sphere was

[1] This is the first mention of Divine Providence (*ʿināya*), so that it would seem either that the author is quoting from some other work; or, as is more probable, he is using notes of his lectures. He has not, however, given us the running comments of the lecturer.

[2] I owe the reference to *Sur*. 29. 9 to Professor Nicholson.

reached. This the Active Intelligence, which is the giver of forms in this world, rotates. By means of the heavenly intelligences and movements of the spheres, the elements came into being; by their means the compounds and lastly the human soul, because existence began from the noblest and descended by stages to the vilest, viz. matter; then it began from the vilest until it reached the noblest, viz. the reasonable human soul.

It may be said to them: Did these lower forms of existence, in the various shapes and species in which they are seen now, come into being in a moment or in order? If in a moment, then the order which they affirm (*var.* he called into existence) in the existence of things is false. If they happened in order one after the other, how can essential precedence between the first caused and the last caused be substantiated?

We ask, What is the temporal relation between the first and last thing caused if they are essentially timeless, albeit the human soul had a beginning? What, too, is the relation of the soul's beginning to the first intelligence, for if between them infinite souls had originated in infinite time, the infinite would be shut in between two limits, and that is absurd. If they were finite, their argument that phenomena are infinite is false; for if celestial movements were infinite, 45
terrestial objects would be infinite also, so the theory refutes itself.

They differ, too, about the order in the beginning of things. Some say the order was (prime) matter (*ʿunṣur*), intelligence, soul, body; others say intelligence, soul, matter (*hayyūlā* = ὕλη), the spheres, the elements (*ʿanāṣir*), the compounds.

Proclus argued that the Creator (*al-bāriʾ*) was essentially generous; the cause of the world's existence was His generosity; and His generosity was eternal. Therefore the world was eternal. He could not be generous at one time and ungenerous at another, for that would involve alteration in His essence. There could be no impediment in the way of the emanation of His generosity, for if there were, His generosity would not result from His essence, because an essential restraint would operate eternally, whereas generosity in the production of things has been established. And if the restraint came from an external source, that source would be the impelling force of the necessarily existent One who cannot be impelled to act or restrained from acting.

Further he said that the Creator (*al-ṣāniʿ*) must either have created eternally *in actu* or *in potentia*. If the former, then the created is caused eternally: if the latter, the potential cannot emerge into actual without external aid which must be other than the essence of the thing itself, so it follows that the Creator's essence must change. And that is false.[1]

[1] A comparison with the fuller text of this passage in the *Milal* will make the meaning plainer. I have inserted the variant readings in the footnotes to the text.

46 Again, he said, No (primal) cause can suffer movement and change, for it is only a cause in respect of its own essence not by way of (activity) received from another. If the cause is eternal essentially, so is the effect.

Answer. Why speak of God's generosity when it is admitted that it is not an essential attribute additional to His essence, but an active one? With you the attributes are either negations like *qadīm*, which is the denial of beginning; or relations (*iḍāfāt*) like *al-khāliq* the Creator, and *al-rāziq* the sustainer in our terminology, and the originator (*al-mubdi'*) and the first cause in yours. God has no attributes outside these two categories. Generosity belongs to the relative not to the negative class, so that there is no difference between the meaning of the Originator and the Generous, for both mean the doer. It is as though you said, 'He creates through His essence', which is the question in dispute.

The opponent says He does not create by His essence, and His activity is not eternal, which is the point at issue. You change the word activity to generosity and make it the proof of the argument. If generosity is the equivalent of activity and bringing into being, then when he says: There was a time when He was generous and there was a time when He was not generous, it is the same as his saying: There was a time when He created and a time when He did not create; and that is the point of the controversy.

47 The difficulty can be solved in two ways. First, operation is impossible before time was, not as regards the agent, but as regards the operation itself, inasmuch as its existence is inconceivable. Activity has a beginning; timeless eternity (*azal*) has not; therefore there can be no connexion between them. God is generous inasmuch as His generosity can be conceived. To say that an individual who comes into being in our time must always have existed because the Creator is essentially generous is to make oneself ridiculous. The timeless existence of a particular thing (*al-maujūd al-mu'ayyan*) is impossible, and the impossibility of a thing's existence is the impediment to the emanation of existence, but not so that the impediment can exercise impulsion or compulsion (of itself): on the contrary it is impossible *per se*. Similarly, if God had created things in order, or everything at once without any order, our opponents would say it was impossible; yet it would not militate against God's being generous. This resembles the doctrine of the Mutakallim that we may ascribe to God power over what can exist, but as to what cannot possibly exist you must not say that God has no power over it, but that the impossible *per se* is not capable of being willed (*ghair maqdūr*)[1] and so its existence is inconceivable.

[1] Or, not an object meet for the exercise of God's power.

This answer applies also to their assertion that if He was not a Creator and He became one, He was first a potential and then an actual Creator, and so his essence changed. We say that He was not eternally a Creator, because operation in eternity is impossible; and if a thing is essentially and in itself impossible it cannot be an object of God's power, and so it is not created. But if it is impossible for
some other reason which ceases to operate, then it becomes an object 48
of God's power and may be created. Eternal creation is impossible because eternity has no beginning and creation has. Union between them is impossible. . . .

With regard to the assertion that He is a cause essentially, the meaning of His being a cause is that He is an originator of the existence of something. It is impossible that the effect should exist together (timelessly) with the cause, for that would disrupt their relation. We deny their coexistence in time, for that would necessitate the existence of the (first) cause in time, subject to change, and that is impossible. The Creator's existence is essential and underived; the existence of the world is derived from Him, and the derivation must always precede in existence.

Secondly, we say: How do you know that God must be generous essentially? They reply: Because what He does is more perfect than what He does not do.

Reply. Suppose the contrary were true what would your answer be, for what you say is not a necessary proposition of a subject whose perfection is in itself and not in another? What God does is not done for a purpose (*gharḍ*) nor in order that He may receive praise, nor
for any reason involving a reciprocal relation. If an object's perfec- 49
tion were in itself, and another object's perfection were derived from something else, obviously the former would be superior to the latter. Now that which is defective unless it does something, is not perfect in its essence, but is defective and finds its perfection in something outside itself and cannot rightly be said to be necessarily existent in its essence.

What is the meaning of 'If He was not a Creator He became one and innovation resulted'? If it means that innovation occurred outside the divine essence it is admitted, but within the divine essence it is inadmissible; it is the point in dispute.

Ambiguity, too, underlies their saying 'He was a Creator potentially'. Potentiality (*quwwa*) can mean abstract preparedness (*istiʿdād*) or power (*qudra*). The former is not to be predicated of God, though the latter is admissible. Here is the point in dispute. But there is no need to postulate something to bring a thing from potentiality to actuality.

Proclus' saying that no cause can suffer movement or change, for it is only a cause in respect of its essence, is inadmissible; moreover, it is false on his own premisses in the case of the First Intelligence, for it does not suffer movement and change and it is not a cause in respect of its essence, but is the thing caused by the necessary existent one, and a cause in respect of its being necessary through him not *per se.* The same holds true of the separate intelligences.

50 [Shahrastānī]. The easiest and best way of proving the temporal origin of the world is as follows: we establish that human souls are finite in number, therefore human beings must be. From this it follows that things of composite nature are temporal and finite, and so are the circular movements which unite the elements. Thus the movements and the celestial movers must be temporal, and so the universe as a whole is of time.

We assert that an actually existent number, if it were actually infinite, would not be susceptible of plus or minus, for nothing can be bigger than an infinite quantity. The infinite cannot be doubled by the infinite. What is finite from one aspect is finite from all aspects. Now human souls are actually susceptible of increase and decrease. At the present day a certain number of human beings exist, each having a soul. If those souls are added to the souls which survive of past individuals the former will be less and the latter greater by the addition and so it will always be. The relation of the past to the total at any given present is the relation of the less to the more. Thus the infinite cannot actually exist.

It might be thought that things which come into being in sequence
51 are infinite in an unbroken line (lit. first before last and last after first) and that if they have no end they must needs have had no beginning. Though this opinion is intellectually a mistake the fancy often eyes it with approval. But if the supposition concerned infinite objects existing together instead of in sequence, actual not potential, they would have to be free from plus and minus as aforesaid, whereas they are not. Everything composed actually of units is subject to plus and minus, and therefore cannot be infinite.[1]

52 When we say that the infinite number is a subjectivity we mean that the mind is unable to conceive an end to it. Just as a pure number can be known without being tied to a thing counted, so the half and quarter can be known without reference to the infinite, but it is impossible to assert that infinite numbers exist, for everything existent is numbered and finite.[1] The universe had a beginning, and the supposition of a precedent non-existence is mere fancy like the supposition of a vacuum beyond the universe in which the universe

[1] I have passed over the repetition of arguments which have been advanced before.

may reside. In fact the vacuum is the spatial counterpart of the supposition of temporal non-existence.

Questions as to whether there are worlds infinite beyond this one are ridiculous. It might as well be asked if this world were preceded by an infinite number of worlds. Before the world there existed 53
naught but the Producer of its existence, its Originator, prior in creation and origination, not prior in essential causation or time. He is *above* the world in origination and unimpeded action, not in essential and local 'aboveness'.

CHAPTER II

THAT ALL THINGS THAT EXIST HAD A BEGINNING THROUGH GOD'S 54
ORIGINATION. HEREIN IS A REFUTATION OF THE DOCTRINES OF THE MU'TAZILA, DUALISTS, AND NATURAL PHILOSOPHERS, AND A PROOF OF *KASB*, AND THE DIFFERENCE BETWEEN *KASB* AND *ĪJĀD* AND *KHALQ*.

ALL theists agree that it is God that gives existence to all existent things.[1] He is the sole Creator. The philosophers asserted the possibility of a thing proceeding from (a source) other than God, with the condition that the existence of that other rests on the existence of something else which goes back to the necessarily existent. They differ as to whether more than one can proceed from it, though most of them say No. Then they differ about that one. Some said it is intelligence; others it is prime matter, then intelligence. They differ as to what proceeds from the first caused. Some say it is soul; others say it is another intelligence and a soul and a sphere, i.e. body; and 55
thus there proceeds from every intelligence an intelligence until that Active Intelligence which turns the sphere of the moon, the giver of forms.

Some of the older philosophers asserted the possibility of a plural thing proceeding from the necessary existent. I have written about these theories in my *Milal*. . . .

The Mu'tazila Qadarites assert that man's will has an influence in bringing into existence and origination in movement and quiescence. . . .

The philosophers agree with us that no body or bodily faculty can 56
originate a body; and the Majūs agree with us that darkness cannot have originated through the originating action of light. The Mu'tazila

[1] From now onwards I have translated much more freely, summarizing the arguments as much as possible.

agree with us that man's power is inadequate to originate bodies, colours, &c., but they differ as to the secondary causes (*mutawalladāt*).

I have appended this question to the discussion about the temporary origin of the world because when it has been proved that the contingent rests on the giver of existence and that *ījād* means giving existence, then everything is contingent resting on God's *ījād* in respect of its existence. Intermediaries are preparatory dispositions, not causes.

'Against the philosophers we argue that everything which exists through something else is contingent in respect of essence; if it were able to produce anything it would produce it in respect of its existing through another, or in respect of its being contingent in its essence, or in both respects at the same time. But it cannot produce in respect of its being existent through another except in conjunction with its essence, seeing that the essence of one is not free from the essence of the other, and its existence cannot escape from its reality, which is
57 contingent existence. The nature of contingency is privative, so that if it had influence on existence the influence would be in conjunction with privation—which is absurd.'

'I have drawn this proof from the doctrine of the philosophers on the subject of body, i.e. that it cannot influence body by way of bringing into being. Body is composed of matter and form, so that if it exerted influence it would be in conjunction with matter; and matter has a privative nature, so that it is impossible that it should bring anything into existence. The body also cannot possibly bring into existence. Thus contingent existence is as matter, and the soul of existence is as form. Just as body exercises no influence in respect of its form except in conjunction with matter, so that which exists through another—the contingent—exercises no influence in respect of its existence except in conjunction with contingent existence. Therefore there is no real bringer into existence except[1] the necessary existent.' . . .

Objection. The contingent merely causes, or brings into being, something else by virtue of the relationship of its existence through another. Simply regard it as existent without reference to contingency and non-existence, because contingency has vanished with the coming of being and necessity has come in the place of contingency, and we can ignore contingency altogether. Thus influence is not exercised in conjunction with contingency.

Answer. But if existence *qua* existence can exercise influence without regard to contingency and possibility, then let the existence of

[1] I omit *bi-wujūd*. If it is to be retained, it would be best to read *mūjad* instead of *mūjid*.

everything exercise influence so that intellect has no better claim to causation than soul or body, and body influences body in respect of its form. For existence does not differ in so far as it is existence.

If it be argued that the First Intelligence only causes something 58
else in virtue of relationships (*iʿtibārat*) of its essence. In respect of its existence through the necessary existent it causes an intelligence or soul, and in respect of the potentiality in its essence it causes a body, i.e. form and matter: your attempt to shun the aspect of contingency is vain, because the aspect of necessity is connected with the existence of intelligence and soul, and the aspect of contingency is connected with the existence of form and matter. We have laboured this point because only one can proceed from the One. If two so proceeded they would come from two different aspects (*jihataini*).[1] If it could be established that the One had two aspects, plurality in His essence would result.

Answer. If the (First) Intelligence caused (another) Intelligence or soul inasmuch as it was necessary through another, the (first) body would have caused (another) body or a soul inasmuch as it was necessary through another; for the notion of necessity through another does not differ. . . . The fact that the body is material does not make production impossible in that it is necessary through another. . . . On this ground you ought to argue that a body can produce a body or a
bodily form. But you agree that that is impossible. 59

We say: Here are four correlatives: intelligence, soul, sphere, and matter, which are substances differing in their real natures, which require four other correlatives differing in nature. On you is the onus of asserting that the First Caused had these real natures, for otherwise it would follow that a plurality should have proceeded from one thing which to you is absurd. Also you must prove that these correlative relationships are not (mere) relations and negations. For if plurality of relations and negations does not cause plurality in essence, does it cause things at all? For the necessary's existence is one in every respect, not becoming plural in relations or negations, and the negative and relative attributes do not cause pluralities: if they did, everything would be in the same relation to the necessary existent, without intermediaries, which according to you is absurd. Thus they are on the horns of a dilemma. If they assert that the First Caused had different causal qualities they contradict their dogma 'only one can proceed from one': and if they say these qualities are relative or negative they are compelled to postulate plural correlatives in the necessary existent, which also contradicts their tenets.

[1] A difficult word to render. Aspects implying different '*sides*' are meant, not mere view-points. On the argument generally see *The Legacy of Islam*, p. 257 f.

60 'If a correlative contains different species, so must its counterpart, so really you are positing two things: its being necessary through another, and its being possible in its essence. Its being necessary through another caused intelligence and soul, and its being possible in essence caused form and matter. Thus you have posited the procession of two self-subsistent substances from one thing (*wajh*). Here is another contradiction.'

The shrewdest of them endeavour to avoid the difficulty by accounting for plurality in the First Intelligence by the relationship of its essence, not by what it derived from another, on the ground that contingency is essential to it, not from another, while its existence is not essential but from another, and so plurality was not derived from the necessary existent.

Upon my life when Intelligence appeared there appeared ready made four relations: its being necessary through another, its being intelligence, its being one in essence, and its being contingent in essence! Inasmuch as it was intelligence it caused intelligence, *qua* existence through the necessary existent it caused soul, inasmuch as it was one it caused form, and inasmuch as it was contingent it caused matter. Since these relationships were different realities, substances of different species were caused. . . . But this is mere sophistry.'

61 Here follows the argument that the necessary existent cannot be freed from the relations which are postulated of the first caused. The philosophers explain the plurality of forms as due to the number of receivers or carriers, though the forms are said to emanate from the Active Intelligence, whose qualities do not multiply with the infinite variety of forms. They ought to apply the same reasoning to the necessary existent as to the Active Intelligence.

62 They say that intelligence as applied to the First Intelligence is a negative predication; but how can a negation have any relation to the existence of an intellectual substance (*jauhar*)? And why not include form and the categories as well as matter in the negations, and then everything would be in the same relation to the necessary existent?

Again, why is existence through another more fitting to cause soul than being free from matter? If you transposed the terms and made necessity through another the cause of intelligence, and freedom from matter the cause of soul, what nonsense would result!

'You assert four relationships of the First Intelligence who is yet one in essence, and you say that his oneness caused soul and body.
63 Then what is derived from the Creator[1] and what has he of his own essence? If he only has potentiality[2] of existence from his own

[1] The necessary existent is identified with Allah.

[2] *Imkān* sometimes means contingency and sometimes potentiality.

essence then three relationships are left. If these are derived from the First they demand three correlatives, the necessary existent being one in every respect; while if they are of his own essence, i.e. necessary accompaniments (*lawāzim*) of his essence (of the First Intelligence) your assertion that that which he has of his essence is only potentiality is contradicted. Potentiality can only be related to matter because the nature of matter is privative. Matter is capable of receiving form, and potentiality has a similar nature because it is capable of receiving existence. So form is left without a cause.

'It is astonishing that body, composed of matter and form, cannot cause its like; and something whose existence is through another and is in itself potential should cause intellectual substances different in species and should be unable to participate in matter notwithstanding that potentiality exists only in the mind, while matter has existence in the external world! From these objections it can be realized that there is no necessity for the intermediate agents which have been postulated as the cause of things.'

Here follows a criticism of the arbitrary assignment of four relations to the First Intelligence. Why did not the series continue to 64
multiply by four? Why only nine intelligences and four elements? How are the unceasing movements of the stars and the change and flux of the sub-lunar world to be explained? The vast scheme of the universe will not fit into their plan and can only lead to belief in an omniscient omnipotent Creator. The foregoing is sufficient to refute the philosophers who follow Aristotle.

The Majūs are concerned with two questions: the cause of the 65
mingling of light and darkness and the way to free one from the other. Some say: Light thought an evil thought and darkness came into being adhering to particles of light; thus darkness had a temporal origin.

It was objected that if light was pure good, what was the cause of 66
the evil thought? If it happened in itself, why did not darkness happen in itself? If it happened in light, then how did light originate the root of evil and source of corruption? If all the world's corruption is to be attributed to darkness and darkness to thought, then thought is the source of evil and corruption.

It is remarkable that they shrank from attributing individual evil to light though they had to attribute universal evil to it.

To those who hold the pre-existence of darkness it is sufficient to say that two absolutely contradictory things in nature cannot be mixed save by force: if their essences could be mixed, their contradictoriness would have ceased. Further, darkness must either be, or not be, a real thing. If its existence is real, it is the equal of light in existence, and distinction between them must be denied in all respects.[1] Similarly, if it is its equal in pre-existence and oneness, it is *qua* existence good. On the other hand, if it is not a real thing, it cannot be pre-existent nor can it form an opposite[2] to its contrary. And how can the existence of the world result from a mingling of it (with light)?[3]

67 Again: If the darkness is pre-existent the origin of the world is a mixture; if the mixture is good, then good has resulted from evil: if evil, then vice versa. If the mixture was good, the freedom from mixture would be evil because it is its opposite: if it was evil vice versa. So whichever view is taken either good is the source of evil or evil is the source of good!

The mingling of two simple substances would produce one nature, whereas the world contains different species and individuals which could not possibly come from a mixture of two simple things.

In dealing with the Muʿtazila we will first mention the way in which the orthodox attribute everything to God's creative power.

1. The phenomenal world contains clear indications of the wisdom
68 of its architect; and since the order of nature manifestly comes from a perfect agent it must be the work of the wisdom of that agent. Man's knowledge is never entirely in line with what man does: it is general not detailed. The operation of (natural) order indicates that the agent is other than he, and one whose knowledge is all embracing. Such was al-Ashʿarī's system as expounded in his books, and applied to the actions of the ignorant.[4]

This argument, however, is not confined to the ignorant but applies also to the knower (*ʿālim*); for his knowledge does not fully encompass his action. Just as it is impossible to initiate and invent in complete ignorance and unawareness of the thing to be initiated so it is impossible where any unawareness is present; cf. *Sur*. 67.14.

Objection. This argument does not demonstrate the impossibility of the origin of action by the will of man. For man's complete comprehension of an action is not impossible, and if the connexion of man's knowledge with an action is conceived as from all aspects you
69 must admit the possibility of an act through man's will from all aspects, because the intelligent and perfect ordering it displays is proof of the agent's knowledge. But according to you this is inadmissible, so your inference that man's knowledge is to be denied is

[1] *Sc.* inasmuch as both are 'things'.
[2] The Berlin MS. has 'equal'.
[3] Repetitions have been omitted.
[4] *al-ghāfil*, he who does not know fully what he does: 'unawareness' would seem to be a mental state midway between knowledge and ignorance. However the glossator of al-Sanūsī's *Tauḥīd* defines it as 'complete absence of knowledge about a thing'.

vain. The power by which knowledge is connected with an action must be created by man. With us complete knowledge about an action is not a condition; but knowledge of the root of its existence is a condition of (man's) being an agent and the one does not destroy the other.[1]

Answer. Our object was not to demonstrate the impossibility of an act through man's will, but to deny that the creature was the creator of his actions for which he will be rewarded and punished. If he were such a creator, the excellence of his work would indicate his knowledge: but it does not. He is not a creator because, if he were, he would know what he created from every aspect: but he does not, so he is not a creator. . . .

Knowledge of action is (*a*) necessary (*ḍarūrī*); (*b*) reasoned (*naẓarī*). 70
Sometimes more and more acquired knowledge is necessary so that an infinite chain of discovery and reasoning would be required to attain a required operation.

Some of the philosophers thought that production came from knowledge, so that if man knew the manifold aspects of operation, universal and particular, time, place, &c., he could produce and create. Thence they argued that the Creator's knowledge of his essence is the origin of the existence of the first act. They distinguished between active and passive knowledge. Man has need of will and instruments, &c., because his knowledge is passive. Therefore the theologians all agree that knowledge follows the knowable and is related to it as it is: it (knowledge) does not acquire it (the knowable) as an attribute and it (knowledge) does not acquire an attribute from it (the knowable).

2. A second way of demonstrating the impossibility of man's power being capable of giving existence. If man's power were capable of bringing anything into existence, it could produce anything consisting of substance and accident, because existence embraces all
existent things. Substance is not superior to accident because it 71
exists, but because it is self-subsistent, &c. Our opponents maintain that self-subsistence, spatial content, &c., are attributes which follow origination (*ḥudūth*) and are not indications of power. As for the terms the thing-ness, individuality, substantiality, the accidental, they are in their opinion names of species latent in non-existence,[2] and are not indications of power. . . .

But the same inability to produce things is found in different persons in different degrees, so that Zaid can move what ʿAmr cannot.

[1] I take this to mean that knowledge of all aspects and consequences of an act is not a necessary condition of man's free will, but that he must consciously perform an act if it is to fall within his *qudra*.

[2] *thābita fi'l-ʿadam*.

Our opponents say that as power[1] itself embraces all man's powers they are equal in capability.[2] Similarly, existence itself embraces all existent things so that they must necessarily be equal in receiving capability; but it can be admitted that capability does not follow power itself, but it differs in relation to different individuals.

But (say we) capability of power must either be universal and not
72 differ in relation to different objects as aforesaid, or be particular; and there is no proof of the particularization of one object as opposed to another: the course of nature as we know it shows no anomaly in man's power.

Objection. You yourselves have admitted that man's power is connected with some objects and not with others, and you call the connexion (*taʿalluq*) 'acquisition' (*kasb*). The particularization you mention in the connexion and 'acquisition' we attribute to particularization in production (*ījād*). It is extraordinary that you should deny man's power when you assert his connexion (with an act). Why don't you admit the possible universality of this connexion so that it can apply to everything, substance or accident? For if you particularize the connexion while denying (its) influence, do not think it strange if we particularize the connexion while asserting (its) influence.

Reply. We assert connexion between man's power and the object of it, but we are not committed to a theory that *taʿalluq* is of universal application since we do not ascribe to it influence in producing or originating anything as you do and are bound to do. Our master al-Ashʿarī denied that man's power had any capability in reference
73 to existence or any attribute of existence. Al-Bāqillānī (d. 403) did allow it a certain influence, as we shall explain; but he kept it clear of existence and thus avoided its universal application. He pointed out the necessary difference between voluntary and involuntary movement, e.g. sneezing, a difference which does not reside in the movements themselves. One is within one's power and is willed; the other is not. Therefore, either it must be said that power is connected with one of them with a connexion of knowledge without any influence at all—which would be equivalent to denying the difference between voluntary and involuntary, because to deny influence is the same as to deny connexion so far as the movements themselves are concerned and we only find a difference in something additional to their existence and the states[3] of their existence. Or it must be said that power is connected with one of them with an influence. The

[1] Reading *ḥaqīqatu'l-qudra* to correspond with *ḥaqīqatu'l-wujūd*.

[2] Capability is perhaps too strong: *salāḥiyya* means suitability, fitness, 'convenience'.

[3] See further, Chapter VI.

influence must either be referred to existence and coming into being or to a quality of existence. The first is wrong, because if it could affect one thing it could affect everything and so it is clear that the influence is another quality which is a state additional to existence.

He said that according to our opponent God's powerfulness only exercised influence in a state, viz. existence, because all the general and special qualities, substantial, accidental and the like, are relegated by him to non-existence so that only one state 'coming into being' (*ḥudūth*) is left. 'Grant me, then, one state in reference to man's 74
power,' said he. His companions replied that he had introduced a term unknown in name or meaning. Never mind, said he, if I cannot find a special name for my term. If aspects and relationships can be asserted of one act and all of them attributed to one quality affecting it, like 'happening'[1] it is evidence of power and the choice between alternatives; for it shows that will and knowledge have been present. Our opponent says that the categories good and bad, commanded and forbidden, are qualities added to existence, some essential to the act, others due to will, just as the qualities which follow coming into existence like substance being susceptible of accidents. Now if he can postulate qualities which are states and relationships additional to existence to which 'powerfulness' does not attach, they being intelligible, why cannot I postulate an intelligible influence to man's power? Take movement as an example. It is the name of a genus embracing species and kind or the name of a species with distinct peculiarities. Movements are of various kinds, e.g. writing, speech, handicraft; and each kind has subdivisions. The fact that handicraft 75
and writing are distinct from each other is due to a state in each movement not to the movement itself. Similarly with voluntary and involuntary movement. So that state can be attributed to the creature as an acquisition[2] and action (*kasban wafiʿlan*). . . . If a divine command is attached to the act and it happens accordingly, it is called 'service' and 'obedience'. If a prohibition, the contrary; and the aspect (*wajh*) is the commandment which earns reward or punishment. Our opponent admits that action is rewarded because it is good or bad not because it is something that exists. Goodness and badness are states additional to action and existence.

Here the Qāḍī was nearer the just view, for he (the opponent) attributed to the creature those acts for which he would not be rewarded or punished, while he theoretically requited that which lies outside men's power. But the Qāḍī specified (*a*) what it is that is not requited and posited it as God's act and (*b*) what is man's act and acquisition and is requited.

[1] Apparently he uses *wuqūʿ* as synonymous with *ḥudūth*.
[2] *V.s.*

The Qāḍī was not really at variance with his colleagues. Act has intellectual aspects and relationships of a general and specific character . . . but in itself it is not made up of these aspects, but they are all
76 of them derived from the agent. Itself it is but potential. Its existence is derived from its producer generally. If it is writing it is derived from its writer in a particular aspect. The two ways can be distinguished intellectually but not by the senses: one is production and initiation in a general sense; the other is acquisition and action —the special relation to the quality. The action with reference to its existence needs one to bring it into existence and it also needs a writer and a speaker if the act is writing or speech. The producer's essence or attribute is not altered when the produced comes into existence: he knows all the aspects of the act. But he who acquires (the power to act) suffers change of essence and attribute when the acquisition takes place; his knowledge does not embrace all the aspects (*jihāt*) of the act.

The eternal power is too exalted to possess a capacity confined to special aspects of (man's) actions, while man's power is too lowly to possess a capacity embracing all aspects of action. . . . Man's special and varying capacity is confined to certain objects whereas the capacity of God's power is one and unvarying, with one connexion,
77 namely existence. You must not confine God's capacity within man's limitations nor ascribe God's perfection to man's capacity. You must not say of the giver of existence He is the writer, speaker, &c., nor of the one who acquires power he is the giver of existence, the Creator, &c.

The difference between creation (*khalq*) and acquisition (*kasb*) is that creation is that which is brought into existence in such a way that the producer is unaffected by the act which he acquires as a quality and does not acquire a quality from it and he knows every aspect of his action. Acquisition is that which is willed by man's will; (or, within man's power). Man is affected by his acquisition. He acquires it as a quality and acquires a quality from it. He only knows one aspect of what he does.

This confirms what al-Ustādh[1] said, namely that every act which
78 comes about by co-operation is an acquisition to the one who asks for help. This actually takes place when the individual asserts that he was not alone in his act. This is what Abū Bakr meant when he said that acquisition means that power is connected with it in one respect but not in all respects; but creation is the originating of the thing itself and its production from non-existence. There is therefore no difference between them and the Qāḍī, except that what they

[1] I.e. Abū Isḥāq al-Isfarā'inī.

called aspect (*wajh*) and relationship (*iʿtibār*) he called quality and state.

Al-Ashʿarī held that man's power had no influence at all, other than the creature's belief that his action was facilitated by sound limbs and capacity and power, all of which come from God.

Al-Juwainī went too far in asserting that man could confer existence, though he did not say that in so doing man was independent of an antecedent chain of causes which ended in the Creator. He only followed the philosophers in their doctrine of a causal chain and the influence of celestial intermediaries, in an endeavour to avoid the folly of absolute determination (*jabr*). Of all forms of this doctrine the compulsion of an infinite chain of causes is the worst. For all matter is prepared for a special form: all the forms emanate from the Giver of form and assume matter by compulsion, so that choice 79
and power over alternatives is compulsion. Men's acts are the result of all-powerful causes and are requited by absolute determination. Everything is the result of a prevenient cause. But intermediaries only prepare; they do not create; their nature is contingent.

The Muʿtazila asserted that a man feels intuitively that a thing happens or does not happen according to his will. He can move or not move. Unless he had the power to produce what he wanted, this feeling would be inexplicable. You agree with us when you distinguish between voluntary and involuntary movements. Now either the difference resides in movements themselves in that they happen one by the power of the agent and the other by another agent's power, or in a quality in the agent who has power over one and not over the other. If he has power over it, then he must influence what he wills, and the influence must be in existence, because the act takes place in existence, not in another quality. Your predication of *kasb* is un- 80
intelligible: either it is an existent something or not. If it is something, then you have admitted that man does exercise influence in existence; if it is not something, it is nothing! They asserted that to posit power without influence was to deny power. Its connexion with its object was like that of knowledge with the knowable.

Reply. Here we flatly contradict your appeal to intuitive feeling. Involuntary acts are not due to man's impulsion, yet according to you he brings them into existence. Many accidents, like the colours which come through dyeing, are due to man's impulsion, yet according to you he does not bring them into existence.

We agree that man is conscious of the difference between the 81
voluntary and involuntary, but as we have explained this is due to a quality in the subject or to a condition of the movement. But the senses are not conscious of bringing anything into existence. We

have found another source for the two movements and states other than 'existence'. Is it not the case that those of your party who say that the non-existent is a thing do not refer the difference to the accidental and the power of movement in that they are within man's power, for they are internal[1] qualities latent in non-existence, nor to the need of a substrate, for they are qualities which follow existence in time. Therefore we do not refer them to existence for they are evidence of the eternal will, but rather to that which you regard as worthy of reward and punishment. . . . A man does not feel the impulse to bring something into being, but rather the impulse to stand or sit and so on. These characteristics of actions are outside and distinct from existence. You can call them aspects and relationships if you like. . . .

82 The connexion (*taʿalluq*) of God's power is universal, whereas man's power is particular. The act is decreed by God before man's power is brought into contact with it. Thus a dual nature is latent in every action—the potential and the actual production. The connexion of man's power does not destroy these two natures. Existence—indifferent as it is to good or bad—is to be attributed to God as its Creator; the taking over (*kasb*) of the act whether good or evil is to be related to man. There is no question of two creators, but rather of two agents working from different aspects, or of two distinct decrees which must be referred to their proper and distinct authors.

We differ from you entirely when you assert that man's actions are within his power, because most of them are not and result in frustrating his intention, e.g. moving one's finger in a straight line without
83 deviating to right or left or hitting a target. Man's power falls short of the impulse which impels him to action. Some other source must be sought.

The second point on which they relied in asserting that man had power over his actions was the relevance of the sacred law. Unless man was an independent agent then commandments were mere folly and even contradictory. Commandments demand something which is possible from mankind. If action is impossible they are absurd and
84 so are the rewards and punishments in the law. In fact the commandments might as well be addressed to fools as to wise men!

Apart from any question of sacred law it is our custom to lay commands and prohibitions on one another and to attribute good and evil to deliberate choice, rewarding one and punishing the other. If any sophist would dispute this, let him submit to insult and blows.

[1] This I take to be the meaning of *ṣifāt nafsiyya thābita fī 'lʿadam*. Fanārī on Ījī iv. 75. 7 (quoted by Horten) says that such a quality cannot be understood by analogy with anything else.

If he feels resentment and physical pain and is moved to retaliate he thereby admits that he has felt something, otherwise why be angry and attribute (responsible) action to his assailant! If he proceeds to retaliate he admits that he has judged the act to be worthy of punishment and recompense. . . .

Reply. We do not admit the validity of your argument as to the 85
relevance of law, because the (bringing into) existence which you claim as man's prerogative is the point in dispute. For existence *qua* existence is neither good nor bad, commanded nor forbidden. Moreover, the law knows other categories, e.g. what must and what must not be done. If you say that what is commanded is an aspect of existence deserving praise or blame we agree, but that aspect cannot be brought under man's power because, according to you, it is a quality attaching to the act after it has been performed. Therefore the thing commanded is not subordinate to man's power.

If it be said that that which is decreed is the existence of the act and that the aspect which is obligatory on man is not that which is commanded, we reply that you have not grappled with the difficulty. . . .

What is the difference, pray, between a commandment not within 86
the power of the creature nor of any one else, and one not within the power of the creature from the aspect of what has been commanded, and within another's power from the point of view of what has not been commanded?

The first proposition resembles absolute predestination. Such people are Qadarites in that they say origin and existence are within the power of the creature; and Jabrites in that they say that the thing the creature is commanded to do is not within his power to 'acquire' or to do.—i.e. 'Blind in whichever eye you like', as the saying runs! . . .

The law attains its objects by punishment and reward according to a person's power. If a man is paid to dye clothes white and he returns them black he is punished. The subject of the divine law is that which is within his power. . . .

We have explained that the influence which man's power exerts 87
is an aspect (*wajh*) or condition of the act similar to that which you ascribe to the Almighty will. Does the law say 'bring (or don't bring) into existence' or does it say 'worship God and associate nought with Him'? The aspect of worship which is a specific designation of action becomes worship by command . . . related to man's power. Why should you not accept another relation (*iḍāfa*) in which we believe, which is similar to what you believe? . . .

We differ in that we say that existence is something that 'is followed', fundamental. It is an expression for essence (*dhāt*) and the thing itself (*ʿain*) and we relate it with all its qualities to God; while to the creature we attribute what cannot be related to God. Thus it cannot be said 'God fasted', 'God prayed', and so on. His qualities are unchanged by his actions, and nothing in creation is outside his knowledge. Man on the contrary acquires names from all his actions and his essence changes through his acts and he does not understand all his acts. This is what al-Isfarā'inī meant when he said: Man acts with a helper. God[1] acts without a helper.

88 As for al-Ashʿarī, he denied that man's power had any influence. Consequently the answer to these arguments is difficult. However, he did allow a certain facility and ability (*tamakkun*) which a man feels himself to possess, namely soundness of body and a belief in the course of nature. Whenever a man resolves to do a thing God creates for him power and capacity commensurate with that act which he originates in him, and the man is described with the epithet proper to the character of the action. . . .

Further, the same authority that imposes commands contains prayers for divine help; cf. *Sur.* 1. If man were able to fulfil the law by his own power he would not have to ask God's help. Opponents say that the words 'God favours whom He will in guiding them'[2] refer to the creation of man's power which can choose between alternatives; but this view destroys the doctrine of grace and guidance; cf. *Sur.* 12. 14.

What makes this doctrine just is man's feeling that he needs a
89 helper although he feels capable of the act. He is conscious of a lack of independence in all that he does or does not do. He can speculate but not arrive at knowledge: he can move his members, but if he wished to do so without employing the connecting muscles he could not. Yet our opponents say man's power can choose alternatives and man is independent in producing and initiating action. God's share in man's action is the creation of this power in man.

The truth lies in admitting ability (*al-tamakkun*), facility (*al-taʿattī*) and capacity (*al-istiṭāʿa*) for the act, so far as they can rightly be related to the creature in a way which corresponds with his power and capacity. At the same time man's poverty of resource (*iftiqār*) and need of external help must be asserted, while it must be denied that he has independence or self-determination. . . .

[1] The reading of B. and P., 'Man is an agent; God is only called an agent' (*bi-maʿna* for *bi-muʿīn*), is attractive; but O. is supported by Shahrastānī's concluding peroration on p. 89.

[2] *Sur.* 17. 39.

CHAPTER III 90

THE DIVINE UNITY

OUR school maintains that the One means that which is not susceptible of division. His essence cannot be divided nor accept associate. The Creator is one in His Essence without division, and one in His Attributes without a like. . . .

The philosophers asserted that we could not speak of parts of quantity or definition within the Necessary Existent and that no 'parts' actually existed. He was inconceivable except as one in every respect, and there could not be two objects both necessary *per se*. 91
Consequently they denied the attributes or, if they spoke of them, it was in a different sense. No sect really believes in two gods. . . .

A proof that two gods could not exist: suppose one wished to move 92
an object and the other wished it to stay where it was. Then either both would succeed and the object would move and rest at the same time! or, both would fail and divine impotence would be manifest; or one would succeed and the other fail, so that the latter could not be a god. On the other hand, suppose they agreed to exercise power and will in a certain act: either they would be associated in the act of production—which is one event[1] in which only one can act—or one would act and the other would not.

Again, either they must have similar or different essential attri- 93
butes. If they were different, only one could have divine attributes. On the other hand, if they were the same, the one would not differ from the other in reality and characteristics, for their reality would be one, but in conditions (*lawāzim*) additional to reality like subject, place, and time, all of which destroy the idea of divinity.[2]

One black man is not different from another in his blackness but as a different subject of blackness or different in time. Thus it can be seen that mutual resemblance within the godhead is inconceivable.

Again, the one who tipped the scale from potential to actual being must have been independent or he was no god. He wished to designate 94
with being when he tipped the scale. If another shared in the act, then the first lost his independence. On the other hand, if the second god did not participate in creation he was deficient in power and no god. His will would be mere desire and wish.

Objection. Your hypothesis of one god willing an object to move

[1] *qaḍiyya*; or proposition.

[2] The argument, as the example which follows shows, is that if the two *ex hypothesi* gods were really one and the same there would be no ground for asserting that they were two. Consequently the idea of a *mahall* must be introduced together with time and place in which difference can be exhibited.

while the other wills it to stand still is inconceivable, because will follows knowledge and knowledge follows the knowable. Therefore if the knowable is movement it follows of necessity that the thing willed is movement. The supposition of contradiction in knowledge is inconceivable and consequently in will also. Now as the foundation of the argument from mutual opposition within the godhead rests on the positing, or rather supposition of, a real contradiction and that is impossible, it is folly to uphold the argument.

The Schoolmen[1] say that movement and rest are naturally possible[2]
95 and if power is adequate and the supposition of contradiction in will is intellectually conceivable, we treat the supposition as if it were established. Fact and supposition are the same so far as impossibility is concerned, e.g. the supposition of a colour or other accident subsisting in the essence of God takes the place of demonstration.[3] Knowledge does not remove the possible from the category (*qaḍiyya*) of the possible for the contrary of the known is a possibly existent genus.

For my part, I say, If *A* knew that the object would move by his will and power would *B* know that it would move by *his* will and power or by some one else's? If *A* knew it as something existent through his will and power, then *B*'s knowledge would be ignorance; and vice versa *B*'s knowledge would be dependent on the act of *A*. The supposition that the god *A* willed and had power over the act of *B* is impossible because the very notion of will is specifying (*takhṣīṣ*) and of power giving existence and origination, and if they depend on the activity of another they cease to retain their specific reality. . . . Therefore the meaning of the operation (*fā'iliyya*) of God is that when He knows the existence of a thing at a particular time He wills it according to His knowledge and gives it being by His power according to His will without any alteration of his essence or attributes. It could be said with some plausibility that its creation necessarily resulted, but we do not use the term *necessary* because we wish to avoid all appearance of asserting essential causation which would rob the Deity of perfection.

We only know the contingent by a necessary intellectual proposi-
96 tion. We know the dependence of all things on an omniscient and omnipotent God by virtue of the need of the contingent. If we suppose that two gods are actually perfect in power, self-determination, and creation, and equality in essential and operative attributes so that each is a producer by his own power, will, and knowledge, mutual opposition in operation must ensue. But if one submits to the other

[1] Lit. The Companions (*al-aṣḥāb*).

[2] The crucial words 'at the same time' are omitted, though no doubt the disputants intend them to be understood.

[3] *taḥqīq*.

their relation is that of slave and god. On the other hand, if each is independent within his own sphere, both have need of a god perfect in all respects.

Therefore the idea of two completely independent creators[1] is intellectually inconceivable. The same is true of dual potentates, knowers, and willers. Nor can there be two beings equal in all respects without one being distinguished from the other in reference to this or that, or place or time, or in a special operation or anything which indicates a different origin or scope. Therefore we maintain that the existence of the One is proved by (His) acts. The same objection against three or more gods holds.

Now the works of the creation point to the existence of one Creator, 97
and if a second be supposed there must either be specific proof of his existence or it must be permissible to assert that just as there is no proof of his existence, so there is no proof against it. If there were proof that another omniscient had created another world that would lead to impotence in the two gods as has been explained. . . .

Again, if there are more gods than one, they must be confined to a known number, so a power that so confined them is necessitated. For quantity in number is the same as quantity in space which requires a determinant. But if they were not confined to a known number, an infinite number (of gods) confined in existence without co-ordination would be necessitated and this is ridiculous. In fine, to assert the possibility of the existence of a thing of which there is no proof is the mere exercise of supposition; a logical possibility is not a god.

Distinguish carefully between the assumption of the absurd in word or hypothesis and the assertion that it is possible logically or in fact (*ʿaqdan*). The aforesaid assumption in books is a mere verbal hypothesis of the impossible which cannot be refuted by reason. 98

Objection. We find good and evil, order and disorder, in the universe. The existence of universal good points to one who wills it, and the existence of evil points to another will. Just as you cannot find a person willing good and evil in a specific action, so it is impossible to say that one God wills good and evil absolutely. Thus direct opposition in operation points to two opposing agents. As you have inferred that if another God were with Allah 'Heaven and earth would fall into disorder',[2] we for our part infer the existence of two gods from the patent disorder that actually does exist.

The Answer of the Mutakallimūn.[3] Existence itself is either entirely good or neither good nor evil. The latter are correlatives. A thing may be good in relation to one thing and evil in relation to another.

[1] Var. 'objects'.

[2] *Sur.* 73. 23.

[3] I omit the reiteration of the argument of *imkān*.

99 Good and evil exist in reference to positive and negative commandments. This, too, is our answer to the Mu'tazilites who say that if God wills evil He must be evil. Evil is only related to Him in that it exists, and existence *qua* existence is not evil. He wills a thing in the sense that something is designated by existence and not non-existence by way of an attribute and with certain possibilities and not others. But God does not will evil in reality.

Our answer to the Dualists. Good and evil are found separate and also mingled. The world of the angels is the world of pure goodness, and the world of unmixed evil is the world of the devils. The world of men is the world of mingled good and evil. So why have you not posited a third (god) to whom the mingling can be attributed? . . .

100 *The answer of the Theological Philosophers.*[1] If we suppose two necessary existent gods, one would have to have a specific difference so that necessary existence would be the genus of which each would be a species. The necessary-existent can only be One. His existence is His necessity, and His necessity His reality, and His reality His Oneness, and His Oneness His peculiar property and uniqueness[2] without distinguishing necessity from existence nor existence from quiddity and reality. Therefore they denied that the Creator possessed attributes additional to His essence.

101 They said that evil meant only non-existence[3] or imperfect existence, and non-existence comes within the universal decree by accident not by essence. The primary intention in creation is existence. Logical division is existence which is pure good; or existence which is followed by evil. The existence of pure evil is impossible, nay, the existence which is mostly evil is similarly (impossible). So that there is no existence which an existence little in evil follows that is more evil than its existence.[4] Thus evil enters into existence by a secondary intention. . . .

Al-Ka'bī said to suppose two self-subsistent beings not differing from one another in time or place and without a real characteristic by which one differs from the other is impossible. The controversialist may say this is the point in dispute which you explain in your own way and elevate your explanation into a proof; for many savants have postulated intellectual substances of pure intellect, . . . self-subsistent and distinguished from one another by real characteristics
102 and there is nothing repugnant to reason in the theory.

[1] I omit the reiteration of the argument of *imkān*.

[2] *ta'ayyun* is defined by Jurjānī as that which distinguishes a thing from something else in such a way that nothing shares the distinction.

[3] Or 'privation'.

[4] The meaning seems to be that degrees of evil do not exist; imperfect realization of existence is better than non-existence.

CHAPTER IV

THE REFUTATION OF ANTHROPOMORPHISM 103

ORTHODOX teaching is that nothing is like God, and He is like nothing; cf. *Sur*. 42. 9. He is not substance, body, accident; he is not local, temporal, receptive of accidents, or the subject (*locus*) of temporal phenomena.

The Shī'ite *Ghāliyya*[1] liken the Creator to the created. The Mughīriyya, the Bayāniyya, and the Sabāiyya[2] and the Hāshimiyya and their followers said that God has a form like the form of men; and the anthropomorphists among the Ṣifātiyya taught the same, relying on the tradition of the Prophet: 'God created Adam according to the form of the Compassionate' and its variant: 'according to His form'. 104

The Ghāliyya said that a certain person was God, or that a part of God was incarnate in him, slavishly following the Nazarenes and Incarnationists of every community. Some of the Karrāmiyya even said that He was a substance and a body, that He lived above the earth[3] and that He was the *locus* of temporal events. They said that when God created a substance the will that it should exist was originated[4] in His essence. Sometimes they avoided the expression 'was originated'[4] and said that the will that it should be came into existence in him and the word Be![5] When the thing created was visible or audible God heard or saw, and so the five temporal attributes (corresponding to the senses) came into being in Him. Sometimes they avoided saying 'incarnation' and '*locus*' though they employed the word *ḥādith* 'originated'. They distinguished between will (*mashī'a*) and volition (*irāda*) on the ground that the former is eternal and the latter temporal. Therefore they distinguished between Making to Be and Made to Be (*takwīn* and *mukawwan*), origination and originated, creation and created. For creation is a temporal thing in his essence and the created is separated. So *takwīn* means God's command (*qaul*) Be,[6] the Command subsisting in His essence while the Made to Be is separated.

Similarly God's speech (*kalām*) is qualities originated with Him—expressions composed of consonants and vowels according to some, of consonants only according to others, so it is temporal, not eternal 105

[1] Bigots or exaggerators, cf. *Milal*, p. 132, line 3.

[2] Possibly the marginal reading *Sabāiyya* is a gloss. Bayāniyya is the correct reading. The founder taught that he was the *bayān* of *Sur*. 3. 132.

[3] Lit. 'that he was in an upward direction'.

[4] Perhaps the consonants should be read '*aḥdatha*', 'he originated'.

[5] In Arabic K.N.

[6] See note 5.

and not an originated thing.[1] They hold that it is impossible that the qualities which originated in His essence should be annihilated.

Muḥammad ibn al-Haiṣam occupied himself with this question in a way worthy of mention except in the question of originated things. In this he could not free himself from his original dependence[2] on the teaching of his master Abū ʿAbd Allāh al-Karrām.

Refutation. We say that if God were circumscribed by form and shape altering through a new quality in His essence he would be of time and capable of being other than He is—in fact if He were not God, a God would be required to make Him what He is.

106 *Objection.* Why find fault with those who say that the dimension peculiar to God is a limit necessary for Him according to His essence? He needs none to specify it. Dimensions in the world of creation need a determinant because they are possible and subject to God's power. But if there is no power above God He has no connexion with contingency. Do we not agree that there are eight qualities? Is this number necessary to Him or can there be another? If you say there must be eight we reply that that limit being necessary to Him no difference can be asserted between a limit to the number of His qualities and a limit to His essence. On the other hand, if you say God may have another quality we ask what is the cause of the limitation? Thus there is need of a determinant according to your argument.

Answer. Dimensions are the same in this world and the next so far as logical possibility and need of a determinant go. If we suppose a dimension similar to that in this world it still requires a determinant. Contingency in possible things does not rest upon the hypothesis of power over them; on the contrary the knowledge of that is plain to the intellect. . . . We only need to assume power
107 in causing one possibility and not another. It is not necessary in the conception of possibility itself. This is a fine point which many *mutakallimūn* have missed.

As to the limiting of the divine attributes to eight, many refused to apply number to them at all. They said God's activity points to His being a mighty one, a willer, a knower. The law speaks of knowledge, will, and power. We confine ourselves to these qualities. The question, Can God have another quality? can be answered in different ways: (*a*) logical possibilities are not in question. We confine ourselves to God's qualities as revealed by creation; (*b*) it is possible logically but the law has not revealed aught.

[1] See Macdonald, p. 335.

[2] The MSS. O. and P. seem perfectly clear at this point. Professor Nicholson, in a letter, suggests reading *ishkal* 'in its original perplexity' with the comment that the following is then hard to explain. I think it is possible that *tikal* (for *ittikal*) is intended, though there is no authority for this form in the lexicons.

Others differed as to the essential attributes of which the reality of a thing in this world is composed, and the accidental dimensions which have no place in the establishing of the reality of a thing.
Essential attributes are not ascribed to a thing in relation to the 108
agent, but belong to it without a cause. Differing dimensions are to be ascribed to the agent for he made them for it with a cause.

Others said: If we suppose another quality it must either be praiseworthy or blameworthy. If it is praiseworthy the lack of it now is a deficiency and the Creator already possesses the attributes of perfection: if it is blameworthy the lack of it is necessary. Therefore there cannot be an attribute additional to the essential ones.

Can God have a specific quality which we cannot grasp? This is a different question from the first, and this, too, received different answers. Some said: He cannot have a special characteristic because He is in essence and qualities distinct from created things and His essence knows no limit in time or place, nor is it divisible actually or hypothetically. If (your) object were to establish a specific characteristic it would lie in the fact that he is distinct from all things.

Others said: His special attribute is divinity which is incomprehensible. Every intelligible entity must be distinguished from its
fellow by a special attribute and all that has been just said is negative. 109
You cannot distinguish one thing from another by negations, so that you must have a positive attribute otherwise you have destroyed its reality. So, if God has a special attribute can we grasp it? The Imam al-Ḥaramain said No, others said Yes. Ḍirar ibn ʿAmr said Yes, by a sixth sense in visions.

Objection. If two self-subsistent objects be supposed they must either be side by side or separate and so in local relation to each other. From this they argued that God must either be in the world or external to it. 'Within' *per se* necessitates proximity and contact, and 'without' *per se* necessitates separation and direction. They often used much equivocation in their arguments, saying: We agree that God has an essence and attributes. The attributes do not all stand in the same place (*ḥaith*) as each other nor are they spatially related,
because that which subsists in another is not susceptible of space, but 110
they all subsist in His essence, i.e. in the place where His essence is. The distinction between essence and qualities is that the essence has a place of its own so that the qualities are in reference to it while the qualities have not. The word *ḥaith* cannot be used of the qualities. The existence of another self-subsistent entity would in no way affect this.... Thus direction by which the Deity can be located can be asserted.

The Qurān asserts that God is situated on high, 'He is the Mighty one *above* His servants'. We assert direction, therefore, as an intellectual and revealed truth. We infer from the text that 'above' is the noblest direction, and therefore we raise hands and hearts on high whither the lord of the prophets ascended.

Answer. All this has arisen from the ambiguity of the word 'self-subsistent'. Of God it means independent of subject (*locus*) and
111 space; of substance it means independent of subject only. Thus you have made the point at issue your proof, seizing on an ambiguity in the word in defiance of its meaning. If we were to suppose a being independent of subject and space and one needing space, so that they must either be in contact or separate, the supposition would be ridiculous, for how can local limitations apply to one who does not occupy space?

Similarly 'within' and 'without'[1] cannot apply to God but to the necessary qualities of spatial objects. But it may be said with truth that God is in the world in the sense that His knowledge and will (operate there) and external to the world in holiness and transcendence, cf. *Sur*. 18. 6 and 4. 57, &c.

112 The verses which point to the nearness of God are more numerous than those which speak of His distance above us. It is just as foolish to imagine that God has a local existence separated from the world by finite or infinite distance as it is to suppose that His existence is in finite or infinite time.

As to the pretence of the Karrāmiyya and Ṣifātiyya that God's qualities subsist in 'the place' of His essence it may be said that we do not mean what they mean by subsistence. We mean that God may be described by them (the qualities) but a description need not
113 require that the described is localized. *Ḥaith*, 'in respect of', is a logical relation, so that all the terms they have used in this discussion are equivocal.

Dimension and direction are limiting laws in regard to bodies, so that if an actually infinite body could be imagined direction in reference to it would have no meaning, so there would be no up or down. . . . If bodies were circular and revolving directions would be constantly changed according to the course of the circumference and the part circumscribed, and up and down would conform to the axis and the circumference. If the world be conceived as circular either as an hypothesis corresponding to the truth or not, it could be said that God was in a (certain) direction from the world, whereas He must needs encircle it, otherwise a part of the direction would escape Him. According to them He is above the whole world, which is ridiculous,

[1] *V.s.*, p. 45.

for it would necessitate that He be 'above' as to those on the earth at the North Pole and below as to those at the South Pole; nay, but some would be above Him and some below Him, which thing is impossible.

As to the raising hearts and hands on high and the prophet's ascension, it corresponds to the abasement of head and hands to the ground. God's throne is the Qibla of petition and earth the mosque of prayer. . . .

The Karrāmiyya hold that temporal phenomena subsist within the 114
divine essence; in fact production in time (*iḥdāth*) is a name for the attributes which originate in God's essence, e.g. the will to specify an act with existence; the utterances like Be! As for his other utterances such as stories of past or future events, laws, &c., they originate in his essence by his eternal will (*qudra*) and do not belong to production-in-time in a thing. . . .

According to Muḥammad ibn al-Haiṣam production is volition and influence (*īthār*) and that is conditioned by speech according to the divine law. . . . Most of the Karrāmiyya held that with every originated thing five qualities originated in God's essence, viz. volition, K, N, audition and vision, though they had posited a pre-existent will connected with the phenomenon, the originated, the act of origination, and creation. Then they said these temporal things do not become attributes of God. He is a creator by his creativeness (*khāliqiyya*) not by creation; a willer by his will-ing-ness
(*muridiyya*) not by will; a speaker by his speakingness. These must 115
remain for ever. They can never pass away after they have existed in His essence.

The Mutakallimūn answer:[1] If a thing of time inhered in God which had not always so inhered He would have suffered change, and some one must have brought the change about. If He had no attributes and then acquired them you must either deny the attribution or deny the alteration (as we do). . . . The distinctions made between
qualities in the opponents' special terminology is logically inadmis- 116
sible. Attributives are attributives however expressed. . . . For our purpose they are the same and so far as the reality of the (being) described is concerned they do not differ.[2]

If the existence of the temporal could be conceived without origination either it originated of itself, or by His power, or by an eternal will. . . .

If it is said it originated itself, logical thought is violated, for 117

[1] It is interesting to note that the author identifies himself here with the *mutakallimūn* (unless, of course, the words introduced by 'we' are a quotation).

[2] There follows the tedious argument of the *murajjiḥ* (*v.s.*, p. 6).

what was not and then became would need a producer. Again, if it (the *ḥādith*) could be originated by God's will or power, then why could not all originated things (*muḥdathāt*) have been so originated, seeing that there is no difference between the *ḥādith* and the *muḥdath* in that both were not and then became. The difference between these two words is a matter of grammar (one intransitive and the other transitive), not philosophy. . . .

The philosophers,[1] taking up the adversary's argument, said that every essence which has not originated has an idea (or reality *maʿna*); then before its inception there originated in it receptive capacity, suitability, and potentiality; then when reception had originated the capacity was changed into existence and the potentiality into actuality. It follows that in its essence it was a potential reality and then an actual one, i.e. matter and form. They had asserted that before the creation of the world God possessed the properties of matter, namely privative natures,[2] for preparedness and capacity are a
118 *privatio rei*. But the necessary existent is transcendently above potentiality and privation, the source of evil.

It was argued against them: You say that God's speech and will are of the same genus as ours and then that the universe is the object of His speech. In that case our speech K and N should produce the same effect! If it is said His speech occurred through the immediate operation of His power and eternal will and our speech did not; and His speech is essentially His and not another's, it may be replied that if there is this difference His speech is of another genus altogether. But if His speech originated after it had not been, it is like our's and was not related to power after it originated, because its influence was only exercised when it was separated from power, not at the time when it was the object of power; and power only became effective in the production of its essence, not in anything else which was originated by it. . . .

119 Another counter-argument. The letter K of the fiat KN. must either precede the N or they must keep together[3] in being; either at the moment of being or as long as they exist. If K preceded N either it remained or it did not remain in existence. If it remained pronounced and audible it was not KN but K, and while the K had not passed away,[4] the N could not exist, for a K continuously audible with an N is inconceivable. If it did not remain it was annihilated. Yet according to your view that which inheres (*ḥalla*) in God's being cannot perish. If they were joined together[3] then the K was brought

[1] *al-falsafiyyu*, lit. the philosophic one, not *al-failasūf*.
[2] The Aristotelian *steresis* is meant.
[3] *yatalāzamāni*.
[4] We must read *yanʿadim*, though O. and P. plainly have *yataqaddam*.

into existence with the N and cannot be said to have preceded the N! . . .

To the assertion of the Karrāmiyya that God heard and saw what He had not perceived before, so that hearing and seeing for Him began in time, it was replied: Do you really assert that the 120
Creator became what He was not before, viz. a hearer, seer, speaker, and willer so that He was constantly earning a new epithet?[1] If not you contradict your assertion that He heard what He had not heard, &c.

The true answer. You have joined positive and negative in saying God was not thus and became thus in a way that is inadmissible. We do not admit that He did not hear and see; on the contrary He did from all eternity. Novelty (*tajaddud*) resides in the percept, as it does in the knowable and the thing decreed. He did not acquire a quality which He did not possess before; on the contrary the negative applies only to the percepts. Therefore we say the sounds and sights did not exist. But God heard and saw and so they came into existence, so that hearing and sight could treat them as objects. The objective relation (*ta'alluq*) was conditioned by existence not by the subject of the relation (*al-muta'alliq*). Many an objective relation is conditioned by existence, life, intelligence, and maturity, but absence of the condition does not necessitate absence of the subject.[2]

To ascribe to God a quality which He has not always possessed 121
is to impute alteration and novelty to Him. According to you these temporal (changes) remain and the subjective relations pass away. A subjective quality whose relation or attachment comes afterwards is not impossible, e.g. (the divine) knowledge, predestination and will. But to say that God retains a quality whose relation or attachment was prior is impossible. In that case He would have willed the world's existence by a time volition in His essence, and the world would have come into being and (then) passed away, while He would be willing and saying eternally Be! to a thing that now was and now ceased to exist, hearing and seeing that which had passed away!

Those letters which you posit are either bare consonants without vowels (*aṣwāt*) or consonants which articulate vowels. The first cannot be heard or understood, for the true function of a letter is to articulate a vowel. . . . The vowel to the consonant is as the genus to the species and the accident to the colour. . . . A coherent state-

[1] *tajaddud waṣfin lahu.*

[2] The Arabic is straightforward, but the thought is difficult. If I understand the author he means that perception always existed in God. His perception preceded the existence of a thing. When it existed perception came into relation with it; perception was always there, but existence was the condition of the relation, not sight. Therefore God was unaffected by the appearance in time of a visible universe.

ment requires in turn speech, words, consonants, vowels, (palatal) impact, motion.

122 Then forsooth the Creator ought to be a moving body!

One of the Karrāmiyya even asserted that God had a body, saying, 'I mean by that self-subsistence', but that is hypocritical ambiguity. For their leader's tenets were that God is a *locus* of temporal phenomena, speaking with vowels, sitting on a throne on high, and the embellishments of ibn Haiṣam could not deliver him from such heresies, for he did not mean self-subsistence by his anthropomorphism, nor by 'an upward direction' on high, nor by 'settling himself (on the throne)' taking possession of. In fact this is to correct a school of thought which is incorrigible and to strengthen a belief which cannot be supported. How can the shadow be straight[1] when the rod is crooked, or the school be well directed[1] whose master is a fool?

CHAPTER V

The Refutation of those who deny the Divine Attributes

123 *Ta'ṭīl* can be divorcing (*a*) the work (of creation) from the Maker; (*b*) the Maker from the work; (*c*) the Creator from the eternal attributes which subsist in His essence; (*d*) the Creator from the attributes and names in eternity; and (*e*) the plain texts of Qurān and Sunna from the meanings to which they witness.

As to (*a*), I have never heard this argued, save that there is a tradition that a small body of the Materialists said that the universe was originally scattered atoms moving without order, and their fortuitous concourse resulted in the world in its present shape. . . .

124 Man's mind accepts the postulate of a Creator, and the Qurān witnesses thereto.[2] Though they forget Him in times of happiness they turn to Him in affliction. The existence of the Maker is taken for granted in the Law which only reveals God's Unity.

125 The Mutakallimūn deduced the existence of a maker from phenomena—the older ones from the principle of potentiality. For my part I do not think these deductions so important as man's need of a Disposer, the Goal of his desires, the Helper in distress. A man's own need is more apparent to him than an external potentiality's need of a necessary. . . . Apostolic tradition says that God created men with a knowledge of Him, but Satan beguiled them away from that knowledge. That knowledge is man's essential[3] need, and that

[1] There is a double play on the word *istawā* which formed an important text for the anthropomorphists.
[2] The references are inserted in the Arabic text.
[3] Not in the philosophical sense. Lit. 'necessary'.

beguiling of Satan is the delusion that he is independent, and the denial of his need of God.[1] . . .

As to (*b*) the Materialists (*Dahriyya*), who hold that the world pre- 126
existed, say that the pre-existence of the world in eternity implies the divorce of the Maker from His work. This has already been refuted in the discussion on production (*ījād*). Causation is just as impossible as the separation of the Maker from His work. . . . You call your God, cause, and principle, and necessitator which implies two absurd things: (*a*) the validity of the relation between cause and effect, and (*b*) the cause necessitating its effect *per se*. The first intention is the existence of the world . . . through first intention. . . . The higher does not will a thing for the sake of the lower; therefore causation is refuted.

As to (*c*) the divorcing of essential attributes and those consisting of 127
ideas and names and judgements,[2] that is the position of the philosophical theologians. They said that the necessary existent was one in all respects. Parts of quantity and definition, whether in matter of form or anything else had no place in His essence or description. His only term was *Necessary per se*, which necessitates no other meaning but His existence. No attribute can add to the meaning of His essence. All the attributes are either relative: as in our language the Origin of the world and the cause of intelligence; in your language the Creator and sustainer; or negative—in our language One, i.e. not a multiplicity and Intelligent, i.e. free from matter. Sometimes relative and negative are combined as when we say Wise, Willer.

It was argued against them that they had used the word existence ambiguously in applying it to the necessary *per se* and the necessary through another and then said that one of the existences was necessary and the other possible whereas necessity does not come into the notion of existence. . . . They cannot escape this argument by saying
that this use of necessity[3] is equivocal, i.e. in one it is fitting and 128
primary and in the other it is not, for this only strengthens the argument against them.

Another argument against them. You say that He is Origin, Cause, Intelligent, and Intelligible, but there is no connexion between these relations and if you can postulate a plurality of relations the Mutakallim can postulate attributes. To strip God of the latter is to strip Him of the former.

As to (*d*)[4] only a few of the early philosophers went so far. The first

[1] The depth of the author's convictions is nobly expressed in the passage that follows.
[2] See further, Ch. VIII.
[3] The reading of O is preferred.
[4] The Arabic text here should indicate a fresh sub-division by the use of cursive script and another paragraph.

originator was an eternal reality.[1] Being before all things He had no name and we know no name to correspond to His essence. His names come from His actions, He is without form, i.e. He is not knowledge, nor knowable. These latter belong to the first thing caused which is prime matter.[2] Such are the true deniers of attributes.

Some of them are reported to have said He is He. We do not say existent or non-existent, wise or ignorant and so on. Thus too the Shīʿite Ghāliyya and the Bāṭiniyya. There is no doubt that he who postulates a Maker must have a name for Him. But a name common
129 (to man and God) does not imply a common meaning. These men shrank from applying such words as 'existence' to Him because they believed that name and meaning would become equated and because every name has its opposite, e.g. wise and ignorant and they feared by calling him wise 'not ignorant' might be understood.

But we know that though the names are common the real meaning is different and God's names come to us by revelation.

Some of the Shīʿas said it is not possible to deprive God of the 'Beautiful Names' nor is it possible to apply anthropomorphic epithets to Him. We use the names revealed to us but not in the sense of epithet and attribute because ʿAlī used to say 'He cannot be described
130 or limited by definition'. We use the names in the sense of giving: thus He is existent in that He gives existence; powerful and knowing in that He gives knowledge and power, &c. We do not say that He is a Knower *per se* or by knowledge but He is the God of those who know *per se* and of those who know by knowledge.

Muḥammad ibn ʿAlī al-Bāqir said that God was called a Knower because He is the giver of knowledge to those that know, &c. But this is not denial of the attributes. He confined himself to a simple statement without going into the question as to whether the attributes belonged to God's essence or to ideas subsisting in His essence. The Fathers and the Muslim community agreed that everything in man's mind is created by God so that ʿAlī's saying 'He cannot be described' is only to be explained as we have indicated.

CHAPTER VI

States (or Conditions of Things)

131 The theory of states or conditions had never been heard of till Abū Hāshim ibn al-Jubbāʾī (d. 933) published his opinion about them. His father, al-Jubbāʾī, opposed him, but he was supported by al-

[1] *anniyya*, lit. 'that-ness'; Aristotle's ὅτι ἔστι.
[2] *al-ʿunṣur*.

Bāqillānī after some hesitation. Al-Ashʿarī, the head of his school, opposed the theory, as did (most of) his followers, while the Imam al-Ḥaramain first supported and then opposed him.

We will first explain what was meant by a *ḥāl* (state), then set out the arguments for and against, showing how the truth lies now with one side now with another.

Now a *ḥāl* has no real definition by which we can recognize it in such a way as to apply to all *ḥāls* and so that leads to a *ḥāl* having a 132
ḥāl! But they can be divided into (*a*) what causes, i.e. predications of ideas which subsist in essences, and (*b*) what does not cause, i.e. attributes which are not predications of ideas.

As to (*a*) every predication of a cause which subsists in an essence has life as a condition of its existence (*thubūt*) according to Abū Hāshim, e.g. a live thing's being alive, knowing, willing, &c., because its being so is the result of life, so life subsists in a substrate and causes the substrate to be alive, similarly with all the other attributes of which life is a (necessary) condition. These predications are called states, i.e. qualities additional to the ideas which necessitated them. But the Qāḍī (al-Bāqillānī) held that every attribute of an existent thing which cannot be said to be existent is a state whether the necessitating idea be conditioned by life or not, e.g. a live thing's being alive, a moving thing's moving and so on. . . .

As to (*b*) it is every positive attribute of an essence which has no
cause additional to its substance like the spatial need of the atom and 133
its being an object, the accident being accident, colour, &c. In short it is the specific characteristic of a thing whether it be that which distinguishes it from something else or that in which it resembles it, i.e. generic and specific attributes.

States are neither existent nor non-existent; they are not things, nor can they be qualified according to the theory of their supporters. Ibn al-Jubbā'ī held that they were not cognizable separately but only with the essence.

Those who deny states say that things are the same or different according to their individual essences. As to genera and species they are mere names. Sometimes a thing is known from one aspect and unknown from another—and these aspects are intellectual relations which have nothing to do with attributes dubbed states.

The supporters said: Black and white share the categories colour and accident, and differ in the category blackness and whiteness; so that in which they share must be other than that in which they differ or something else. The first is sophistry, the second surrenders the point.

The deniers said: Black and white are merely two incorporeal entities (*ma'nayāni*).[1] They do not share in something that is like an attribute to them, but in a word which indicates genus and species. Universality and sharing therein are not to be referred to an attribute, i.e. a state belonging to black and white, for the two states of the two accidents would share in the 'state of being a state' (*ḥāliyya*); and that sharing does not necessitate the postulate of a state of a state for that would land us in an infinite regress. It is a mere matter of universal and particular.

134 The supporters: Sharing in common and differing are an intellectual category beyond the mere words which were coined to express them.

Those who hold that universals and particulars are mere verbal distinctions deny logical definitions of things and inference. If things were distinguished by their essences and existence, it would be folly to talk of intellectual judgements, and rational demonstration would be impossible.

The opponents. We know intuitively that there is no mean between existence and non-existence, yet you believe that the *ḥāl* is neither existent nor non-existent. When you go on to distinguish existence and latency[2] and apply latency to the *ḥāl* to the exclusion of existence the theory is quite unintelligible. The extraordinary thing is that Ibn al-Jubbā'ī said that the *ḥāl* could not be said to be cognizable or otherwise. Now the goal of induction is the establishing of knowledge about a thing's existence; but if its existence is not conceivable,
135 induction is impossible, and to discuss it is paradoxical.

What do you mean by saying that 'sharing' is an intellectual judgement? If you mean that intellectual relations are concerned, that does not necessitate positive[2] qualities in substances. If you mean that one particular thing has a quality in which something else shares, and another quality which distinguishes it from other things, that is the point at issue; for the individual thing has no associate and the universal has no existence at all.

Further the object of intellectual inquiry is to arrive either at a positive or a negative conclusion while the Ḥālist toys with something between existence and non-existence.

Definition and reality (*al-ḥadd wal-ḥaqīqa*) according to those who deny the theory of states are words for one and the same thing. The definition of a thing is its reality and its reality is that which is peculiar to it *per se*. Everything has its distinguishing peculiarity which attaches to its essence, and nothing shares therein, otherwise it would have no special nature. Universal and particular are mere

[1] *ma'nā* is often used as the opposite of *kam*, the quantitative and corporeal.
[2] *thubūt*. Perhaps 'positive assertion'.

words coined to connect like with like. Essence does not embrace them. On the contrary a thing's existence and its specific description 136
are one and the same.

The supporters. With us the *ḥāl* is a positive thing, but we do not assert without restriction that it is a positive thing existing by itself, for such must be either substance or accident, and this is neither; but it is an intelligible quality of them. A substance (*jauhar*) is known by its substantiality not by its need of space and being receptive of accidents. If the two cognizables differ in one thing the difference is to be referred to the state. Sometimes a thing is known of necessity from one aspect, deductively from another: one knows of necessity that the mover is a mover, then by deduction that he is a mover by a movement. But why do those who reject accidents deny that movement is an accident added to the mover and not deny that he is a mover?

You rejectors agree that movement is a cause of the substance moving: similarly power, knowledge, and all the accidents and ideas. . . .

A cause must either necessitate its essence or something else beyond 137
its essence. The former is ridiculous, as a thing cannot be its own cause and effect. If the latter then that thing is either essence by itself or a quality of essence. It cannot be the former, for that would lead to the cause producing essences and those essences being causes, which is absurd and leads to an endless chain. Thus it is clear that it is a quality of an essence which is the state that we postulate. We do not say that it is existent or knowable by itself; sometimes it can be known with something else and not separately, like contact, contiguity, &c. . . . With regard to your assertion that we are merely dealing with intellectual aspects and relations, we reply: These are not unfettered abstractions but are peculiar to essences; the intellectual aspects attaching to one essence are really states. . . . They are qualities by which substances are described. You call them aspects; we call them states. The two cognizables are distinct though the essence is the same, and the distinction between the two cognizables points to the numerical difference (*taʿaddud*) of the two aspects and states, viz. two real cognizables to which two distinct cognitions attach, one necessary, the other derived. That is not like relative 138
terms, for they are mere words in which there is no real knowledge attaching to a real cognizable.

Your saying 'the individual thing has no associate and the common thing has no existence at all' is folly. The particular *qua* particular has no associate, and the attributes which we postulate are not particular and peculiar, but such as embrace particularizing and universalizing. . . . He who regards the latter as mere words has abrogated intellectual relations. Do not the terms change in different languages and times while the intellectual relations and aspects do not?

Again their words 'The definition and reality and essence of a thing are words for one and the same thing'; and 'things are different through the peculiarity of their essences and nothing shares therein'; granted this be so the peculiarity of the individual is one thing and
139 the peculiarity of the species another. You do not classify the substance according to a peculiar property but *qua* substance absolutely. You have postulated a universal idea common to substances; otherwise every atom would need defining separately and the ordinary predication of substance would not hold, and so we should have to introduce a universal idea into the definition, and that would destroy your thesis that things are only distinguished by their essences, and justify our assertion that definitions are not independent of the universality of words which points to the qualities of the universality and particularity of essences. These qualities are states and aspects and intellectual relations belonging to them—call them what you will so long as you accept the idea and reality of them.

The opponents. Your argument is unsound. The word *ḥāl* embraces the genus of *ḥāls*, and a *ḥāl* is the quality of a thing peculiar to that thing; so either its meaning must be universal and particular or something beyond the word itself and that would lead to the assertion that a *ḥāl* has a *ḥāl* which is absurd. You do not escape by saying that 'the quality cannot be described', for you were the first to postulate a quality of a quality because you made existence, blackness, &c., states of the black; thus you have postulated qualities of qualities, so why not states of states? As to aspects and relations
140 they have an existence in states also. The universal state is one thing and the particular another, yet they are two relations in the state and a state which causes (other) states is one thing and a state which does not cause a state is another. Did not Abū Hāshim postulate a state in the Creator which necessitates his being knowing, willing? And knowingness and willingness are two states. A causal and a non-causal state are different in relation and the difference of the two relations does not necessitate the difference of the two states in reference to the state.

According to them existence in the pre-existent and the temporal, the substance and the accident, is a state indifferently. Thus they had to argue that one thing is concealed in two different things, or that two different things are in one thing, which is ridiculous. Being *qua* being, forsooth, is in what is still to be—a monstrous absurdity.

Again, if existence is a state uniting genera and species, then the

different pluralities must be united in it and the genera must suffer change without existence being affected, which is like the change of forms in matter as the philosophers say without a change in matter. 141
But the analogy is not sound because matter according to them is not free from form. . . . How is it possible to conceive existence, bare, absolute, universal, unchanging, and in what does it inhere? . . .

The truth appears from these discussions, but we do not disclose it yet.

The opponents. How is an unchangeable existence to be conceived whose species change one into the other and the substance becomes accident and vice versa? It would involve the entry of one existence into different genera, and the uniting of different genera and species in one existence.

The supporters. Universality and particularity in the state are like genus-ness and species-ness in the genus and species, because genus-ness in genera is not a genus in the sense that every genus demands a genus (for that) would require an infinite regress. . . . Similarly state-ness (*ḥāliyya*) which attaches to states does not demand a state, for that would require an infinite regress also.

A man who says existence is universal is not bound to say the 142
universal has a universal, nor if he says accidental-ness (*ʿaraḍiyya*) is a genus need he say the genus has a genus. . . .

As to your saying: If existence were one and similar in all objects the presence of one thing in two, or two in one, would result.[1] What holds good of existence and state applies equally against your intellectual relations and aspects. None will deny that existence is common to substance and accident, not only in word but also in meaning. . . .

A universal judgement demands that something must be held in 143
common and such sharing can only be conceivable after the special characteristic of the thing has been identified. A particular assertion is impossible apart from the underlying universal. He who says 'Things differ in their individual essences' cannot apply a universal judgement in a special case.

You accuse us of reversing the genera and of positing one in two and two in one, while we accuse you of abolishing the genera and denying the one in the two. The court is sitting, but who is the judge?

The judge who is familiar with the tenets of both parties[2] says: You who take the negative position are in error (1) because you make universals and particulars mere words and assert that different things differ in their essences and existence, but your statements are self- 144

[1] The words of the opponents' assertion are slightly changed.

[2] I.e. Shahrastānī himself.

contradictory because you adopt a universal judgement when you say that universals are mere words. Abolish words altogether, still intellectual judgements remain. Beasts that have neither speech nor intelligence do not lack this guidance, for they know by nature what herb to eat, and when they see a similar herb they are not assailed by doubt as to whether it is eatable. Had they not formed precisely the same judgement in the second case as in the first, they would not have eaten nor would they shun its opposite were they not acquainted with the genus. Therefore the movers are right in saying that you have shut the door of definition.

I go further and say that you have shut the door of intellectual knowledge and speech. For the mind perceives mankind as a universal whole distinct from the individual. Similarly the accidental is universal to all kinds of accidents, without colouredness or blackness, and this particular black coming into one's mind. This is the immediate percept and the content of the word as it is conceived in the mind; (but it is) not the word itself, because the word (only) explains an idea in the mind. The thing meant does not change with the language in which it is expressed, Arabic, Persian, Hindu, or Greek. No com-
145 plete speech is free of universals, and these universal ideas are the distinguishing mark of human minds (*nufūs*). To deny this is to put oneself outside the pale of humanity and to enter the enclosure reserved for beasts.

(2) Your second error is to ascribe the distinction between species to individual essences—a dreadful mistake, because a thing is only distinguished from something else by its specific attribute. The specific attribute of a thing's species is not the same as that of the essence; for substance[1] differs from accident in needing space absolutely and by way of species, not particularly and individually. The particular substance only differs from (another) particular substance in occupying a particular space, not space absolutely. . . . If substance differed from accident in its existence as it differs from it in occupying space, spatial need would be predicated of accident and substance, because (forsooth) existence and need of space are one, and all idea of resemblance and difference would be abrogated. . . .

146 As to the mistakes of those who postulate states: (1) They postulate of a particular object qualities peculiar to it and qualities in which other things share, and this is sheer folly. For that which is peculiar in a particular thing and that in which something else shares is one in relation to that particular thing; so the existence of a particular accident and its accidental nature, &c., are verbal expressions for that particular thing. If existence is specified by accidental nature

[1] Or atom.

then it is in itself an accident; and if the accidental nature is specified by colouredness (*launiyya*), then it is in itself colour, and similarly colouredness by blackness and blackness by this black. It is not intelligible that a quality should come into existence for one particular thing and actually exist for something else, and so become an individual quality in two things like one black in two substrates and one substance in two places. . . .

(2) They say that the *ḥāl* is neither existent nor non-existent; yet existence with them is a *ḥāl*, so how can it be right to say existence cannot be said to exist? ... They posit cause and effect and say the one 147
causes the other, but how can something which does not exist become a cause?

(3) According to them everything in existence is a state. Give us an example of a state which neither exists nor does not exist, for all-embracing universal existence according to you is a state. . . Therefore there is nothing that is not a *ḥāl*. If you posit a thing and say it is not a *ḥāl*, that thing embraces a universal and a particular, while the particular and the universal according to you is a *ḥāl*. In that case there is nothing but a no-thing and no existence but no-existence, and this is the most stupid theory imaginable.

Now the truth is that a man is conscious of the conception of universal things apart from the words which express them and apart from individual forms. Further, he is conscious of intellectual relations attaching to one thing: these (universals) are either to be referred to the words that define them—a theory which we have refuted—or to the existing individuals—which we have disproved. Therefore it only remains to be said that they are ideas really existent 148
in the mind of man which the intellect perceives. Inasmuch as they are universals with no existence in individuals they are not an existent thing in individuals, accident or colour absolutely; but they are individuals in that the intellect conceives from them a universal idea. A word is formed to correspond with this in such a way that if the word were to perish or be changed the idea logically formed in the mind would not be affected.

Those who deny that there are states err in saying that they are mere words, and are right in saying that what exists as an individual is without universality and relation. Those who assert that there are states are wrong in referring them to qualities in individuals and right in saying that they are intelligible ideas above and beyond the words which express them. They ought to say that they are existent concepts in the mind,[1] non-existent in individuals[1] instead of saying that they are not existent and not-non-existent. No intelligent man

[1-1] The marginal gloss seems correct.

denies these ideas, though some call them mental concepts; others logical suppositions of the intellect; others realities and ideas denoted by words and expressions; others qualities of genera and species. But provided the ideas are clear call them what you will.

These realities and ideas have three relations: their internal relation, their relation to individuals and to the mind. Inasmuch as they exist in individuals they can be treated as individuals and specified,
149 inasmuch as they are conceived in the mind they can be universal, and in relation to themselves they are pure realities neither general nor particular. He who knows these three relations will have no difficulty in the matter of the *ḥāl*; and furthermore the truth about the dispute as to whether the non-existent is a thing will be clear to him.

CHAPTER VII

150 Is the Non-existent a Thing? Of Matter and a Refutation of the Theory that Matter exists without Form

A 'thing' cannot be defined because nothing is so well known and any word that is used to define it involves the notion of 'thing-ness' and existence. . . . It is a mistake to define a thing as 'an existent' (*maujūd*) because existence and thing-ness are the same. Again, it is a mistake to define it as 'that of which something can be predicated' because the words 'that which' have been introduced into the definition.

151 The Ashʿarites do not distinguish between existence, latency, and thing-ness and essence, and individual reality.[1] The Muʿtazilite, al-Shaḥḥām first asserted that the non-existent was a thing, an essence and a reality and claimed for it the relations of existence, e.g. the subsistence of the accident in the substance, &c. Most of the Muʿtazilites followed him although they did not assert the subsistence of the accident in the substance, &c.; but a number of them opposed him. Some merely employed the word thing-ness (of the non-existent), while others held that to be impossible like Abū'l-Hudhayl and Abū-l-Husayn al-Baṣrī; others said the thing is the pre-existent while the temporal is called a thing metaphorically and by extension. But Juhm ibn Ṣafwān held that the thing was the phenomenal and the Creator is He who makes things what they are.[2]

The Negative position. Elementary intelligence assures us that positive and negative assertions are contraries. If you posit a definite thing at a definite moment in a definite mode you cannot deny it in

[1] *wujūd, thubūt, shay'iyya, dhāt,* and *'ayn.*

[2] Lit. 'The thing-er of things.'

the same conditions. If that which is to-be-denied is latent according to those who say that the nonentity is a thing this proposition is abrogated. Put into a syllogism we get the form (Barbara):

All non-entities are to-be-denied.
All to-be-denieds are not-latent.[1]
Therefore all non-entities are not-latent.

The Positive position. Just as denial and assertion are contraries 152
so are existence and non-existence contraries. We say that existence and latency (*thubūt*) are not synonyms nor are the to-be-denied and the non-existent.

The Negative. If you say that latency is a wider term than existence and embraces both entity and non-entity why don't you say that the to-be-denied is a wider term than the non-entity so that a universal attribute becomes a state or aspect of the to-be-denied positively, just as a particular attribute of the non-entity becomes a state or aspect of the non-entity positively? . . .

The Positive. You, too, have attributed universals and particulars to the non-entity since you talk of the necessary, possible, and impossible in relation to it. If the non-entity were not a latent thing
you could not treat it thus. . . . The fact that it is an object of thought 153
and intellectual relation points the same way.

The Negative. We do not assert universals and particulars in non-existence: they are mere expressions and mental suppositions. Moreover, the mental relation with the non-entity is not *qua* non-entity but on the supposition that it exists. Therefore absolute non-existence is a notion resting on the assumption of absolute existence in opposition to particular non-existence, i.e. the non-existence of a particular thing. It can be said of an objective entity that it (no longer) exists or it can be said of a subjective entity, e.g. the Resurrection, that it does not exist. It can be denied in the present, asserted in the future. Non-existence itself is neither universal nor particular, and cannot be known without existence or the assumption of existence. Knowledge has the existent as its object. Then if the non-existence of that thing becomes known it can be denied and it may be said that it is not a thing at the present time. If existence is to be asserted of (non-existent) substances, then it is clear that the
world pre-existed, and there was no beginning to the Creator's 154
activity and no influence. If it is to be denied every to-be-denied with you is a non-entity and every non-entity is latent, so that the argument is turned against you.

[1] *laysa bi-thābit.* It has already been said that the Ash'arites do not distinguish between latency and existence. Therefore it follows that they admitted no mean between existence and non-existence.

We say that God gave the world existence with its substances and accidents, so it may be said He gave existence to its reality and essence[1] or something else. If you say it was the former then, according to you, they were two essential attributes latent in non-existence while the divine power had no connexion with them. . . . If you say He gave existence to something else the same argument applies.

The Positive. What you say about knowledge having the existent or the hypothetical existent as its object is false of God's knowledge of the world's non-existence in eternity, for the world did not exist then, nor could there have been a supposition thereof, because its supposition or any supposition on the part of the Creator would be ridiculous, for supposition implies doubt.

Therefore God's knowledge was of something known, so the non-entity must be a latent thing. When you say that knowledge is connected with the existence of a thing at the time it exists, and it necessitates a knowledge of its non-existence before it existed, you confine knowledge to objects of cognition and objects are finite, and so it follows that intelligibles are finite also—a thesis that you do not hold. . . .

155 As to your saying that existence[2] is to be denied or latent in our system, existence is to be denied and is not latent, and all-to-be-denieds and non-entities are not latent, because impossibilities are to-be-denieds and non-entities, and are not latent things. The key to our system is that the essential qualities of substances and accidents belong to them because they are what they are,[3] not because of any connexion with a Creator. He only enters the mind in connexion with existence because He tipped the scale in favour of existence.

What a thing is in essence preceded its existence, viz. its substantialness and accidentalness, and so it is a thing. What a thing has through omnipotence is its existence and its actuality (*ḥuṣūl*); and what follows its existence is the property of occupying space and receiving accidents. Therefore there is no question of the influence of the Creator's *ījād*, for the influence of (divine) power is in existence alone. The omnipotent only confers existence. The potential only needs the omnipotent in respect of existence.[4] . . .

156 Essential things are not related to the Creator, but what befalls them from existence and actuality is. If the Creator wished to produce a substance the substance must be distinguished from the accident. For if they were indistinguishable in non-existence and the distinction was not a positive[5] thing the Creator's intention to

[1] *'ainahā wa-dhātahā.*
[2] The correct reading must be *al-wujūd.*
[3] *lahā li-dhawātihā.*
[4] Again the tipping of the scale follows.
[5] I.e. latent.

produce a substance could not have been realized without an accident. Specifying a thing by giving it existence is only conceivable if the thing specified is a distinct entity so that substance not accident, movement not rest, results. Hence the real nature of genus and species does not depend on the Creator's activity. If they are not separate things *per se*, *ījād* is inconceivable and variety in actual phenomena must be due to mere chance.

The Negative. The eternal knowledge has all intelligibles as its object; the world's existence, so that it really came to exist; the impossibility of its eternal existence; and the possibility of its existence before it did exist. But the true objective relation (*muta'allaq*) is existence from which all other intelligibles result. You can know
that the Creator is God and that there is no other, but that does not 157
demand a succession of cognitions that every created thing is not God. If you know Zaid is at home you know he is nowhere else and need not know that he is not *chez* 'Omar or Bakr and so *ad infinitum*. It cannot possibly be said that such infinite cognitions are latent things in non-existence, e.g. the absence of Zaid in such and such a place. . . .

As to their assertion that essential qualities are not due to the Creator and that only existence *qua* existence is the object of the divine power, this is something they have heard and not rightly understood.[1]

The Negative. A thing's existence, and its individual reality (*'ain*), 158
its essence, substantiality, and accidentality, in our view are all one. That which (God) brought into existence is the thing's essence, and divine power is connected alike with its essence as it is with its existence, and influences its substantiality as it does its actuality and appearance in time. The distinction between existence and 'thingness' is merely verbal.

These people[1] believe that universals and particulars are mere words or intellectual fictions; but the qualities which follow production, e.g. the substance being susceptible of accident, can be argued against them. For (say they) they are not due to God's power. They do not assert them to be prior to appearance in time, so why do they not argue that all the essential attributes also follow appearances in time? One might reverse the argument and say that the properties of substance were created by God's power and existence followed!

They tried to evade the difficulty of distinctive specifying by saying that if substances and accidents were latent in non-existence *ad infinitum* there could be no real specifying; but this is no answer; it only adds to the difficulty.

[1] These last comments are presumably from the author himself.

Now the truth is that this question is bound up with that of the
159 *ḥāl*. The Muʿtazila have become hopelessly involved in theories which they do not grasp. Sometimes they call the essential realities in genera and species 'states', i.e. qualities and names of entities neither existent nor non-existent: at other times they call them things, i.e. names and states of non-entities. They have mixed philosophy with theology and the doctrine of formless matter, borrowed some logic and some metaphysic, and the result is a house of straw.

We point to a particular substance and ask: Was this substance a positive (latent) corporeal substance before it existed, or was it universal substance, a thing unspecified? If it was this one, nothing
160 else shared in it. If it was absolute substance before it existed, it was not this because that is not this. What is latent in non-existence has no real existence, and what really exists is not latent. . . .[1]

161 The supporters of states maintain that species like substantial-
162 ity, &c. are things (latent)[2] in non-existence because they are the object of knowledge and the known must be a thing. Individuality, substantiality, &c., are states in existence which cannot be known separately nor exist by themselves. But what an object of knowledge in non-existence which is unknown in existence! Had they an intelligent grasp of genera and species they would know that mental images are the quiddities of things in their genera and species which do not demand that they should have a real existence outside the mind. . . .

163 When the Muʿtazila learned from the philosophers that there was a difference between the causes of existence and quiddity they thought that mental concepts were things latent in individuals, so they affirmed that the non-existent was a thing and thought that the existence of genera and species in the mind were states latent in *individua*, that the non-entity was a thing and that the state was latent. It is annoying to hear and answer such absurdities, and unless I had undertaken to explain the various schools of thought in this book I should not have troubled to deal with such things.

(1) The theory that there is formless matter (*hūlē*).

It is said that the first principles are Intelligence, Soul, and Matter, to which some add the Creator, all of them being void of forms. When the first form, i.e. the three dimensions, appeared, there arose a composite body. Before that it had no form, merely the capacity to

[1] Here follow arguments similar to those already advanced.

[2] *thābita*. This word is elusive in meaning. I have sometimes rendered it by 'positive'. It is best defined by the *muthbitūn* themselves. On the whole 'latent' seems to do justice to something that is neither existent nor non-existent, though it comes down on the side of existence somewhat.

receive it. When form appeared actually there came into being the secondary matter. Then when the four modes (heat and cold active, and dampness and dryness passive) adhered to it there arose the four elements (*arkān*), viz. fire, water, air, and earth which are tertiary matter. From these arose the composites to which the accidents of generation (*kaun*) and corruption adhere.

(2) The theory that matter is not free from form. This treats (1) as 164
speculative.

The supporters of (1) argue that it is demonstrable that every body is composed of matter and is subject to addition and subtraction and form and shape; that the subject of addition and subtraction is something lying behind them and exists independently of them while addition does not remain after subtraction and vice versa. Hence an atom without bodily form can receive addition and subtraction at the same time. These adjuncts can cease and so can form and shape so that it is possible for the atom to be void of all forms.[1] Thus a non-composite atom must be the foundation of all composite bodies, for otherwise there would be an endless chain of composites like shirt, cloth, cotton, elements, and prime matter[2] which is *hyle* receptive of forms and modes.

The supporters of (2) object that this is to assume the point at 165
issue. Addition and subtraction are accidents and as such alter and change. That which changes is accident, not substance, and you cannot treat them alike.

The Mutakallim asks why substance is free of all accidents if it is free of one, to which they reply that the self-subsistent is independent of a subject, otherwise it would need an accident as the accident needs it and so there would be no intelligible distinction between them.

The Mutakallim answers that substance cannot be free from all 166
accidents, not because it needs them in its self-subsistence as a substance, but because it is inconceivable unless it is in a definite place.

The supporters of (2) argue: Assume that matter is a self-subsistent substance void of form, and then that it acquires dimension, either dimension must have come suddenly or gradually. But dimension carries with it place and volume, and it must have had the latter before it got the former. If dimension came gradually and by extension then direction is implied, and once more all the categories are present.

The supporters of (1) argue that potentiality preceded the temporal 167

[1] The opponent quotes the argument rather differently, *v.i.*

[2] *'anāṣir*. This has not been mentioned above in (1).

thing's existence and also the matter (*hyle*) in which potentiality resided, though neither potentiality nor *hyle* were eternally pre-existent. . . .

Plato's proof of the temporal origin of the world: The existence of universal objects can be conceived in the mind and outside the mind: they are differing realities with different characteristics like the celestial intelligences.

168 The supporters of (2). If potentiality can only be posited in matter,[1] matter[1] is inconceivable without form, and form subsists in the Giver of form.

[Shahrastānī] If we regard *hyle* as a subsistent object it is either one or many: if it was one and then became two was it (*a*) by the addition of another, or (*b*) by the multiplication of that one without external addition? If (*a*) then they are two substances, one added to the other, and their mutual relation presupposes form. If (*b*) then *hyle* became divisible—at one time having the form of unity, at another the form of plurality, and we are driven to the endless chain. . . .

169 It is clear that *hyle* is never free from form but it actually subsists therein. Form subsists not in *hyle* but in the Giver of form. Matter preserves form by receiving it and form comes into being in *hyle*. Both are substances because body is composed of them and body is a substance. Actual distinction between them is inconceivable: only a logical difference can be drawn.

CHAPTER VIII

Proof that the Propositions connected with the Divine Attributes can be known.

170 The Mutakallims began by asserting that the propositions connected with the divine attributes could be known before they made a like assertion of the attributes themselves. The Muʿtazila, who denied the attributes, admitted the propositions. The Mutakallims adopted (*a*) the method of deduction and induction and (*b*) necessary and intuitive knowledge. Some think it better to begin by affirming that God is powerful (*qādir*); others put knowing (*ʿālim*) first; others put volition (*irāda*) first.

(*a*) The first class argued: He who tips the scale of being must be powerful. Living people can or cannot act. We have examined all the attributes of a living being in the desire to discover the reason

171 why impotence is removed and facility established, and we find only

[1] *mādda* not *hayyūlā* = *hyle*.

the attribute Power or His being Powerful. Similarly we attribute the perfection of creation to His being knowing, and when we find a thing as it is and not something else which it might well be we postulate His being Willing. . . . None of these attributes is possible without their subject being Living. Therefore we say The Powerful One is Living. If we did not employ these adjectives we should have to use their opposites, impotence, ignorance, and death.

Those who deny the divine attributes ask of the Ashʿarites: Why, if you deny the *ḥāl* (*v.s.*) and say that things differ through their essence and existence can you claim anything common (*jamʿ*) between man and God?[1] Again, you will not admit that man is the producer of his actions though you allow a sort of acquired power over action to man. How can there be anything common between him of whom production is inconceivable and him of whom acquisition is inconceivable?

Answer. We do not deny that intellectual modes and relations are 172
common to man and God[1] in cause and effect, &c., for if the mind grasps the intention (*maʿnā*) of one agent's action it can predicate similarly of every agent. Again, we recognize a certain power of activity in human actions, and a distinction between voluntary and involuntary action. But is the influence of a will (*qudra*) on the thing willed production or acquisition?

They asked the Muʿtazila: (1) According to you the agent only influences the act in a state which cannot be said to exist or not to exist. Powerfulness according to you is a state, so how does state produce state?

(2) You give man power in production and regard God's power as a state. . . . If you give both God and man power in origination,
then you must affirm that man's power can produce anything. 173
This is obviously untrue, so how can there be an analogy with the unseen?

Again: You cannot use human analogies and say: 'Building points to a builder: we have investigated the qualities of a builder and find that he must be powerful'. But this is not so because a builder requires instruments—an absurd assumption of Allah. . . .

We say that man's knowledge of the wonders of creation assures 174
him that their Creator must be Knowing, Wise, Powerful, Willing—only a fool could doubt it. There is no need to postulate action in the seen and apply it to the unseen; they are obviously the same.

The Imām al-Ḥaramain answered that God's tipping the scale of being must have been through and according to His essence, or through His essence by way of an attribute, or through an attribute

[1] Lit. the present and the absent, i.e. the two objects of comparison.

beyond His essence. It cannot have been through essence because the essential cause makes no distinction: every effect stands in the same relation to it. Therefore the 'tipping' must have been through a super-essential attribute, or through the essence by way of an attri-
175 bute. Revelation calls this quality Volition. Volition specifies; Power produces. Knowledge effects ordered arrangement. Volition is not connected with a thing until after the Willer becomes a Knower. All these qualities demand Life. . . . (Some of the objections have already been discussed in Chapter I.)

We refer all the attributes to His being a necessary-existent essence in majestic perfection. From Him everything proceeds in perfect
176 arrangement. He receives relative names like Cause, First Principle, Maker; and negative names like The One, Intelligence, The Intelligent, The Necessary.

I say that your cause and first principle could be said of anything that existed *per se* and was the cause of something else. When the first intelligence came into being from the Necessary Existent One was He its cause *per essentiam* or *per accidens*? If the former He was not absolute and independent; if the latter He could not have been the cause of anything else because He was only a cause by second intention.

177 Further, we say that there is no connexion between God's being the first principle and cause, and being necessary in His essence, for the first is relative and the second is a negative term. You cannot refer both back to essence. . . .

178 Since you postulate the correlative[1] as an idea and an accident additional to substance what is the intelligible difference between the relation of father to son and the relation of cause to effect?

For correlative is an idea whose existence is in analogy to something else and has no existence apart from it, like fatherhood in relation to sonship, not like father, who has an existence of his own. His being a cause and origin is an idea whose existence is in relation to the caused, and has no existence apart from it; so with every cause save the first. You say that fatherhood is an idea, viz. an accident additional (to essence) so why do you not say that causality is an idea, an additional accident, so that causation by essence would be a sort of generation.

I have often thought that what the Nazarenes believe of the Father and the Son is really the same as the philosophers' supposition of the Necessitator and Necessitated and the (first) cause and (first)
179 effect. But 'He begetteth not and is not begotten', causeth not nor is He caused. All things stand in relation to Him as slaves to their Lord.

[1] *iḍāfa*.

CHAPTER IX

Proof that the Eternal Attributes can be known

The Mu'tazila said that God was Living, Knowing, Determining 180
per se, not by Life, Knowledge, and Power. They differed as to His being hearing, seeing, willing, speaking (*v.s.*). Abū Hudhail al-'Allāf followed the philosophers in holding that God knows by knowledge which is Himself (*nafsuhu*), but His Self is not to be called Knowledge after the manner of the philosophers who say that He is Intellect, Intelligence, and Intelligible.

The Mu'tazila differed as to whether the predications connected with the divine essence were states of the essence or modes and relationships. Most took the view that they were names and predications attaching to the essence, and states and qualities are not like the essential qualities attaching to a substance and the qualities which follow origination.

Abū Hāshim said they were latent[1] qualities of the essence; and he posited another state which caused these states.

The orthodox Ash'arite upholders of the divine attributes said that 181
God knew by knowledge, was powerful by power, &c., and these qualities were eternally additional to God's essence, being eternal attributes and ideal realities (*ma'ānī*) subsisting in His essence. . . .

The philosophers said that the Necessary Existent *per se* is one in all respects and no qualification or species can be applied to him. Such terms as are used are negations (One means immune from plurality) or relative like Maker, or a compound of both. . . .

We will now set forth the doctrines and arguments of each school 182
in such length that their mistakes will be revealed and the truth be plainly manifest.

Those who posit attributes give four points of contact between the seen and the unseen world, viz. cause, (necessary) condition, indication, and definition. The fact that a person knows is caused by knowledge, and the logical cause is inseparable from the caused; one is inconceivable without the other. If a knower need not have knowledge, knowledge need not have a knower! The adjective knowing requires the quality and vice versa. He who has qualities must be described by them. They extended this argument to cover God's volition and speech, for they are both eternal epithets,[2] not differing in causation, though according to them (i.e. the opponents) they differ in pre-existence and time (*ḥudūth*).

[1] Or, permanent, *v.s.*

[2] I am inclined to think that the original reading may have been *rasamāni*; Jurjānī defines a *rasam* as an epithet which is the same in pre-existence as in eternity

183 The Muʿtazila said that cause and the need of cause applies only to the potential, not to the necessary existent. God's being knowing is necessary; He needs no causation. Every necessary proposition in the seen world is without cause, e.g. the substance's receptivity of accidents and so on. . . . .

Answer. By causation we do not mean production and origination, but logical necessity and a true reciprocal need of nexus. . . .

184 My view is that the distinction between the relation of the possible to the agent in that it may be brought into existence, and the relation of the state of knowing (*ʿalimiyya*) to knowledge in that it may be necessitated should be carefully observed, for they are vastly different.

185 This question touches the *ḥāl* which we have already sufficiently discussed. It only remains to be said that it is admitted that knowledge is the cause of the state of knowing and vice versa. If knowledge exists its subject must be a knower. . . . The opponent will not admit that there is any resemblance between the knowledge of the Creator and the creature save in name, and claims that they are different in every respect.

186 The Ṣifātiyya argued that the Knower's knowing was conditioned by his being alive, whether in this world or the next, and applied the
187 argument to the divine knowledge also. . . . But condition and conditioned are involved in priority in essence though in existence they are necessary complements. . . . You can say 'the Knower became knowing because knowledge subsisted in him'; but not 'Knowledge subsisted in him because he was knowing'. If these predications were the same in essence this difference could not be posited. Similarly we distinguish between man's power (*qudra*) and the object thereof (*maqdūr*). Though capacity accompanies act in existence it is prior to it in essence, so that you can say, 'The act occurred through the capacity' but not 'The capacity occurred through the act'. Thus we treat condition and conditioned, for the subject must be alive first so that knowledge and power can subsist in him; you cannot say knowledge and power (must exist) first so that he may be alive, for that would abrogate the distinction between condition and conditioned. Do not suppose that this distinction is merely verbal. . . .

188 Either talk of cause and condition must be abandoned altogether, and the word necessity as applied to the mental realities must be dropped, and this is the easiest course, . . . or it must be held that knowledge precedes knowingness and that existence in knowledge is primary and more fitting than it is in knowingness: then it may be

so far as prescience is concerned. O. has a *vox nihili*, P. is wanting, and B. omits the word.

affirmed that essence precedes attributes, and that existence in it is primary and more fitting than it is in the attributes . . . the described *qua* essence precedes the attribute, and the attribute *qua* causation precedes the described. This latter course is to be deplored.

The Mutakallimūn disputed as to whether definition was identical with the defined or not, and whether it and the thing itself (*ḥaqīqa*) were one or two things. Those who denied states said that the definition, reality, essence, and individuality (*'ain*) of a thing expressed one idea.

The supporters of the *ḥāl* maintained that definition is merely the 189
words used to explain the characteristics of the defined, which latter is to be distinguished by a peculiarity common to its class; and this peculiarity is a *ḥāl*. There are some things which can be defined while others are indefinable. Most of the Mutakallimūn's definitions are merely substituting a better-known for a less-known word. The logicians have laboured much in this field, but their results are like those of a diligent student of prosody who has no talent for verse. But they may well be excused, for the subject is exceeding difficult.

Our view[1] is that definition is of three kinds: (*a*) verbal explanation of a term, e.g. thing is something that exists (*maujūd*). . . . This has
no value save that the inquirer knows the word better; (*b*) descriptive, 190
i.e. definition of a thing by its necessary accompaniments, e.g. substance, that which is susceptible of accidents; this kind of definition is helpful in some cases; (*c*) true definition which explains a thing's reality and peculiarity, the essentials held in common with other things and those peculiar to itself. . . .

The definition must be better known than the defined, not identical with, nor additional to, it; it must not define the unknown by the unknown. . . .

In reply to the assertion that the definition of Knower as a possessor of knowledge holds good of God and man, it was said that this was not so because the middle term differed in the known and in the
unknown. . . . Moreover, 'possessor of' is sometimes used descrip- 191
tively, sometimes actively and passively, and sometimes of actual possessions as in *Sur*. 40. 15 where there is no question of an attribute subsisting in the divine essence.

The Ṣifātiyya. The divine knowledge and power are sometimes inferred from God's being Wise and Powerful, and sometimes from a thing being known[2] and decreed. Knowledge is connected with the knowable and power with the decreeable and if it is proved that He knows about the knowable He must know by knowledge. Knowledge is comprehension of the knowable and it is impossible that the divine

[1] The author is speaking. [2] Or, knowable (*ma'lūm*).

essence should comprehend or be connected with an objective relation. Therefore the essence must have a comprehending quality which comprehends (and) is connected with things that can be known.

The Muʿtazila said: God's cognition resides in the fact that He is a Knower, not in knowledge nor essence. The only meaning of knowable is that it is not hid from the Knower as it is, so that there is no perceptual or estimative connexion by which it may be transferred either to the Divine Knowledge or the Divine Essence. To say that knowledge is comprehension is tautology. . . .

192 The Ṣifātiyya. There is an obvious difference between a thing's being knowable and its being decreeable. The first is a much larger category, and can be eternal or temporary, necessary, possible, or impossible. The second is confined to the possible. The relation of the knowable to the divine essence is one, and so is the relation of the decreeable.

We say that the relation of the divine essence to the knowable and the decreeable is on the same footing as you say, or that the relation is different. If the former then it would follow that one is not a wider category than the other, and everything that can be known would necessarily be decreed, just as the converse is true. If the latter these two attributes are not related (*muḍāf*) to His essence but to a quality beyond His essence; and that is what revelation calls Knowledge and Power.

The Muʿtazila said that to predicate different aspects of the relationship of a thing did not require that the quality should be other than a unity: a substance was conceivable as occupying space, or
193 self-subsistent and so on, but this was no indication of plurality in essence or attributes, i.e. essences subsisting in the (one essence), nor of plurality of positive states in the essence. Therefore the statement that God is Knowing and Powerful must be similarly understood.

The Ṣifātiyya agreed in part, but added that the fact that substance occupied space and received accidents showed that it entered into relation with volume and accident. Similarly God can be said to be externally existent, one, &c., and these qualities refer to One Reality; but when He is said to be Living, Knowing, Willing, different specific realities are in question . . . and these are of such a nature that one cannot take the place of another. . . . If they were the same His
194 knowledge would be His Power, and even mutual opposites could be united in one subject—a ridiculous assumption.

We say God is Knowing, Powerful. The Muʿaṭṭila say He is not willing and not powerful. Now assertion and denial must refer to essence, attributes, or states. The first is impossible because (essence) is intelligible without being described as knowingness and powerfulness. . . . Knowledge (or, perhaps, the assertion) that God is self-subsistent does not tell us that God knows, and therefore the proof that God is self-subsistent is other than the proof that he knows and wills; nor does the denial of the quality of knowledge convey the denial of His essence, for the Muʿaṭṭila deny that He knows and wills while they confess that they know about His essence. As to states we have disproved them, so that only attributes remain.

The Muʿtazila. You are the first to postulate different realities and separate characteristics in one essence, since you say that God knows by one knowledge which is related to everything knowable. Obviously knowledge about black is not the same as knowledge about white but contradicts it because, according to you, two similars are not united, though sometimes two different cognitions are united in one reality (*ḥaqīqa*). So God's knowledge is virtually different cognitions. Simi- 195
larly God's eternal power is related to decisions beyond mortal power, and they are virtually different acts of power—similarly with volition, hearing, and seeing, but especially speech. This is one eternal attribute, yet it is in its essence command, prohibition, news, and interrogation, threat, and promise. Obviously these are different realities postulated of the one speech. If you say that these realities are to be regarded as aspects and relations (of speech) we say precisely the same of the (distinctions you claim to perceive in) the divine essence. . . . We deny the validity of the analogy of human and 196
divine. . . . Your argument as to the incidence of assertion and denial is not cogent. The anti-Ḥālists refer them to a particular entity, so the assertion of essence absolutely is inconceivable except as a mere form of words, or it refers to an aspect and relationship. When we say He knows we refer to a knowledge by essence according to an aspect and relationship—or, as the Ḥālists would say, according to a state of his being knowing. . . . Assertion and denial, then, do not refer to qualities additional to His essence but to aspects and relationships; and that is how we regard the qualities. Your argument therefore falls to the ground.

The Ṣifātiyya: Knowledge *qua* knowledge is one reality with[1] one characteristic (*khāṣṣiyya*). Cognitions differ in the relationship of their objects and agree in the unity of the subject. That relationship does not exclude knowledge itself from the reality of the state of knowledge (*ʿilmiyya*). . . . Knowledge follows the knowable in existence and non-existence. It does not acquire the knowable as a quality, nor acquire a quality from it. Cognitions in this world differ with the transitory nature of things, but the eternal knowledge is 197

[1] read *wa-lahu* for *wa-laisa*.

virtually different cognitions not virtually separate characteristics. As to speech, we affirm that command and prohibition, &c., are comprised in true speech and they are united in one reality; relationships of that reality differ in regard to their objects. . . . But it is utterly impossible to say . . . that God knows in respect of His willing and vice versa. . . . Attributes which are not . . . additional to[1] God's essence, negative in the sense that 'eternal' means 'without beginning', &c., are contrary to our assertion that knowing means that He has knowledge. . . . The beauty of the universe proves this together with the power which wrought it. But power and knowledge are two mental realities, not united in essence. You Muʿtazila admit this when you say that knowingness is not itself the meaning of powerfulness because one may know of one and be ignorant of the other.

198 Abū Hāshim. . . . There is no real difference between the party of the *Ḥāl* and the *Ṣifāt* except that the *ḥāl* is at variance with the *ṣifāt* because the *ḥāl* cannot be said to be existent or non-existent, while the *ṣifāt* subsist latent in God's essence.

[Shahrastānī][2] But the former are involved in the method (*madhhab*) of the Nazarenes in their doctrine of unity in substance and trinity in personality; but that contradiction does not follow from the method of the Ṣifātiyya.[2] We maintain that there is proof that the Creator knows and wills, and if these words merely express one idea, according to you they must be interchangeable, and the denial of one would carry with it the denial of the other; and so God must have produced the world by knowledge alone! . . . Undoubtedly the Knowing, the Willing, are not words of such universal application as The-Cause-of-Existence, and The Creator, and we perceive intuitively a fundamental difference between them. If they were synonymous we should not feel this difference. . . .

199 The Muʿtazila. We do not deny the existence of these intellectual aspects and relationships of the one essence, nor do we assert the existence of attributes except in respect of these aspects. What we deny is that there are attributes which are essences (*dhawāt*) eternally existent in God's essence. If there were such they would have to be His essence itself or other than His essence. We say they *are* His essence. If they were not they would be of time (which even you would deny); or eternal, and have shared His essence from all eternity,

[1] Lit. 'beyond'.

[2–2] These words are apparently the author's. The meaning is not immediately apparent, but it would seem that the Ṣifātiyya, by insisting that all the divine attributes which are indicative of personality have a distinct existence in The One, exclude the possibility of their being indicative of a trinity of persons. The party of *Ḥāls*, however, asserted that aspects or modes could be predicated of the divine essence itself, and thus approached to the Christian doctrine of hypostases. Cf. *al-Milal*, p. 56.

and so be other gods. For eternity is the specific quality of the Eternal. . . .

They drew on the writings of the philosophers and added somewhat 200
when they argued that the necessary existent was absolutely independent, and that to ascribe an essential attribute to him was to destroy the independence of the quality and the qualified alike. . . .

The Ṣifātiyya. We deny the existence of a qualified without a quality. We deny, too, the relevance of your dilemma, that the attributes are 'either His essence or something else'. That can only be said of two things, one of which can exist without the other, or without the supposition of it. We do not admit that the attributes are 'other', and we do not assert that they are the essence itself.
Those who uphold the theory of states say they are neither existent 201
nor non-existent, and we similarly affirm that the attributes are neither the essence nor other than the essence, for every quiddity[1] is composed of two things, e.g. humanity of animal and reasoning. It would not be right to say that Reason is humanity itself or that it is other than it. A part is never the thing itself nor other than it.

Your words 'If the quality is eternal it must be God' and 'Eternity is the specific quality of God' are bare assertions. Divinity is an essence described by the epithets of perfection, so why should we assert that any and every eternal attribute is God? He who says that eternity is the specific quality of divinity must tell us what the universal is, for the particular can only be conceived when the universal is known. If existence is the universal and eternity the particular, divinity is composed of the universal and the particular. Therefore the particular is either the universal or something else, and we turn your argument as to the eternal attributes against you. As to your argument that if the attributes were subsistent in His essence, His essence would need them and they are virtually accidents and the existence of the described is essentially prior to that of the quality,
we reply . . . that such considerations apply only to substances and 202
accidents; 'need' as applied to timeless eternity is inconceivable.

In reply to the philosophers we say that absolute independence means that God in respect of His essence is independent of place: and in respect of His attributes He has no need of an associate. . . . His independence resides in His perfect attributes, so how can He be said to have need of that of which He is independent? . . . He is independent in His essence and in His attributes. The described does not need the attribute nor the attribute the described. Need could only be established if the attribute were a kind of instrument, which is impossible.

[1] *ḥaqīqa*.

203 The philosophers. . . . The necessary existent is one in all respects. There is no plurality of parts nor of intellectual ideas. If there were His essence would consist of genus and species, and the parts would constitute the whole. The constituent is prior to that which is constituted, and the former cannot be necessary *per se* . . . but in the constituted the ideas which you postulate must either be necessary *per se*, and so there must be two necessary existent ones (which we have shown to be impossible) or not necessary *per se* but subsist in (God's) essence, and we have demonstrated the impossibility of that.[1] . . .

207 [Shahrastānī] We do not affirm that God can be defined, but that he can be described. . . . To ascribe composition, genus, and species, to Him is to use human analogies which cannot apply to His essence. . . .

208 If we say He knows His essence and He knows that which is not His essence, then His knowledge about His essence is not a knowledge about the other object from the aspect in which it is a knowledge about His essence, but the relationship (*iʿtibār*) is different. With you the relationship of the connexion (*iḍāfa*) of the First Intelligence with Him is other than the relationship of the connexion of the Second Intelligence to Him. And if the intellectual relationships and aspects differ you are met with plurality in the essence. We call each relationship an attribute. Your negative Ideas with us are (the attributes of) eternity and oneness . . . your relative (*iḍāfiyya*) Ideas with us are His being Creator, Sustainer, for the idea of creativeness is conceivable from the creation. . . . We have too the ideas of His being Knowing, Willing, Living. They cannot be said to be negative, for not-ignorant is not the same as knowing. . . . A relative name is applied when an agent performs an action. But the existence of the known and the decreed result from God's knowledge and decree and therefore not in the way in which you apply relative terms. (For they
209 say that God's knowledge is active, not passive.) The Mutakallimūn hold that knowledge comes after the knowable. With them (the philosophers) the knowable comes after the knowledge and the decreeable after the decree. Hence they said that the First Intelligence proceeded from Him because He knew about its essence. Therefore if knowledge is neither a negative nor a relative idea, and is not a composite of both of them, it is plain that it must be an attribute of the Described.

The philosopher asserted that the First Principle understands his (own) essence and he understands what his essence causes and his intelligence is *per se*, inasmuch as it is free from matter *per se*. It is

[1] Here follows a repetition of arguments which have already been advanced about the universal character of existence and the particular incidence of necessity.

the cause of the second principle, which is the first (thing) caused,
so that its existence is necessary inasmuch as it understands its
essence. Everything else is caused in the order of existence by it. Its
freedom from matter is a pure negation in which no plurality of
essence is found. . . . Though the First Intelligence is entirely free 210
from matter, yet its essence in relation to his essence is only potential,
and as such its nature is of the non-existent,[1] material order. Its
abstract conception (of itself) does not attain to the rank of the First
Cause, because it is only the greatest of things in regard to perception,
not in regard to perfection.

The Ṣifātiyya. The Creator knows His essence and He knows what results from it either by one or two acts of cognition. If you say that two knowables demand two cognitions you have contradicted your own thesis: if by one cognition, then He knows the essence inasmuch as he knows the consequence and vice versa, so that the essence must be consequence and the consequence essence, because there only results therefrom what actually results according to His knowledge about His essence and He in respect of His essence knows the result. So essence and consequence are brought into existence, or not, by Him. If He knows the essence in a way other than that in which He knows the result relationships are multiplied and the essence is plural with the plurality of aspects and relationships as we shall explain in Chapter X. . . . .

[Shahrastānī] Obviously 'Knower' implies information about the 211
knowable, and when we say 'He is not in matter' that implies that
He is immaterial. These two concepts are utterly different, and for
the life of me I cannot see how one can be the other's very self. . . .
What distinguishes the Necessary from all other essences? For if it
has no particular it has no universal, and if particularization occurs
through the essence, why do you say it is in existence and not necessity? 212
An attribute particularizes, though in deference to the sacred law we
speak of knowledge, power, and will. You agree as to the knowledge and
power, but you say that He knows through His essence and that His
essence is knowledge. If the essence *qua* essence embraces existence,
and particularization only befalls through an attribute, every existent
universal to be particularized must have an existent specific, so that
the duality of universal and particular would follow, whether or not
one is genus and the other species. If you claim that specific differences are sometimes negative and a negative does not necessitate
duality, you fall into the mistake of some of your logicians who
think that a negation can be essentially a specific difference. . . . But 213
a specific difference must be a positive thing.

[1] Or 'privative'.

The solution lies in resolving the ambiguity of language. We have to use the word existence ambiguously . . . whereas strictly it cannot be applied to God in the sense that it is applied to all existing phenomena. This ambiguity affects the names of all his attributes. . . . But you cannot affirm this and then resort to logical division based on the commonly accepted use of terms. You might as well divide the term *ʿain* into eye, sun, and fountain.

CHAPTER X

Concerning the Eternal Knowledge in Particular; that it is Eternally One, embracing all that is Knowable, both Universals and Particulars.

215 Jahm b. Ṣafwān and Hishām b. al Ḥakam posited in the godhead temporary cognitions about the knowable which constantly change. These conditions were not in a substrate. They agreed that God knows eternally what will be, and knowledge about the future is not the same as knowledge about the present.

The early philosophers asserted that God only knows His essence and from His knowledge of His essence there arose of necessity existent things which are not known by him, i.e. they have no form with Him separately or as a whole. Some said He knows universals, but not particulars: others that He knows both. . . .

We reply to the Jahmiyya that if God originated knowledge for
216 Himself either it must be in His essence or in a substrate, or not in either. Origination essentially demands alteration; and origination in a substrate would demand that the substrate should be of time; while origination not in a substrate would demand the denial of God's specifying. . . .

To consider the meaning of 'not in a substrate' . . . if it applies to the essence of knowledge it must apply to all knowledge; if it applies to something additional to the essence of knowledge it must be the work of an agent,[1] and if that were admitted it could be argued that no accident needs a substrate, which is contrary to experience. . . .

217 Hishām. God knew eternally that the world would exist. When it came into being did His knowledge remain knowledge that it would exist or not? If it did not, then His knowledge or perception[2] suffered change, either in His essence or in a substrate, or not in His essence and not in a substrate. The first is impossible . . . and so is the second . . . so he must have originated the knowledge not in a substrate. If His knowledge that the world would be, remained un-

[1] I.e. discursive. [2] *ḥukm*, the intellectual perception of relations is meant.

changed in its original connexion then it was ignorance and not knowledge at all.

You derive the belief that God has knowledge from his being knowing; and we derive the belief that His knowledge receives new additions from His being a Knower of new things. Therefore to say that eternally He knew the world is absurd. It was not known to exist in eternity, but it became known to exist at a definite time. Therefore God did not know in eternity that it existed; He knew it at the time it happened. Therefore His knowledge changed. If we know that Zaid will come to-morrow that is not knowledge that he has come.

Al-Ashʿarī.[1] There are no changes or novelties in God's perception, 218
state, or quality. His knowledge is one eternal knowledge, embracing all that is and will be knowable. . . . There is no difference between its relation to things in eternity and things that happen at different times. His essence is not affected by the advent of the knowable, as
it is not affected by changes in time. The nature of knowledge is to 219
follow the knowable, without acquiring a quality from it nor acquiring it as a quality;[2] and though knowables differ and multiply they are one in being knowable. The way in which they differ is nothing to do with knowledge about them, but is peculiar to themselves. They are known because knowledge comes into contact with them but that does not alter. The same argument applies to all the eternal attributes. . . . We do not say that God knows the existent and the non-existent simultaneously for that is absurd; but He knows each in its own time, and knowledge that a thing will be is precisely knowledge of its being in the time that it actually comes into being. . . .

If we knew of a certainty that Zaid would come to-morrow and could suppose with our opponents that such knowledge could remain, and then Zaid came, there would be no new knowledge and no need of it, seeing that it had preceded his coming. What was known had happened.

Their argument that we find a difference between the state of our
knowledge before and at the advent of Zaid and that this difference 220
lies in new knowledge applies only to the creature. In God there is no difference between the decreed (*muqaddar*), the established, the accomplished, and the expected. All cognitions are alike to Him. . . .

A cogent argument against them was this: are these new cognitions knowable before they come into existence, or are they not an object of knowledge? If they were knowable was it by eternal knowledge and cognitive power, or by other cognitions which preceded their

[1] I am unable to verify this reference to al-Ashʿarī.
[2] This is a formula which constantly recurs.

existence? If the former then our answer that everything is known by eternal knowledge is your answer about the new cognitions. If the latter, then those cognitions would need other cognitions, and so an endless chain would result.

221 The Muʿtazila. God knows eternally through His essence about the future, and the relation of His essence, or the mode of His knowingness to the knowable in the future is the same as to the knowable in the present. We know the future on the assumption that it will exist, the present as something actually existent. There is no impossibility in the assumption of knowledge (about a past state of things) persisting and the same knowledge holding two knowables either as to human or divine knowledge.[1]...

223 [Shahrastānī] We do not use the words Intelligence and Intelligent of God, but change them to Knowledge and Knower, in deference to revelation. The Mutakallim infers God's knowledge from the order
224 in nature, but this way is not open to you, because you say that (divine) knowledge does not embrace singulars, whereas ordered arrangement can only be asserted of singulars, which can be perceived. As for universals they exist as suppositions of the mind. You are therefore in the position that the order is not knowable in the way that order requires, and what is knowable shows no trace of order.

The philosophers replied that God was free from matter, and all relation with it. He is not veiled from His essence. It is matter that forms the veil, and God, who is transcendent above matter, knows Himself in Himself.

Answer.... But what has the denial of matter to do with God's knowledge?...

225 Avicenna said: Everything that is free from matter is Intelligence in its essence. Every abstract quiddity can be linked with another abstract quiddity and may be intelligible, i.e. impressed (*murtasama*) on another quiddity. The impression of it is its union, and Intelligence has no meaning but the union of one abstract quiddity with another. Therefore if an abstract quiddity is impressed on our intellectual faculty, the impression itself therein is its knowledge and perception of it, and that is intelligence and abstract thought (*taʿaqqul*). If there were need of any form other than the impressed one, there would be an infinite regress. Therefore if the union itself is intelligence it

[1] Here follows a long extract from 'the philosophers'. It is really from Avicenna's *Ilāhiyyat*, p. 588. (The only printed edition ceases to number the pages after 554.) It is to be found in Shahrastānī's *Milal*, and a translation is given in Haarbrücker, ii. 256. The passage is also to be found in the *Najāt*, Cairo, 1331, p. 403. There is nothing to indicate that the author departs from his text in the middle of p. 222, line 15.

follows that every abstract quiddity could from its essence be intelligent.

[Shahrastānī] All you have done is to treat the union (*muqārana*) as a middle term. No doubt you do not mean corporeal union, nor the union of substance and accident, nor of form and matter. But as you have explained, you mean conveying an image,[1] and impressing; and by these two latter you mean abstract thought. But this is to assume the point at issue. You might as well have said the proof that He knows is that His essence could be impressed with a form, i.e. be knowing. The inference that God is intelligent because He is 226
intelligible is absurd. . .

(*a*) Does His knowledge come into connexion with His essence (and) then that knowledge come into connexion with what He knows as it happens; or (*b*) does His knowledge come into connexion with His essence and another cognition come into connexion with what He knows? According to (*a*) it must be said that He only knows His essence because no form is present with Him except His essence, and His intellect has no impression but its own thinking. For you say that Intelligence is the union of quiddities and that the union is the impression of one quiddity on another, so that on this showing nothing can be united to God's existence but His existence. And no impression can be made on His thought but His thought. All accidents, being separated from His essence, must be the object of its thought (*maʿqūliyyatahā*) separate from the object of the thought of His essence. As to (*b*) plurality would result. For if His knowledge of 227
His essence and of the First Intelligence were one from one aspect that would necessitate that His essence was the First Intelligence and vice versa. If they were not so from one aspect then the aspects (*wujūh*) of the divine essence would be many. Again, if His intelligence and knowledge are active, and not passive, it would follow that every object of cognition would be passive to Him, while He would be the object of cognition to His own knowledge. What a conclusion!

Avicenna. God's knowledge of things is necessary, because He knows His essence. . . . The First Intelligence's knowledge of God is 228
not necessary because it knows its essence, for its origin preceded its essence: it is not a consequence of it. . . . The known is not the knower, nor a result of it, so it must be additional to the knower. Thus plurality came into being.

[Shahrastānī] You distinguish between His knowledge of His essence and His knowledge about things, calling one essential and the other necessary knowledge. Do you mean by necessary cognitions things knowable by Him by one knowledge necessarily, which is

[1] *tamthīl.*

229 correct; or do you mean other cognitions necessary to His knowledge about His essence? In what subject are these cognitions, and how are they connected with knowables? . . . But 'Naught in Heaven or
230 Earth is hid from Him' (*Sur.* 3. 4). . . . God's knowledge, like His other attributes, is perfect, and not reached by induction and reflection as ours is. Nothing is hid from Him, whether universal or singular truths, essential or accidental. To distinguish between them is to postulate plurality of relation and aspect and effect.

Those who affirm that the knowledge of the First Caused about the First (Cause) is not necessary to its knowledge about its own essence, because the origin of the first caused preceded its essence, so that knowledge of what preceded its essence is not necessary to its knowledge about its essence, and so is another separate knowledge, follow Avicenna in asserting that he who knows something of his need does not necessarily know what he needs, because what he needs preceded his essence . . . but he only knows it by another knowledge.[1] This is not so. But (though) knowledge often results from knowledge it does not follow that a thing knowable results from a knowable. Avicenna fell into this mistake because he believed that the existence
231 of the first caused resulted from the first cause's knowledge of it, and his knowledge about it was the result of the first cause's knowledge of its own essence. . . . He contradicted his fundamental principle that 'from one only one can proceed', and it did not avail him to plead that one was *per se* and the other from its cause. . . .

To those who say that God knows things universally . . . we reply that all singulars demand a universal proper to them. . . . Universals increase with the classes of singulars. If God only knows the singular from its universal, so that knowledge of the universal does not change while knowledge of the singular does change it follows that knowledge about its universal must be plural, as it is of its singular. If all
232 universals were united in one that one universal would be the only knowable, and it would be necessary to Him in His existence. Thus knowledge about it would be necessary to the knowledge about His own essence, and so we get back to the position of those who say that He only knows His essence. . . .

Again, God's knowledge is not conditional upon happenings and events as when we say there will be an eclipse of the moon if such and such conditions are fulfilled.

The Ṣifātiyya said that the difficulty in the schools had arisen through adding the notions of past, present, and future to knowledge,

[1] See *The Legacy of Islam*, pp. 258-9. This acute criticism of the dominant theory of the kosmos and its relation to the Creator deserves to be read *in extenso*. I have had to reduce it to as small a compass as possible.

and thinking that (God's) knowledge must change with changing events as our knowledge does. . . . But to those who perceive that 233
the eternal knowledge is one this difficulty does not exist.

God's knowledge is one, for if it were many it would multiply with things knowable; and things knowable, necessary, possible, and impossible are infinite, whereas the existent is finite; or it would multiply to a specified number, and this implies one who specifies. The Eternal cannot be specified, so that His knowledge is one . .
though knowables are infinite. The Ashʿarites hold that what God 234
knows about every knowable is infinite, giving as instances the logical possibilities of every knowable, for at any and every moment the phenomenal may be changed. . . .

Objection. . . . What difference is there in a specified number of cognitions and one knowledge—one who specifies the number is
required. God's cognitions are either general or specific. If general 235
in that He knows the infinite then it is one knowledge of one knowable; and what is specified therein remains unknown: if specific in that the things knowable are distinguished in His cognizance by their special characteristic then it is impossible to reconcile specifying with the denial of finitude.

The Ṣifātiyya. By the connexions of God's knowledge we do not mean those of sense and conceptual imagery . . . but we mean that the eternal attribute is capable of perceiving what is presented to it in a way that is not *per impossibile.* That capacity is called connexion (*taʿalluq*); and the aspect of presentation for perception is called object of connexion (*mutaʿallaq*). Both are infinite. . . . The eternal knowledge is a quality meet to perceive what is presented to it as a possibility . . . and the eternal power is a quality meet to give existence to what is presented to it as a possibility. Thus the meaning of presentation is mode of possibility. . . . The meaning of that to which presentation is made is capacity either to perceive
or to bring into existence. It is generally believed that the changing 236
forms that matter constantly receives are infinite and proceed from the Giver of form whose essence is one, yet by way of a quality it has the capacity of emanating. . . . The presentation of possibility to power is as the disposition of matter to receive form; and the capacity of the quality such as perception and bringing into existence is as the capacity of the Giver to emanate form. . . . Capacity as applied to the Eternal is metaphorical; of the temporal it is real. . . . God comprehends all possibilities by one faculty, namely capacity of knowledge like perception, and gives them being by a faculty the capacity of power; specifies them by a faculty of will, and acts as He pleases by commandment and by a faculty, namely the capacity of speech. We

do not mean by this capacity the power of disposition in matter which Aristotle imagined, but perfection in every attribute. Whether
237 these faculties and properties are found together in one attribute or in one essence caused such difficulty to the scholastics that al-Bāqillānī declined to discuss the matter and took refuge in the authority of revelation.

CHAPTER XI

On the Divine Will

238 Three questions are involved: (1) Does God will in reality? (2) Is His will pre-existent and not of time? (3) Is it related to everything?

As to (1) al-Naẓẓām and al-Kaʿbī said No. They said that willing meant creating; and willing men's acts meant commanding them, while eternal will meant eternal knowledge. Al-Najjār said that willing meant 'not compelled and not disapproving'; while al-Jāḥiẓ denied volition altogether and said that if the doer knows what he
239 is doing and acts deliberately[1] then he wills. If he inclines towards the act of another agent that inclination is called volition. Volition, however, is not a genus composed of accidents.[2]

Refutation of al-Jāḥiẓ. Your distinctions apply to men's senses only. Man sometimes acts according to his volition; sometimes he does not: often he wills the act of another without inclining towards it in desire just as he may will his own acts when they are distasteful, e.g. taking medicine. It is folly to argue that will is knowledge, for knowledge is concerned only with the knowable without influencing it in any way. Knowledge . . . is connected with the eternal without affecting it, whilst will is connected only with that which is temporal and subject to change, and does influence it.

Refutation of al-Kaʿbī and al-Naẓẓām. . . . The fact that man acts in a certain way and not otherwise is a proof of volition, and purpose, and the argument holds of God's works. . . .

240 Al-Kaʿbī replied that this proof only held good of man's acts. His limited knowledge is tied to time and circumstance. But God's knowledge coexists with power . . . so that volition is unnecessary, and He has no need of purpose. Indeed volition must either precede or coexist with acts in time; if it precedes, it is resolution, a quality only conceivable in one who hesitates. If volition accompanies action then either it is or is not a novelty in His essence or in a subject. But this is absurd, so it is clear that there is no meaning to volition as applied to the Eternal, save that He is Knowing, Powerful, Active.

[1] Lit. 'without carelessness'. [2] This passage is better expressed in the *Milal*.

Answer. Knowledge follows the knowable whether it comprehends 241
every aspect of it or not. . . . To divide knowledge into a determinant and a non-determinant is to follow the philosophers in their Active Knowledge. . . . Knowledge produces the order of the universe; will determines its characteristics, and power brings it into existence. . . . If man's knowledge were unlimited he would still need will in exercising choice. . . . According to the Ṣifātiyya knowledge follows the event, it does not cause it; power causes it and does not specify it; volition specifies it according to God's knowledge. The eternal attribute precedes the temporal object of volition, but this is not resolution, for resolution is the settling of a question after hesitation. If
willing were but desiring, then knowing would be but believing 242
and thinking. . . . To know is not necessarily to will, and to will is not necessarily to have power to do; but he who has done a thing has had power over it, and so has willed it; and if he has willed it he knows it; so will follows knowledge in such a way that it can be conceived that one knows and does not will, while the converse is inconceivable.

Refutation of al-Najjār. To say that willing means 'not compelled' is to substitute a negative for a positive proposition. . . . Many a man is not impotent, and yet is not powerful, . . . and many will while reluctant, as in taking medicine. . . . Proof of God's will is that things are as they are when they might be otherwise. How can the inference therefrom be evaded? 'Not compelled' is to
be inferred from His power, not from His will to make things as 243
they are.

(2). God wills by an Eternal Will. God wills either in Himself[1] or by a will. If it is established that He wills by a will either the will must be eternal or temporal. If it is temporal it must either be temporal in His essence, or in a subject, or not in His essence, and not in a
subject. . . . Reasons why these views are impossible. . . . If it be 244
objected that there is no relation between the temporal and the eternal we point to equivocation. . . . By saying that the Eternal is not in a subject we mean 'not in a place', while by 'the divine will is not in a place' we mean not in a spatial object.[2] There is no common ground here.

The Muʿtazila. Volitions which are not in a subject are contrary 245
to the accepted meaning of accidents and ideas, and only dire neces-

[1] 'self' (*nafs*) not 'essence' (*dhāt*) is the word used.

[2] *mutamakkin*. It is interesting to observe that Ibn Ḥazm, p. 25, defines the words *lā mutamakkin* as 'not in a place' (*makān*), so that the difference which is made much of here must either be a later refinement as the context suggests; or, as Ibn Ḥazm was an individualist possessing little sympathy with metaphysical subtleties, be one that he would not countenance.

sity has brought about the assertion of such, inasmuch as[1] the divine will cannot be denied with al-Kaʿbī, for that would necessitate that all acts would be purposeless as the Natural Philosophers hold. . . . It cannot be asserted that God wills by His essence, because the essential attributes must be universal, and that would necessitate that God wills crimes and evils. Nor can an eternal will be asserted, for that would involve the existence of two Gods. Nor a temporal will subsisting in God's essence, nor in any other essence. Thus it is clear that it is not in a subject.

However we do not despise the theory of the philosophers who posit separate intelligences attaching to bodies, self-subsistent, the origin of phenomena; nor the theory of temporal cognitions not in a subject propounded by Jahm and Hishām; nor a speech (*taklīm*) not in a subject asserted by the Ashʿarites; for the speech in God's essence was not conveyed to Moses' hearing, and what Moses heard was not in a subject.

246 The Ashʿariyya. But if you say that a speaker is the agent of speech, admit that a willer is the agent of will. There is no comparison
247 between your theory and the philosophers' theory of separate intelligences, for they posit self-subsistent substances receptive of ideas, although they do not assert that they are spatial. But you posit volitions of temporal phenomena, namely accidents not in a substrate, thereby robbing them of the specific qualities of accidents, and not making them substances. . . .

Your reference to Ashʿarī is fundamentally unsound, for according
248 to him God's speech is audible by men, as He (will be) visible to men; and that does not involve conveying or alteration or ceasing. You have gone round the schools picking up ideas with the meanest results.

(3). As to the question of the relation of God's will to everything the Muʿtazila who hold that God's volitions are in time say that God wills His particular acts in the sense that He purposes to create them according to His knowledge. His will precedes the act by a moment. He wills that the good acts of His servants should come to pass and that the evil should not. What is neither good nor bad, obligatory nor forbidden, He neither wills nor disapproves of. Will[2] and disapproval can precede such acts in time. . . .

The earliest of them said that temporal volition necessitates a thing willed, and they specified causation (*ījāb*) by intention to produce action. They did not mean by causation the cause producing the effect, nor secondary causation. Will, they said, does not produce

[1] The correct reading must be *min qablu* instead of *qīla*. Unfortunately this page is one of a batch of manuscript collations which were lost in the post between Beyrout and Oxford.

[2] The sense of *irāda* is weakened almost to wish.

secondary effects, for they held that the divine power necessitates its object by means of cause. Therefore if will produced secondary effects by means of cause the thing willed would rest on two causes and the phenomenon of two objects of power would involve two Powerful Ones.

The Muʿtazila said that if the eternal attribute were related at all 249
it would be so universally. If the will were eternal it would have as its object all its own volitions and all the volitions of men. Therefore if Zaid wanted one thing and ʿAmr its opposite it would necessitate God's willing two opposites at the same time. . . .

The Ashʿariyya said that the eternal attribute must be related to everything, or its universal relation must be with that which is properly its object. . . . The first is impossible if the economy of the divine attributes of knowledge, power, and will are considered. The divine knowledge is universal, power is of more limited application and will still less. Will confers specific existence and is concerned with its renewal from moment to moment.[1]

As to the relation of eternal will to two opposites at the same time[2] they denied the proposition altogether, for what befalls is what God knows will befall. It is the object of will and He is the willer. What 250
He knows will not befall is not willed. He who wanted it to happen was the wisher. The eternal will can be related to both. . . .

The eternal will is only related to a phenomenon from one aspect, namely the momentary, inasmuch as the phenomenon is continually specified with existence; and the two wills (of Zaid and ʿAmr) share in continual re-creation and are related to the divine will by way of re-creation and specification, and in this respect are not opposites. If it be said that the divine will is related to both wills, . . . and to one object of will, namely the one that happens according to knowledge, and is related to the non-occurrence of the other, i.e. the will that one should happen and dislike of the other that is correct, cf. *Sur*. 2. 181.

The Muʿtazila. If God's will is related to everything He wills evil, 251
whereas the Qurān 32. 40 says He does not. If He wills evil He is evil.

The Ashʿariyya. . . . It does not follow. He who wills to know does not necessarily know. . . . Man's will is sometimes necessary, sometimes acquired.[3] . . . The first is not ethical, the second is. . . . Therefore no parallel can be drawn between man's will and God's will.

[1] For the Muslim doctrine of continuous re-creation see an interesting article by D. B. Macdonald in *Isis*, ix (1927), 326 f.

[2] These words ought to form the beginning of a new paragraph in the Arabic text. See note on p. 86.

[3] I.e. according to the theory that man's will is only apparent. He acquires the faculty of willing because God creates in him the consciousness of free will.

252 The relation of the eternal will to man's acts is not in respect of the commandments . . . nor by way of acquisition: but in respect of its specifying phenomena by existence instead of non-existence each moment, fixing its dimensions. Thus it is neither good nor evil. . . . Existence which God wills is good. . . . But existence so far as man is concerned is a mere quality of his action in reference to his power, capacity, time, place, and obligation; and in this way is not willed nor decreed by God.

We have proved that God creates men's actions . . . and he creates by choice and will, not by nature and essence. He wills and chooses renewal of existence and new phenomena and *qua* existence it is all good. He wills good (and as to evil inasmuch as it is existent, it partakes of good and from that aspect is good and is willed, so that pure evil does not really exist. God wills existence)[1] and He wills good while man wills good and evil. The Wise[2] said evil comes within
253 the divine will *per accidens*, not through essence, and by second intention; for evil according to them is either privation of existence or privation of the perfection of existence. Existence and the perfection of existence is the primary intention. Sometimes existence is primary perfection and goes on to a secondary perfection: sometimes it is absolute as in the case of the separate intelligences. . . . That which is in a primary, i.e. potential, state of perfection until it actually reaches the second perfection meets with conditions which either help or hinder its advance. Now the eternal will and the divine providence are related to both, but to one by way of inclusion and secondary intention; . . . to the other by way of disposition and origin (*aṣāla*) and essence, i.e. willed and intended by a primary intention. Thus rain descends for the general good of the world and is good absolutely, but if it destroys the house of an old woman . . . that is relatively evil, but not intrinsically (*bil aṣāla*) and is a secondary not a primary intention. The existence of universal good along with singular evil is philosophically better than a state in which there is no universal good and no singular evil. . . .

254 The Muʿtazila. If God commands a thing He wills it, and if He forbids it He dislikes it. The proof is that command requires performance and will demands that the thing shall be specified with existence. To require a thing and its opposite is absurd, so that to say that Allah commanded Abū Jahl to believe and willed him not to believe would involve command and will being at variance, which is absurd. On this principle your analogy from the divine knowledge is excluded. God may command and know that the command will

[1] These words are inserted (by the original hand) in the margin of O.
[2] *al-ḥukamā*, i.e. the Islamic philosophers.

not be obeyed, because knowledge makes no demands on others, whereas will does.

The Ashʿariyya. We do not admit that every one who commands 255
a thing wills its performance, unless he also knows that it will be performed.... The theory of will opposed to knowledge is destructive of the distinctive character of will which is to specify things....

Some objectors said that what was contrary to the known was not decreed, so how could it be willed, as knowledge is universal and will particular.

[Shahrastānī] My opinion is that he who orders a thing does not will it in so far as it is ordered, whether it be obedience or anything else when he knows that it will be performed; or whether the reverse. For the act commanded is acquired by the performer, and we have explained that that accounts for the epithets worshipper, pilgrim, &c. The act is not related to the Creator in this way nor does He will it in this way; but it is related to Him by way of creation from moment to moment, and specific determination; and the action not being an act of the willer is not an object of will to him. So far as man is concerned his act which we call acquisition and which takes place
in agreement with divine knowledge and command is willed and 256
approved, by which I mean willed by creation from moment to moment, and specific determination, and approved by praise and reward; while what takes place in agreement with knowledge and contrary to command is willed and not approved, by which I mean willed by creation from moment to moment: disapproved by blame and punishment. He who masters this nicety is secure against Qadariyya and Jabriyya. Thus Allah wills things not in respect of their being good or evil, but in respect of their being specified with existence instead of non-existence, and being of a certain size and time.... If man had no power over anything his act would be created from moment to moment, specified by the divine will irrespective of good and evil.... All acts good and evil are willed by God and make
for the good of the world, cf. *Sur.* 2. 181.... The eternal will is only 257
related to those things which are constantly renewed, and all such things are the work of God ... and are not to be referred to men.... God's will specifies His actions in reality, not in the way in which it is related to man, and His command specifies men's actions really, not in the way in which it is related to Him, so that the relation of command and will is not necessarily reciprocal, though it sometimes is.

Abu-l Ḥusain adduced examples of will conflicting with command,
e.g. when God ordered Abraham to sacrifice his son and willed that 258
he should not do so; for had He willed it Abraham would have done it. But we will not stop to consider such puerilities.

The Muʿtazilites seized upon the literal meaning of such texts as 'He likes not ingratitude in His creatures', 39. 9[1] to which the
259 Ashʿariyya replied with allegorical and specific explanations. Thus God's will or love is not related to disobedient acts as such, just as His power is not related to men's works inasmuch as they acquire them. To take these texts in order. 'He likes not ingratitude' means he does not like it so far as religion and law are concerned, for it brings evils in its train. This meaning is strengthened by the fact that pleasure and anger are opposites. Anger is used of blame, and punishment hereafter, and similarly pleasure of praise now and reward hereafter. . . .

260 The philosophers. The world order moves towards Good, because it proceeds from the origin of good, and the good is what everything desires. . . . When the first being knew the perfect good *in potentia* . . . it emanated from him . . . and that is the eternal providence and will.
261 Thus good came within the divine decree essentially not accidentally while evil came accidentally. . . . Evil may be said to be deficiency like ignorance and impotence, or like pain and sickness, or like fornication and theft. In fine evil *per se* is privation, i.e. the loss of a thing's true and perfect nature. Evil absolutely does not exist, except in speech and thought. Accidental evil exists *in potentia*, because of matter. It begins through a certain disposition (*hai'a*) which prevents its proper receptiveness of the perfection towards which it moves. The pernicious result is due not to a privative act of the Agent, but to the unreceptiveness of the object; thus arise bad
262 morals, the dominion of the bestial over the human mind, giving rise to evil practices and corrupt beliefs; or the evil influence may come from without as from parents and teachers. . . . Evil, coming in thus, accidentally, is rightly rewarded with destruction because of the existence of the opposing cause. . . . When evil is mixed with good it is most proper that it should be brought into existence, for its non-existence would be a greater evil than its existence . . . otherwise
263 a universal good would be lost in the interest of a particular evil. . . . A good example is fire. . . . Any other interpretation involves the error of the Dualists.

The Mutakallimūn. Our only controversy is concerning the good things which are related to man's acts and acquisition like corrupt
264 beliefs and evil practices. . . . Are they due to our will and not to God's? There is no dispute as to whether dangerous beasts and terrors from the sky, plagues, &c., with all their attendant miseries are good or evil. . . . Ignoring the particular question as to whether these things have aught of good in them we keep to the universal. You

[1] I have omitted other texts cited.

say that everything proceeds from the one . . . and argue about first and second intentions. But what is the difference between evils accidentally necessitated in the universe, and the universe coming into being necessarily? For in that case nothing in existence is necessitated *per se* so that anything else can be necessitated *per accidens*. To say that everything desires the good contradicts your principle so far as concerns the divine will. For God does not desire the good, but everything desires Him, for He is pure good. He is the desired, not the desirer . . .[1]

[Shahrastānī] We see the corporeal world full of trials, famine, 266
pestilence, and wars . . . persisting in ignorance and corrupt beliefs, the majority living evil lives, lust and anger prevailing over the mind and intellect, so that you can hardly find one in any country holding[2] the divine wisdom which you regard as the *imitatio dei*, or a remnant obeying the church's[3] laws which we regard as a copy of the divine commands. Most of them as it is written are 'deaf, dumb and blind and do not understand', 7. 100. How then can your philosophers maintain that the evil that is in the world does not exist, when the facts contradict you?

Wherever we find nature and the divine determination prevailing over human choice and acquisition happiness prevails; but wherever human choice and acquisition prevail evil prevails, so that we return to the position that there is no evil in God's works; and if evil is to be found therein it is relative to one thing and not to another. Evil only enters into men's voluntary acts, and they, in so far as they are
linked to the will of God, are good; but if linked to man's acquisition 267
they acquire the name of evil.[4] Nevertheless the existence of devils and their leader Satan as revealed by the scriptures cannot be denied. . . . The early doctors asserted that every singular in this world existed as a universal in the next . . . so singular evil in this world had its universal counterpart. Thus the Magi postulated two principles, the source of good and evil respectively. See further my *Milal*.

CHAPTER XII

That the Creator speaks with an Eternal Speech

All Muslims hold that God speaks with a speech: only the philo- 268
sophers, Ṣābians, and Deists deny that. Theologians prove the thesis

[1] Here *murād* and *murīd* have an unusual nuance.

[2] B. has 'taking refuge in'.

[3] *shar'iyya*.

[4] This would seem to mean that man's will, if surrendered to God, will produce good; but if his free will is exercised apart from God's will evil must result. Shahrastānī has not stated this explicitly perhaps because it conflicts with the orthodox doctrine.

in different ways, thus the Ash'arites say that reason demands that God must be alive, and it is proper to a living being to speak . . . otherwise He must be said to be dumb. Further a king is obeyed, and the idea of king involves positive and negative commands. As the differences in the world of phenomena indicate His power and knowledge, so the differences in commands and prohibitions indicate
269 His (explicit) commandment. . . .

Al-Isfarā'inī said: the order of the universe proves God's knowledge. It is impossible that He should know a thing and not announce it, for knowledge and announcement are necessary correlatives. It is impossible to conceive the existence of one without the other. He who has no power of relating cannot communicate his knowledge. It is well known that law, instruction, narrative, warning, guidance, and teaching,[1] become Him, so that He must have speech and speaking to convey them.

[Shahrastānī] Either He speaks to Himself (which none holds) or He speaks with a speech which must be either temporal or eternal. If temporal it must either have originated in His essence, as the Karrāmiyya whom we have already refuted hold, or in a substrate as the Mu'tazila say; or not in a substrate as nobody believes. . . .
270 Now if speech resided in a substrate that would be the agent of speech. . . . Hence the only possibility is that God speaks with an eternal speech.

The philosophers and Ṣābians[2] replied that the statement that a living person must either be said to speak or be dumb was a bare assertion without proof apart from human analogies . . . which the Asha'rites were fond of extending to all the divine attributes. . . . The argument that either a proposition or its contrary must hold true of God is ridiculous. A living person has five senses, but you would not say that either God smells or He does not. . . . We treat seeing, hearing, and speech in the same way. Many a quality which is perfection in us would be a defect in God. . . .

271 We agree that God is a king whose commands are to be obeyed, but his commands are not verbal but factual (*fi'lī*), i.e. by way of making the creature know by compulsion[3] that he must perform the act commanded. To ensure this God creates in the creature *certain*[4]

[1] These terms summarize the contents of the Qurān.

[2] The reading of B. must be followed.

[3] I think the true reading must be *jabran*, not *khabaran* (B. could be read with *j* against O.'s *kh*). Though it would, of course, be possible to hold that man's intuitive necessary knowledge of right and wrong was *khabar*, the argument favours compulsion; cf. line 11.

[4] *ḍarūrī*, i.e. (*a*) the knowledge of the senses and (*b*) immediate knowledge, e.g. that two opposites cannot be true.

knowledge that the matter must be thus. Discussion as to whether God speaks with a speech which He creates in a substrate or speaks eternally with a speech that can be heard at one time and not at another is sheer nonsense, because giving liberty or forcing obedience takes the place of speaking. . . . *Sur.* 41. 10: 'Then He said to heaven and earth: come ye two willingly or unwillingly. They said we come willingly'. This is not verbal speaking, but divine compulsion. . . . Cf. also 19. 42: 'Our speaking to a thing when we will it is Be! and it is'. Speech addressed to the non-existent is impossible.

Again, if God speaks it must either be or not be with human speech; 272
if the latter, it must belong either to the tongue or the heart (*nafsānī*). The first is impossible, composed as it is of letters and sounds made by the impact of members of a body. . . . If He creates His speech in a substrate His speech is not speaking but action. . . . Moreover, that substrate would have to possess a man's frame and so be a man . . . and this would lead to incarnationism. If the substrate had no organs
of speech, sounds and not speech would result, like rustling and 273
rippling and thunder; but these are not speech. Nor can mental speech be admitted, for whether it be a mental concept of words normally used by the tongue in Arabic or any other language the mind holds the image of words; or something that is embedded in the very nature of the mind—distinctions and reflections which the tongue can express—it must be denied of God. . . .

Thus it follows that what lies outside the genus of human speech cannot be used as an argument in reference to human speech. . . . And your argument that every one who knows perceives in himself the news of what has become known to him is excluded; for if it is true of man it is not true of God. Similarly the argument that a king must be the author of commandments does not hold good of God.

The Mutakallimūn. Our method is to employ human analogies: 274
from the laws (of nature) we infer (God's) knowledge; from actual events His power; and from the determination of possibilities His will. Similarly we infer from man's incumbent duties that God commands and prohibits, cf. *Sur.* 7. 52. Laws demand fulfilment, and demand is an intelligible concept outside knowledge, power, and will . . . knowledge is connected with the knowable; it does not
demand it . . . power is simply capacity to produce, and is connected 275
with the possible . . . will is capacity to determine possibilities . . . . We have demonstrated that some things are willed and not commanded, and vice versa. Will is only properly connected with the act of the willer; demand and command with the act of another. . . . Thus laws cannot be included under the attributes of knowledge,

power, and will, and so we refer them to speech. Revelation refers to them as commands and addresses.

Further, man's voluntary acts are threefold: (1) mental, the free exercise of his intellect and thought; (2) vocal, the free exercise of his soul and his tongue; (3) active, the free exercise of his bodily powers. On all these God has laid commandments. The mental embraces the true, the spurious . . . the vocal embraces truth and lying, . . . wisdom and folly; the active embraces good and evil,
276 obedience and disobedience. It has been proved that the Creator is wise and just and has the sentence and judgement in regard to all these movements. That judgement must either be an act or a speech. An act is impossible because every act is preceded by its judgement. But that act is a proof of his judgement, and his judgement is inferred from his act. . . . We admit that freedom of action (*taṣrīf*) in fact, takes the place of laws in words so far as man's involuntary acts are concerned, but the voluntary acts call for judgement. So then every act and giving of freedom by the Creator points to His judgement and claim (upon man).

Now we[1] say action points to the knowledge, power, and will of the agent and in so far as it vacillates between the permitted and the forbidden categories it points to the Creator's judgement which is sometimes a positive, sometimes a negative command. . . .

The assertion that God speaks rests upon the possibility of His sending apostles. He who denies that God speaks must deny that He
277 sends apostles. He who recognizes the possibility of God's sending an apostle, his messages being God's commands and prohibitions, and attributes them to a work which He does in a substrate in that it can be understood from that work that God likes or dislikes certain actions . . . has admitted our point. . . .

There are two kinds of judgement: first command and prohibition; and secondly threats and promises. To deny this is to deny the
278 sovereignty of God, and man's eternal recompense, and to falsify the proposition of divine wisdom.

There are animal souls which only employ one sense for communicating: others use mere sounds without intelligible[2] words; others intelligible noises until we find words composed of letters properly arranged. This is an indication of rational souls. Not every rank is of the same genus as its predecessor, . . . but it may be hazarded that spiritual souls and angels exist in a similar hierarchy of mutual understanding. As rational speech is not that of birds and beasts, so the speech of angels is not as ours. . . . If we carry the analogy into

[1] Apparently the speaker is Shahrastānī.

[2] Intelligible to an ordinary human being.

the unseen we say that He to whom belongs 'the creation and the 279
command' is above commands uttered by mortal tongues and the thoughts of men's minds, and that He in His oneness thinks and hears in a way that utterly transcends our thought and speech. . . . Further, why do you admit that the Giver of intelligence is intelligent and the author of beginning is powerful, and deny that the Giver of speech is a speaker? Why treat speech differently from the other attributes? . . .

The Muʿtazila. We agree that God is a speaker, but a real speaker is one who makes speech, so that God is a maker of speech in a substrate . . . because if, as you say, a speaker is one in whom speech
subsists it must either subsist eternally or temporally. If it were 280
eternal there would be two eternals. . . . What makes the eternity of speech impossible is that if the speech which is command and prohibition were eternal God would have had to lay commands on Himself. . . . There can be no possible doubt that the words 'we sent Noah to his people' (*Sur.* 7. 56) when (*ex hypothesi*) there was no Noah and no people is a report of what did not exist, an impossibility, and a lie. The words 'take off thy shoes' addressed to Moses when he did not exist . . . is speech with the non-existent, and how can a nonentity be addressed? Therefore all commands and narratives in the Qurān must be speech originated at the time the person addressed was spoken to. Therefore the speech is in time.

If, as the Karrāmiyya say, the speech originated in His essence He is a *locus* of novelties, and that is false. It must have originated in a subject, for speech is a sound articulated and formed in a body, so it is plain that it is in a body.

The Ashʿariyya. How would you maintain against a Ṣābian or a philosopher that God speaks, if His speech is an act like the rest of
His acts . . . and what proof is there that He speaks through another? 281
How do you differ from those who say that He creates an intelligible act or that speech is ascribed to Him metaphorically?

The Muʿtazila. The proof lies in the miracles which confirm the veracity of the prophets who claim to speak in the name of God.

Response. You cannot argue this because you have said that if God had not sent an apostle the intelligent person would be bound to recognize God, and God would have had to reward him. But if God did not send an apostle how can you maintain that He speaks. You say that speech is an act of God, but how can you prove that He did that particular act? You say that the divine will is created not in a substrate, and that speech is created in a substrate. . . . What is the difference?

[Shahrastānī] Speech has a meaning whether it be in words, or 282

sounds, or a mental quality and an intellectual reasoning without words; and every meaning which subsists in a substrate gives its name to the substrate. Inasmuch as the meaning is created it can be said to be made, and inasmuch as it is a meaning subsisting in a substrate . . . the substrate can be described by it. . . . But to say that the meaning of God's being a Maker is the meaning of His being described as a Speaker is absurd. . . . Speech, according to the opponent, is composed of consonants and vowels (or sounds); sound is a wider term than speech. All speech is sound according to him, yet all sound is not speech. Yet are we to call the Creator a sounder
284 because He creates sound in a substrate?[1]... To refute their statement that a speaker is he who makes speech: suppose God created in a sick man the words 'I stand and I sit' either the speaker is their creator, in which case the Creator says 'I stand and I sit'; or it is the man himself. In that case gone is their argument that a speaker is not he in whom speech subsists, but the maker of the speech.

Again, there are miracles of speech which God created in stones and beasts, e.g. the poisoned sheep cried: 'Eat me not for I am
285 poisoned'[2] and the pebbles in the prophet's hand glorified God. All this was God's doing. The speaker, according to them, is he who makes speech, so God must have been speaking through them, since He was their maker, and that is impossible.

The Najjāriyya agree with the Ashʿariyya that God creates men's works, so they are bound to say that He speaks with their speech because He is the maker of it. . . . The mighty is he who has power over two opposites. Therefore if they say a speaker is he who makes speech, they must say that the silent is he who makes silence, so that if he created silence in a substrate he was silent. . . .

286 Letters and words would not be called speech unless they had a meaning. Their place is the tongue, but meanings and intelligibles are in the heart.[3] When both are found together a man is called Reasoner and Speaker. If words void of meaning are heard a man is called mad, not a speaker except by metaphor. On the other hand, if we find ideas[4] in the heart without words a man is called a thinker, not a speaker, except by metaphor. The difference is precisely that between a man who professes a belief which he does not hold, and one who holds a belief and does not profess it.

Unless the words corresponded with the thought in the mind there would be no speech. Nay, further, unless the thought in the mind preceded the expression of it on the tongue it could not be expressed.

[1] I have omitted this strife about the words.
[2] Cf. al-Dārimī, Intr., p. 10.
[3] *janān.*
[4] *maʿānī.* Here the same word, as often, does duty for 'meaning' and 'idea'.

This is obvious of us, but what is to be said in reference to God? Does He create words in a substrate and give an indication of their meaning or not? They must have a meaning, and wherein does it reside? Not in God's knowledge, for that makes no demands[1]. . . nor 287
in His will, for though that can be supposed to make demands it cannot include narrative, interrogation, threats, and promises (which are contained in the Qurān); nor can it be His power, for nothing could be more remote from that which makes demands on others. . . . Therefore it must be in a speech. It now remains to debate whether this speech is one or many: eternal or temporal.

CHAPTER XIII

That God's Speech is One

The Ashʿariyya hold that God's speech is one, embracing commands, 288
narrative, interrogation, &c.

The Karrāmiyya hold that God's speech in the sense of power over speech is one idea; and in the sense of speaking (*qaul*) is many ideas, subsisting in His essence, and that they are audible sayings and words preserved which originate in His essence when He speaks: they cannot pass away or cease.

The Muʿtazila hold that speech consists of an ordered arrangement of words whether in this world or the next; they are created and subsist in a temporal substrate. When God gives them existence they are heard in the substrate, and as they come into being so they cease to exist.

Al-Jubbā'ī said that speech human and divine required the organs of speech: his son Abū Hāshim said 'not divine speech'.

The Ashʿariyya said that as it was proved that speech was an idea 289
subsisting in God's essence, as God's knowledge, power, and will was one, so must His speech be one. . . . If our opponents agreed that man's speech is an idea in the mind corresponding to the words on the tongue and that God's speech is an idea subsisting in His essence corresponding to the words which we read with the tongue and write they would agree on the unity of the idea; but as the word speech is used ambiguously we cannot reach a common basis. What they call speech the Ashʿariyya agree is plural, created in time: what the Ashʿariyya call speech they deny altogether. In this discussion the opponent takes only a negative and destructive position.

The Muʿtazila: it is impossible that God's speech should be one, and (also) commands, interrogations, &c., for these are different 290

[1] Sc. as the Qurān does.

realities and separate specifics. It is impossible that one thing with one reality should embrace different specifics. You can have one idea embracing many ideas like genus and species, e.g. humanity; but these have only subjective existence. It is impossible that one thing which is different things should exist objectively, for that would abolish the realities as the Sophists do. The relation of command, &c., to speech is as the relation of power, will, black, and movement, to one thing, for they are all realities, and that is absurd. You can say that speech is a generic term containing species although genus has no existence without different species, and species has no existence without individuals with different accidents; accident has no existence without different species, e.g. colour, which again must be specified, e.g. black; for accident has no essence apart from the
291 substance in which it subsists. . . . But you have posited speech subsisting in God's essence as one reality which is in itself command, prohibition, &c., and this is absurd.

The Ashʿariyya. . . . According to al-Ashʿarī speech is one attribute with one peculiar property. The categories of speech are characteristics or necessary accompaniments (*lawāzim*) of that attribute. The divine knowledge is one attribute and not many because knowables are many; . . . nor is speech plural because speech has many relations. Command and prohibitions are descriptions of speech, not parts (*aqsām*) of speech. . . . The fact that speech embraces many meanings is not to be compared with the division of the accident into different classes. The parts and the descriptions of a thing are not
292 one and the same. The divisions of mortal speech are descriptions of God's speech. Thus an idea is sometimes one in essence with descriptions viz. rational relations: then the rational relations are sometimes in respect of connexions, sometimes in respect of necessary accompaniments. Is not will sometimes pleasure and sometimes anger? . . . Thus speech is sometimes command and sometimes prohibition . . . yet it is one in essence, its names changing with its relation.[1]. . . .

293 The philosophers who are most vehement in denying the eternal speech and its uniqueness postulate an intelligence one in essence and existence from which different forms infinite emanate. Their emanation is like the relation (*taʿalluq*) of the Mutakallimūn . . . the difference in speech is like the difference of emanation in the forms. Compare, too, their doctrine that the first principle does not multiply with the multiplicity of objects and qualities. . . .

294 The Muʿtazila. . . . Command and prohibition are opposites with different specific qualities which cannot be posited of one speech. We

[1] Arguments about the *ḥāl*, advanced already, have been omitted.

do not deny that one thing can have different names . . . but we do
deny that one thing can have different specific qualities. The fact
that speech is command and prohibition is not established by its
relation, but it is a specific of the speech itself from whatever point of
view. . . . A speech that is in itself both command and prohibition is
impossible. . . . It is incorrect to say that speech is different in descriptions and not in divisions, for command, prohibition, &c., are divisions 295
of speech. Speech embraces them like a genus. . . . It is sheer nonsense to say 'the divisions of mortal speech are descriptions of God's
speech'. How can realities change and intelligibles vary? . . .

But perhaps a philosopher would say that as Intelligence is one so
the emanation from it is one, but the receivers and carriers are diverse
and so the emanation differs with the different receiver (*mafīḍ*); e.g.
when the sun shines on pieces of glass of different colours each piece
displays its proper colour. The forms are many but the diversity proceeds from the receiver not the emanator. But you posit one speech
which is as a matter of fact a plurality of different properties and in
which the diversity resides, so that there is no analogy. . . . 296

The divine essence is one and its perfection is not in attributes.
He is above all names and attributes: these can only be predicated
of Him in respect of the traces of His activity. . . .

The Ashʿariyya. We do not assert different realities . . . of the one
speech. . . . If we were to say that something was commanded and
forbidden at the same time that would be absurd.[1] . . But it does not
follow that differences which do not involve contradiction are im- 297
possible . . .; consider for example the various properties of the substance. . . . Just as the eternal knowledge embraces diverse cognitions 298
as a universal without plurality of essence or difference in its property
so the eternal speech embraces all speech. . . . This is what we mean
by 'divisions (or parts) of mortal speech are like descriptions of divine
speech'. . . . Imperatives, aorists, and futures are divisions which deal
only with aspects and relationships because the eternal speech is one
without plurality. . . . Before Adam's creation mention is made of
the caliphate in the future: 'Behold I am about to appoint in the
earth a caliph' (2. 28). After Noah's mission and long after his
generation the past tense is used 'We sent Noah to his people' (7. 57).[2]
When Moses is mentioned before he existed it is on the model of news
about the future:[3] when he is mentioned in the Wady al-Muqaddas
it is on the model of the imperative 'Take off thy shoes'. All these

[1] The text in the three MSS. differs considerably here.

[2] The first quotation is of God's speech to the angels before the world was created; the second was spoken to Muhammad himself.

[3] I.e. the prophetic perfect common in the Hebrew prophets.

differences are to be regarded as explanations of the speech which is
299 in accord with what is known (to God).

If we could conceive that we possessed an intellectual speech preceding the existence of the person addressed and remaining throughout the ages, the object of the speech would be in one unchanging reality while what expressed the speech would be in different parts. If we could conceive that we possessed an intellectual speech corresponding exactly to an intellectual comprehension exalted above age and time so that its relation to past, present, and future was the same, any difference would not be due to plurality of characteristics of meanings in its essence, but to that which is altered by time. Does not the Qurān speak about what will happen in the resurrection? (5. 116). Does He not refer to the future in the past tense when as yet there is no resurrection? . . . Real and eternal speech being exalted above time can speak of the future as though it were the past. . . .

300 How can they conceive the descent of spiritual beings and their becoming individualized in corporeal beings as revelation records 'We sent unto her our spirit and it appeared (*tamaththala*) to her in the likeness of a mortal' (19. 17)? How does the Mutakallim explain this? That the spirit was annihilated and the individual brought into existence? That is not resembling something. Or that the spirit makes use of an existing person—that again is not *tamaththul* but metempsychosis. If he cannot explain appearing in the shape and likeness how can he conceive the eternal command appearing now in the likeness of Arabic, now of Syriac, so that it must be said to be the speech of God? . . . That which clothed[1] Gabriel changes, but his reality by reason of which he is Gabriel is unchangeable. Similarly with the speech of God. . . .

301 The Muʿtazila. If you posit an eternal speech either you assert that God's speech was command, news, &c., in eternity, or you do not. If you do you are absurd for the following reasons:

(1) A command must apply to somebody, and there was nobody in eternity to be addressed . . . and it is impossible that the non-existent should be the object of a command.

(2) Speech with oneself without a second person is ridiculous in this life (from which you draw an analogy) and to call to a person who has no existence is too foolish to be ascribed to the wise.

(3) The speech[2] with Moses is different from that with the prophet and so is the manner of it. It is impossible that one meaning which is

[1] *libās*.

[2] *khiṭāb* not *kalām*, because the former would normally require the presence of the *mukhāṭab* or person addressed.

in itself speech should be with one person with one meaning and manner and with another person with another meaning and manner and then the two speeches be one thing and one meaning.

(4) The two reports of the conditions of the two communities differ with their differing conditions. How can two different conditions be described by one report? And how can they be command, &c.? If you assert that speech is one you abolish its divisions without 302
which it is unintelligible. . . . The story of Joseph and his brethren is other than the story of Adam and Noah, &c., and how can the report of what happened to one person be the very same as that which happened to another? Commands laid upon people in the time of Noah were peculiar to that age. . . . How can you maintain that narratives are one when they differ in each case; or that commands are one when they alter from time to time? How can you assert connexion between the meaning of news about past or future which makes no demands and the meaning of the imperative? News has no imperative and the imperative no news. True they belong to the category of speech, but they differ in species. . . . But you can't refer speech with its divisions and species to news or to commands. . . . 303
Nor can you refer the difference and plurality therein to the words (*ʿibārāt*) . . . for these correspond with the meanings they express . . . and so the meanings are plural as the words are. . . .

As to your argument from the spiritual being assuming the likeness of the corporeal being and the angel taking the form of a man being like the (divine) idea appearing in words (*ʿibarat*) this to us is folly. For what is 'assuming the likeness' and 'taking the shape'; and how is there an appearance? . . . In our view Gabriel is an ethereal being[1] who became gross and visible to human sight, like diaphanous vapour which is invisible and becomes thickened and visible as clouds; or we hold that the one entity is annihilated and the other produced without the assuming of another appearance or personality. One substance cannot become many substances except by adding other substances to itself; and by substances we understand the spatial which is not patient of interpenetration, so your thesis is meaningless.

The Ashʿariyya. Al-Kilābi said that God's speech in eternity is only said to be command, &c., when the persons addressed are existent, and their presence is a condition of responsible obligation. So when God created man and made them to understand His speech 304
in these categories they can be ascribed to Him. They are to Him as active attributes. . . .

Al-Ashʿarī held that God's speech was eternally command, prohibition, &c., and that the non-existent was the object of an eternal

[1] *shakhs laṭīf*.

command as though it actually existed. . . . If a non-existent thing can be commanded why should not the person commanded be non-existent? . . . We are bound by laws commanded in the prophet's time, and if law can precede a person's existence by even one year why should it not do so eternally?

[Shahrastānī] The fact is that this difficulty of the relation of God to
305 what was non-existent in eternity affects all the divine attributes. Did not God decree and know eternally when the world was non-existent? Then how can knowledge and power be related to a pure negation? (1) On the assumption of existence? Then how is assumption conceivable in reference to God? . . . (2) Or were power and knowledge related to what really existed existence being circumscribed and finite? (3) Or it must be accepted that knowledge is a quality capable of perceiving all that is laid before it, and power capable of producing all that is meet to exist. These categories are infinite. Thus we maintain that what God can know and decree is infinite, and we believe that God's cognitions and decrees are infinite, and that is only conceivable in what does not but may exist. The relation in reference to the subject of the relation is to be referred to the universal capacity of the quality; in reference to the object of the relation to the capacity of the known and decreed. . . . We argue similarly as to God's hearing and seeing. . . . Neither hearing nor seeing can be connected with the non-existent, but they only become perceptible by the divine quality when perception is meet, i.e. in a state of existence alone, not beforehand. Thus the divine command is related to the thing commanded. . . .

306 As to their assertion that a speech which has no parts is unintelligible we say that the Mutakallimūn confine them to six; others add other parts like the vocative and so on. . . . The interrogative is inconceivable of God in the sense of asking for information. . . . 'Am I not your Lord' (7. 171) is simply a figurative way of making a person see that the case is thus. The commands are statements connected with reward and punishment just as vocatives are statements, e.g.
307 'O Zaid' which means I call Zaid. . . . As it is possible to relegate all categories of speech to two without impairing the verity of speech so they can be reduced to one as we assert. Revelation calls it 'command' in the words 'Our command is one' (54. 50) . . . and in the words 'Are not the creation and the command His?' (7. 53). There is the opposition as between word and deed from which it can be induced that God's command is uncreate. Were it created the words 'Are not the creation and the command His?' would be mere supposition. . . . Moreover, the Qurān shows that command precedes creation (16. 42), a precedence which is only conceivable in eternity in

reference to the first phenomenon. Thus it is established that God's speech is one. . . .

Different meanings are like different cognitions which one know- 308
ledge comprehends. Similarly different reports and commands though they demand different words and meanings are comprehended by one idea,[1] i.e. the Real Eternal Speech.[2] Differences in time make no more difference to speech itself than does the different state of cognitions which exist and will exist to knowledge itself. This idea is difficult to grasp because our experience is the reverse.

But if we consider the way in which the mind grasps a concept and we abstract it from corporeal matter and fanciful images in the mind we obtain a universal intellectual perception, which does not alter with time. . . . Again, communications received by way of a vision in a dream would take more than a day to describe though they were perceived in less than a moment, and the subject would know that he 309
saw and heard as it were one thing and one subject of communication (*maʿnā*). . . . Similarly the mind perceives the solution of a complicated question in an instant, but the tongue and pen need endless explanations to convey it. . . . The intellect is a unity of perception, and the mind is one in speech;[3] plurality is to be conceived only in the world of sense. . . .

The Muʿtazila. Before this difference arose Muslims agreed that the Qurān was the word of God, composed of chapters and verses . . . and words read and heard . . . and that it was a miracle of the prophet, proving his veracity. . . . The early Fathers used to say 'O Lord of 310
the Mighty Qurān', 'O Lord of Ṭā hā'. . . . The name Qurān was given because it was an assembling together as in the phrase 'The she-camel collected (*qara'at*) her milk in her udder'; and assembling can only be truly predicated of that which is separate. But such things may not be said of the Eternal Word of God.

The community has agreed that the word of God is among us. We read[4] it with our tongues, feel it with our hands, see it with our eyes, and hear it with our ears (9. 6). But how can such terms be applied to the eternal quality?

The Ashʿariyya. You were the first to upset this consensus. With you God's speech is words that He initiated in a substrate that existed and passed away. What we write is our own work, and what we read is what we have acquired. . . . What is among us is not the

[1] *maʿnā*. [2] *qaul*.

[3] O. appears to have *qubūl*, reception; but *qaul* is to be preferred.

[4] Reading and reciting are synonymous in Arabic. The ability to read silently is comparatively modern. If I remember rightly St. Augustine was astonished to see St. Ambrose reading without moving his lips. Thus here, 'reading with the tongue' is correct.

speech of God, nor was it a speech of God's; it is not a miracle, nor do we read and hear it. . . . What we read is only something like it, or about it, as one recites the poetry of the long dead Imru'l-Qais. . . .

311 [Shahrastānī] We do not deny that a book . . . is not eternal, but the question is as to whether the words therein are an eternal quality, one and not many. It is agreed that the speech of God is not that which our vocal organs produce, but a meaning beyond that. And we believe that that meaning is one, eternal: you that it is like ours,
312 many, temporal. . . . Obviously the word Qurān is being applied both to the reading and that which is read. . . .

The true answer is that the verses which Gabriel brought to the apostle are called[1] the speech of God, just as the person in whose likeness Gabriel appeared is called Gabriel, so that it can be said 'This is God's speech and this is Gabriel.'. . . In each case it is the revealing agent (*muẓhir*) which is referred to. You say 'Your speech is right and wrong', and you don't mean the expression[2] apart from the meaning, but the expression as the revealing agent of the meaning, for true and false are in meaning, right and wrong in words. One can be sound and the other unsound. Sometimes the expression is mentioned when the meaning is meant. Thus: This is God's speech, and, God's speech is among us: let none touch it but the purified. 'It is for us to collect it and read it'[3] refers to the expression, while 'Then it is for us to explain it' (75. 17) refers to the meaning. If the book *qua* book were the Qurān he would not have said in another verse 'purified pages wherein are upright books' (98. 3); so that now the
313 Qurān is in a book and now the book in the Qurān. . . . Honouring the book because of what is written in it is like honouring a house for the sake of the householder.

The Fathers and the Ḥanbalites said: Agreement has established that what is between the two covers is the word of God, and what we read and write is the very speech of God. Therefore the words and letters are themselves the speech of God. Since the speech of God is uncreate the words must be eternal, uncreate. In the earliest days they disputed about the eternity and novelty . . . but now it is the novelty of the letters and words, and the eternity of the speech and command to which the expressions point that are in dispute. The Fathers ascribed pre-existence to these words regardless of any other divine attribute, while the Muʿtazila said they were created in time. . . . Al-Ashʿarī departed from the consensus when he asserted the novelty of the letters, so that what we read is not really the speech of God, but

[1] Here B. alone may be right. [2] Or, more fully, the words in which it is expressed.
[3] It will be remembered that the Muʿtazila affected to regard 'collect' as the meaning of (*qara'a*).

only metaphorically. But why did he not say that revelation asserts that what we read and write is the speech of God, without going into the howness and reality of it?

The Fathers said, 'We do not claim that the letters are eternal.' 314
They suffered terribly at the hands of the Mu'tazila for refusing to admit that the Qurān was created, and that not for letters and sounds which we make and acquire. Nay, they knew that God possesses Speech, Word, and Command, and that His command is other than His creation (cf. 7. 52 and 30. 3, &c.).

Since we have not detailed information about the Fathers' belief 315
that the Qurān is the speech of God it is not legitimate to infer that they meant the reading or the read, the writing or the written. . . . They said that the proof that God had words was the text 'Ended are the words of thy Lord' (6. 115). Sometimes word is mentioned (39. 71); sometimes command: 'Our command is but one' (54. 50). Thus God has one command and many words. Therefore we say His command is pre-existent and His words are eternal, and the words 316
reveal[1] the command, and the spiritual things reveal the words and the corporeal things reveal the spiritual. . . . The words and letters are eternal. God's words are unlike our words. . . . As the letters are the means of the words and the words are the causes of the spiritual beings, and the spiritual beings rule the corporeal, so everything subsists in God's word, preserved in His command. . . . God's speech is not like our speech as we learn from the example of Moses, who heard God's speech as it were the dragging of chains, and the prophet who said[2] concerning revelation 'Sometimes it comes to me like the ringing 317
of a bell. This is the more grievous way. Then he (Gabriel) leaves me and I retain in my memory what he said.'

CHAPTER XIV

On the Reality of Human Speech and Psychic Utterance

Al-Naẓẓam said that speech was an intangible (*laṭīf*) body sent forth 318
by the speaker, which strikes the air and sets it in motion as in waves. The air receives its shape and then strikes the drum of the ear which receives its shape; then it reaches the *khayāl*,[3] whence it is presented to the intellectual faculty[4] and understood. Sometimes he says speech is a movement in an intangible body according to a specified shape. Then he became confused as to whether the shape, when it was

[1] I.e. by being their sphere or theatre.

[2] Bukhārī, 1. 2.

[3] This was said to be the hinder part of the first venter.

[4] *al-fikr al-aqlī*. *Fikra*, according to Avicenna, is a movement. Cf. *Ishārāt*, 127. 7–9.

originated in the air, was one shape which the hearers hear, or many. But he did not understand this and many other of his borrowings from the philosophers.

The philosophers apply the word 'speech' (*nuṭq*) to that of the
tongue and vocal organs so arranged as to express the meaning that
319 is in the mind; also to (*a*) distinctions of the intelligence, (*b*) the think-
ing of the soul, and (*c*) the conceptions of the imagination. These are ideas in man's understanding each with its own relation. If (the ideas) are related to the purely intellectual they are the distinction between true and false—universal abstracts; . . . if to the purely psychic they are reflection and oscillation between the true and false until the middle term is reached and the right indication understood; . . . if to the purely imaginative they are supposing and picturing—sometimes picturing the sensible in the intelligible, and sometimes supposing the intelligible in the sensible. . . .

Speech reaches the drum of the ear where it is perceived and passed
320 on to the imaginative faculty which exercises supposition—thence
the psychic faculty where the soul exercises thought, thence the intelligent faculty which exercises distinction. Thus there is an ascent from sensation to intelligence—from the many to the one.[1]

Abū'l-Hudhayl and al-Shaḥḥām and al-Jubbā'ī maintained that speech was purposeful words[2] heard in noises but not heard in writing. The rest of the Muʿtazila disputed as to whether there could be letters without sounds as there were sounds without letters.

Al-Ashʿarī said that speech was an idea subsisting in the human
mind and in the speaker himself (*dhāt*); it was not in letters and
sounds.[3] What the intelligent man revolves in his mind is speaking
321 (*qaul*). He hesitated whether to call the words formed with the
tongue real or metaphorical speech. If the former, then psychic utterance could only be called speech equivocally.

The Ashʿariyya. A man finds speech going on within himself—
recounting what he has seen or heard in the past, or conversations
with others as though they were still present, or meditations as to
what ought to be done. . . . Supposition, reflection, &c., are (only)
322 words for psychic speech. Though his mental faculty[4] be empty of
every idea . . . psychic conversation (*ḥadīth*) goes on even in sleep. . . . The Muʿtazila held that before revelation men perceived in themselves two promptings,[5] one inviting them to a grateful recognition of their maker, the other to a denial of the same. . . . These two impulses give

[1] I have shortened this section very considerably.

[2] *mufīda*, lit. 'profitable'.

[3] I.e. practically consonants and vowels.

[4] *dhihn*, i.e. the faculty of the soul (*nafs*) which can embrace the external and internal senses and is provided to acquire cognitions. See al-Jurjānī.

[5] *khāṭir* is a difficult word to render.

information about the soul's speech and conversation, so how can they deny it? Moreover, all men's processes of logical reasoning are psychic conversation. Often he takes a pen and writes it down with- 323
out uttering a word. . . . The meaning of words differs in different places: the intellectual content does not. Thus the meaning of Allah is precisely the meaning of *Khudha* and *Tangri* and *Sirbāwand*,[1] and so on. This psychic speech of man distinguishes him from the beast.

The Muʿtazila. We do not deny the promptings of man's heart. They may be metaphorical or real psychic conversations, but they do not determine the tongue's expression. .. He who knows no Arabic never thinks of an Arabic word, the same may be said of him who is ignorant of Persian; but the man who knows both languages talks to 324
himself in either, so obviously they (*sc.* the promptings) are questionings[2] and conversations which follow the expressions a man learns in his childhood. The expressions are the roots (*uṣūl*) from which they proceed, so that if we suppose a man to be without these expressions he is dumb and unable to speak. Yet we cannot doubt that though he is without language his intellect understands every intelligible, though he has never heard anything. Therefore real speech is composed of properly arranged words uttered by the tongue. . . . He who has power over speech is a speaker: he who has not is dumb; and consequently speech is not a genus or class in itself with an intellectual existence like the other ideas, but it differs conventionally, so that if people liked to agree on signs and nods mutual understanding could be attained in that way. . . . A proof that God calls the warbling of birds, the sounds of insects,[3] the creeping of ants Speech and Speaking. Solomon said (27. 16) 'We have been taught the speech of birds', 'the hoopoe said', &c. Even the mineral world is metaphorically said to speak 'O ye mountains', &c. (34. 10). 'The thunder tells forth 325
his praise' (13. 14). What is meant is that all these point to their maker's existence. . . . It all proves that speech is not a kind of accident with an intellectual existence, but it is an utterance in the

[1] The first three are the names of God in Arabic, Persian, and old Turkish. The fourth (variant *Sirnāwand*) I am unable to identify. The languages which the author has explicitly mentioned (p. 319) are Arabic, Persian, Hindi, Greek, Syriac, and Hebrew. The first two are accounted for, and none of the last three can be referred to. Professor Gibb has kindly consulted his colleagues at the London School of Oriental Studies, and tells me that they think the word is 'the title *bhagavān* given very commonly to Buddha in the combination Śri-bhagavān, or possibly Śri-bhagavant "bounteous one" though exact confirmation of the title is lacking'. Other suggestions are that the 'Dailami and Gīlānī names ending in -āwand are meant (Minorsky) or Śri-mant, in dialect Śri-vant, a common title of Vishnu'. I cannot find any helpful parallel in the index to al-Bīrūnī's *India*.

[2] *taqdīrāt*, or, perhaps, determinations.

[3] *ḥukl*. The margin writes 'that which has no speech'. Damīrī in his *Ḥayāt al-Ḥayawān*, does not recognize this creature as an individual animal.

tongue with a conventional meaning which mankind may or may not possess and still remain man. For he is distinguished from beast by form and shape; not by soul and intellect, and utterance and speaking. You Ashʿarites follow the philosophers in defining speech as psychic utterance, as you follow them in defining man as a speaking animal, making speech his specific difference. . . . Hence you ought to say that the speaking soul is man . . . and the body is its instrument and mould: then it would follow that God's commands would lie upon the soul and spirit, not the body, and that the resurrection would be for souls and spirits. But here you leave the path of orthodoxy.

The Ashʿariyya. The human mind perceives meanings beyond
326 those of intellectual distinguishing, and mental images. . . . Every rational being is bound to use his reason until he attains a knowledge of the uniqueness of his Maker by deduction and inference; but this is only possible after long mental processes involving psychic speech in Arabic or Persian expressed by the tongue, if the man can speak; by indication and signs if he is dumb. That which happens in the imagination, the soul, and the intellect respectively is not the same. He who can distinguish between these relations can easily imagine psychic speech and the doctrine that that idea is a genus or species of ideas whose reality does not differ; and that which is in the imagination[1] and tongue is not a real stable genus and species, but differs as convention dictates among different persons and in different places. This is not real speech. . . . The ideas in the soul are existent verities which the soul ponders over with its essential speech and intellectual (power) of distinguishing. . . .

327 As to their saying 'if people liked to agree on signs and words, mutual understanding would ensue' this exactly proves our point that lingual speech is figurative speech. Understanding is psychic speech apart from intellectual knowledge. . . . The speech and signs of men refer to psychic speech as opposed to the sounds made by animals. . . .
328 As to what the Qurān says of the speech of animals (1) either God gave them intelligence and a real speech properly articulated as a miracle for the prophet concerned; or (2) he laid speech upon their tongues (they being unaware of it), and the prophet understood it . . . as when the shoulder of mutton cried out 'Don't eat me'. The assertion that it would follow that the soul was a spiritual substance without a body does not deserve an answer. . . .

The philosophers hold that the human soul in the sense that beasts and plants share in it is the first perfection[2] of a natural body, i.e. one

[1] *V.s.*, p. 105, note 3.
[2] Professor Nicholson reminds me that al-Jurjānī explains that this term can be illustrated by the example of the relation of the shape of the sword to the iron:

organically alive potentially; in the sense that men and angels share in it it is a substance without a body; it is the first perfection of a natural body moving it spontaneously from a rational (*natqī*) intellectual source potentially and actually. That which is actual is the distinguishing mark of the angelic soul while the potential belongs to man. Thus speech (*nuṭq*) is a specific attribute in either case. They 329
said that the substantiality of the soul must be asserted before you give it a reasoning speech, and though al-Ash'arī agreed with the Mu'tazila in denying that soul and spirit were substance, but an accident[1] which does not remain for two moments, i.e. life only; yet he was like a Mu'tazil in agreeing with our natural philosophers that the soul was not a spiritual substance insusceptible to change, but that it is a body susceptible to generation and corruption and an accident which follows mingling. There is no difference between their saying 'It changes from moment to moment' and their saying 'It does not remain for two moments', i.e. it exists from moment to moment.

The philosophical theologians infer the existence of the soul from its activities; . . . its hesitation in intellectual judgements and its search for causes; . . . its production of the latent powers of others as 330
when a teacher educates the soul of his pupil from potential to actual capacity to write. . . . Animals do not possess this peculiar property. What they know they know by nature. . . . Further, every bodily faculty is limited in its effects. But the intellectual faculty of the soul is infinite. . . . Therefore it is impossible that its essence and faculties should be corporeal. Its special property is that it perceives itself 331
through itself.[2] . . . It is not a bodily or psychic instrument. It is perceiver and perceived . . . nothing veils it from itself. It is not like the senses for they do not perceive themselves through themselves, nor like that which perceives by an instrument so that if the instrument is damaged the perception fails. . . . Another proof that the soul is not a body nor a bodily faculty is that abstract universal knowledge cannot inhere in a body. . . .

Matter does not enter into sensation but the representation which 332
corresponds to it is impressed on it and the imaginative faculty forms an abstraction of it. Sense appropriates it when it is present; the imaginative faculty when it is absent, and thought forms an abstraction of it, but as a particular and personal thing. The intellect forms one universal abstraction apart from all material associations. . . .

'second perfection' would lie in the inseparable accidents, e.g. the sword being cutting.

[1] The other reading 'without an accident', &c., may be right, but the following clause makes it improbable.

[2] *dhāt*.

Thus the reasoning soul cannot be divided into parts nor be composed of matter and form. . . .

333 Human souls differ from bodies and their faculties and other mingled souls in their movements from potential, theoretical, and practical capacity to perfection; as the matter of their material intelligence[1] is different from the matter of other bodies, so their movements from potential to actual are different. Corporeal matter assumes the form of three dimensions; psychic matter assumes the form of conditions, the derived intellect,[2] the intellect in property,[3] and the intellect *in actu*, in that order. . . .

A further condition is found during sleep when events of years and
334 very long conversations which it would take volumes to record pass in a moment of time. . . . It might be thought that these are like forms seen in a mirror, but that is not so because such dreams are of successive events, not of simultaneous visions. . . . Now if the body or one of its faculties was the *locus* of these perceptions the sequence and succession of phenomena would demand time and priority and posteriority, so it is clear that the soul is not a body and its essential perceptions are not those of bodily senses. . . . It is superior to time and place. . . . This condition is not peculiar to sleep but belongs also to wakefulness. Its properties are that it can receive the impressions
335 of cognitions one by one, or altogether, and can perceive the answer to a difficult question in an instant. . . . Thus it is clear that the soul is not of those bodies which can be defined . . . nor is its speech that of the tongue which changes with people and country; it is the very root of humanity.

All these propositions were objected to:[4]

336 (1) What is the meaning of this 'perfection' which you posit of natural organic bodies potentially endowed with life? Is it part of a body, an accident, or something beyond the body? Of men and angels you say it is a substance beyond the body. But in the way in which perfection is common to beasts and plants it is not common to angels. . . . You have used the word perfection ambiguously meaning actuality and existence, ultimate completeness, soundness. . . . Such things should not occur in definition. . . .

337 (2) We agree with what you say about the soul's activities, but

[1] Al-Jurjānī defines *'aql hayyūlānī* as the pure capacity to grasp intelligibles. It is called material after the manner of prime matter which is free from form.

[2] The derived intellect (*mustafād*) has in its consciousness deductive knowledge or processes which it has already employed.

[3] *malaka*. The knowledge of necessary propositions (*habitus primorum principiorum cogitabilium*) with the psychic capacity to 'acquire' deductive knowledge.

[4] Shahrastānī himself appears to be the author of these criticisms. He usually claims the last word in the chapter for himself, and cf. 'we say' under the third objection.

what would you reply to one who ascribed them all to the perfection of man's composition? . . . The wonders of nature are due to properties in mixed and composite bodies. . . . All the properties that you mention can be attributed to perfect composition alone, save one, 338
and that is the soul's grasp of universals. . . .

(3) You argue as though every accident which inheres in a substrate must necessarily be subject to division with the division of the substrate, but we do not admit that this is necessary. Accidents of contact and composition dissolve with the division of their substrates—others remain in the part as they remained in the whole. . . . We say that if the division of the substrate necessitates the division of the accident, then the unity of the accident demands the unity of the substrate. . . . A point is an accident and it is indivisible, so you must posit a substrate for it, one in essence indivisible as to the body, and its bodily substrate must be indivisible. . . .

Does the one universal idea which the intellect grasps remain with 339
it in its memory actually for ever or can the intellect be utterly unmindful of it? . . . It is common experience that man is unmindful of intelligibles once attained. Yet they remain preserved in the memory which is a bodily faculty. If it can preserve them universally, why cannot a bodily faculty actuate them universally? . . . Or are they preserved in the separated intelligence which works upon it (the memory) by way of emanation and gives it the first form itself, thus reminding it of what it had forgotten? Two difficulties here arise. First, how is the distinct form impressed on the essence of the giver of forms separately so that one man receives one form and another man another while the giver of forms preserves the whole in distinct and separate ways . . . yet remains one in essence and universal in relation? It is an utter impossibility. Secondly, if your conception of memory is right it must apply also to the first perception, so that you assert that he that perceives universals is the Agent Intellect, just as it is he that remembers (preserves); and the human soul does no more than arrange what is presented to it. . . . Thus man comprehends with a comprehension in the essence of the agent intellect just as he remembers with a memory in the same. So the passive intellect is his actually, as the active intellect is actually from him (the agent intellect); and the relation of particular intelligences to him . . . is like the relation of the internal senses to man's intellect. But here 340
we touch a most difficult question between us and the philosophers, which will be dealt with elsewhere, if God will.

CHAPTER XV

Concerning our Knowledge that the Creator is Hearing, Seeing

341 Al-Ka'bī and the scholars of Baghdad said that the meaning of God's being seeing, hearing, was that he knew about sights and sounds, but not in a way that added anything to His being Knowing about the knowable. In this the followers of al-Najjār agreed. The Mu'tazila, too, who said that He hears and sees according to His essence. Those who said that the meaning is that He lives, contradict al-Ka'bī, like al-Jubbā'ī and his son. Others said that it means He perceives sights and sounds. . . .

Al-Ash'arī said He hears with hearing and sees with sight, and they
342 are two qualities subsisting in His essence additional to His being knowing. His proof was that if God cannot be called a seer and a hearer the opposite must be affirmed. . . . If God is alive sight and hearing must be ascribed to Him or He would be deficient; for they are attributes of praise. God has described Himself thus. . . .

343 Al-Ka'bī said that he did not admit that sight and hearing were perceptions additional to God's knowledge. A man's perception of what he hears and sees is in his mind,[1] and intelligence. His sight does not sense the thing seen, but the seer senses and the hearer senses, not the ears.[2] This is real knowledge; and since a man gets it by sight the sight is called sense. But it is the knower who perceives and his perception is not additional to his knowledge.

The proof of this is that a man who knows a thing by report and afterwards sees it finds a difference in the state (of his knowledge) but not a difference of genus or class, but of general and particular, but
344 the soul's consciousness is the same in both cases. If the perceiver perceived by perception it would follow that when his sense rang with sound, slave-girls would be singing before him, drums would beat and horns would blow; . . . he would see far-off friends and overlook those at his elbow. But this is not the case. Al-Jubbā'ī said if a living being has a sound body, he is called hearer (and) seer; there is no other meaning to perception, human or divine. A sound essence perceives all that is presented to it whether resemblances or contraries: it perceives black as it perceives white. If it perceived by a perception it could perceive some things and not others that confront a perceiver, just as we can know one thing and not another.

They said[3] that if perception were admitted of men it could not be

[1] Lit. 'heart'. [2] Perhaps the words 'and eyes' have dropped out.
[3] It is not said who the speakers were; presumably al-Jubbā'ī and his school.

admitted that the mere being alive was its governing principle. Another condition must be a sound body, and another condition of sight must be light between the seer and the seen and an open space between the hearer and the sound. Smell, touch, and taste require 345 bodily contact, and therefore must be denied of God, while the other two senses require conditions other than life for real perception. . . . Thus your position is untenable.

Al-Ashʿarī said that perceptions, i.e. cognitions as a result of information received and actual vision, were a different genus. . . . Knowledge can be of non-entities, perception cannot. . . . Al-Kaʿbī gave no meaning to perception. . . . Al-Ashʿarī said it was a genus of cognitions. On this theory God hears and sees with two perceptions which are particular cognitions beyond His being Knowing. . . . Those who take the other view say that if knowledge of a thing combines with other knowledge of it and the object of the cognitive process becomes united therein and the two cognitions are equal in the soul's attributes, difference between them is inconceivable.

Yet we do find a difference between knowledge and perception when we see something we have only heard of before . . . and we 346 know that the two genera are different. . . . If a blind man comprehended all that a man with sight comprehends he would obtain all knowledge except the perception. Therefore the perception is additional to knowledge. . . .

Those who will have no analogy drawn from the human frame hold it possible that God should create vision in the mind and knowledge in the sight. In that case knowledge is confused with perception, and it would follow that the hearer would hear with sight and none of the senses would have their distinctive character as God has given it them. . . .

In answer to al-Jubbā'ī's definition of seeing and hearing as meaning 'A living one without a defect' it was said many a person with sight and hearing was defective in other ways. If the denial of defect is to stand in the place of perception, then that defect must exclude perception, so Jubbā'ī in denying perception virtually affirmed it. . . . 347 'Without a defect' is pure negation and its perception by sense is inconceivable. The difference between the two states of perception (*v.s.*) and the non-existence of perception cannot be referred to pure non-existence, for in that case the difference would not-exist; for difference in non-existence and the non-existence of difference are one and the same. There is a necessary difference between a man's being a hearer and a seer though they both imply that he is alive. Therefore they must be referred to something additional to his being alive, otherwise the necessary difference would not exist. . . .

Some asserted that all the attributes of perfection are summed up in His being Living, and the defective attributes are denied in the words 'without a defect'. . . . The analogy of the human frame is
348 false, for it would require that the Creator should possess it.

It is remarkable that they carried this analogy so far as to talk of rays of light which are luminous bodies sent forth from the sight to the object of vision . . . and of reflection as in a mirror.

349 Reasons for the absurdity of this view, and also for the view that a form is transferred from the object to the sight.

350 Is perception the perception of a form in the perceiver's sense corresponding to the external form, or is it the perception of the external without an intermediary form in the sense? Is the place of perception the external sense of eye and ear or are they instruments of the common sense in which real sensation resides, so that contraries can be found together therein while perception remains one? Some think that this is knowledge, seeing that it is within: others that it is a perception more specific than knowledge seeing that its perceiver is external. Again are the five perceptions really different so that their difference is in species or is the difference referable to the percepts? . . . This is the question at issue between the Mutakallimūn and the philosophers.

The Mutakallimūn hold that the five senses embrace five different
351 perceptions. . . . A man sees with his sight . . . as he knows with his mind (heart). The seats of vision, hearing, and knowledge are the sight, the ear, and the heart respectively. The difference between knowledge and perception corresponds to the difference in their respective places. . . . Some senses demand a contact, others do not—only the latter can be predicated of God. This is the theory of those who make a distinction between perception and knowledge. Those who hold that perception is knowledge assert that the locus and the reality of them are the same, except Al-Ashʿarī who said that every perception was knowledge but not every knowledge was perception. Perception was a special knowledge demanding an individual percept and having the existent as its object. Existence of the thing perceived is necessary for perception, but knowledge can deal with the non-existent, the necessary, the possible, and the impossible. He hesitated as to whether all the perceptions were special cognitions or (just) perceptions. His followers did not hold that existence was the governing necessity for perceptions, but contact was the necessary condition.

352 The philosophers explain their theory of sight; the lens of the eye; and how it is that large objects at a distance appear small and small objects at hand appear comparatively large. If perception were in the
353 eye and were connected with the object as it actually is, the thing

would be seen in its actual size and form. A point of flame whirled rapidly round, the sight 'perceives' as a circle while it is actually only a point; and falling rain is seen as a straight line whereas it is actually circular in form. Thus it is established that the true sense is within, not in the external form.[1]

Sight and hearing differ from the other senses in that their percep- 354
tion is other than that which is impressed on them.[2] All these faculties are prepared to receive the emanation which comes from the Giver of forms, for the sense does not originate perception.

The nearest approach to this theory was al-Ashʿarī's method of separating between hearing and seeing and the other three senses. He made physical contact a condition for these latter and asserted the existence of bodily senses, though he did not attribute them to God. When he realized that hearing and sight had a particular internal relation he hesitated as to whether perception was a particular knowledge or another comprehension[3] in the common sense. On his theory the perception by hearing might reside in the sight, and the seeing
perception in the hearing. It is generally held (*al-qaum*) that they are 355
united in the common sense so that the seen is read and the read is seen. In reality of perception there is no difference and they have one locus. The Muʿtazilite theory of perceptions is confused....

CHAPTER XVI

That the Vision of God is an Intellectual Possibility and a Dogma of Revelation

356

No Muslim has asserted the possibility of vision in the sense that rays from the eye can reach His essence or that the vision is of the senses. Dogmatic theologians differ as to whether vision is a perception beyond knowledge or a special knowledge as mentioned in the preceding chapter. The Muʿtazila, claiming that a human organism is necessary for sight, deny the vision of God absolutely. Al-Ashʿarī asserted that it was possible and must be believed. He hesitated[4] as to whether it was a special cognition, i.e. connected only with an existing thing, or a perception virtually the same as knowledge in its

[1] Here follows the physical theory of hearing which has already been given—see p. 105.

[2] Here follows the theory of taste, smell, and touch.

[3] *Maʿnā*, medium of perception. Ibn Ḥazm, iii. 3 defines *idrāk* as a *maʿnā* added to sight and vision, namely the idea of comprehension which is not in sight and vision. *Idrāk*, he says, is to be denied of God in this world and the next.

[4] This 'hesitation' to which Shahrastānī refers more than once was perhaps to be found in the three monographs which al-Ashʿarī devoted to the subject of the *visio Dei*. See Spitta, p. 66.

connexion, i.e. not affecting, or being affected by, the object of vision. . . .

358 Abū Isḥāq took much the same view save that he called vision a *maʿnā* which neither affects, nor is affected by, the thing seen. It is virtually the same as knowledge, unlike the other senses. . . .

We have shown above that visual perception does not require the junction of rays of light with the object of vision nor the separation of anything from the seer.[1] Therefore there is no question of influence in either direction, so that *maʿnā* is like knowledge or *maʿnā* is a genus of knowledge. Agreement has already been reached on the possibility of our knowing about God. This is as far as we can go in asserting the intellectual possibility of the vision of God.

The Muʿtazila raised five objections:

359 (1) You have found in that which exists a valid cause for vision . . . and if you say that vision is a special knowledge or an idea in the place (*ḥukm*) of knowledge . . . then you have not sought a valid cause for knowledge . . . so why do you seek it for vision? Say either that vision has the same objects as knowledge or that there is no cause and no valid ground for it.

(2) No argument from the *ḥāl* is permissible in your case because you Ashʿarites deny it and refer the categories of the universal and particular, separation and sharing, to mere relationships. . . .

(3) We cannot admit that vision has as its object pure substance and pure accident, . . . since you cannot subtract colour from the substance seen . . . nor can you see all accidents. . . .

360 (4) As the visible is more specific than the knowable and vision is connected with the known according to the attribute of existence so we say that it is connected with the existent according to the attribute of origination. . . .

361 (5) Vision is one of the five senses. Do you say that they are all connected with the existent and existence makes them valid, or that vision is a peculiar property connected with every object? The first involves the heresy that God can be heard, smelt, tasted, and felt—the second it is incumbent on you to demonstrate. That sight does not affect and is not affected by the thing seen is the question in dispute. . . .

The Ashʿariyya replied to (1): We are not alone in seeking a valid cause for vision, for you yourselves find it in colour and that which is subject to colour. We ask what is the common ground for these two categories of substance and accident being visible. It is not in their being substance and accident. . . .

[1] P. has 'the seen'. Avicenna uses the words *ittiṣāl* and *infiṣāl* of the conjunction and opposition respectively of the stars, *Najāt*, 393.

As to (2) it may apply to al-Ashʿarī's school but the Qāḍī Abū Bakr, 362
who is my guide in this matter, held the theory of states so that the objection falls to the ground. . . .

As to (3) . . . A man sees a person afar off but he cannot tell what 363
his colour or shape is; afterwards these become plain. Therefore colour and shape are not the same as body to the sight. What is it which unites these in perception? . . .

As to (4) we reply that existence in time cannot be the valid cause 364
either on your arguing or ours. For some accidents are not visible, and if existence in time were the cause of a thing being visible everything that existed in time would be visible. With al-Ashʿarī the existing in time is an existence preceded by non-existence. The latter can influence nothing, so only existence remains as the cause (of an object being visible). . . .

As to (5) we say . . . that the five senses have different properties 365
and perceptions and no sense shares in another's peculiar property. None of them is connected with substance and accident in one uniform way, but all of them are connected with accidents. A condition of their connexion is bodily contact except in the case of hearing and seeing. . . .

Scholars differed as to the valid cause of hearing.[1] Some said it was 366
existence; others, existence in relation to the audible being speech. Speech is sometimes a meaning in words, sometimes a psychic utterance. Both can be heard.

We have already asserted that there is a psychic speech which has no language. Similarly we assert that there is a psychic audition without language—sometimes it comes through an intermediary and a veil, but not always. 'No mortal can expect that God will speak to him except by inspiration or from behind a veil, or by sending an apostle' (42. 50). Inspiration, then, is without intermediary and veil, as He says 'He inspired His servant', or as the prophet himself put it 'He blew into my heart' (*v.l.* spirit). Sometimes it came from behind a veil as to Moses, 'And his Lord spake to him'; and sometimes by the intervention of a prophet and a veil as He says 'Or He will send an apostle'.

In fine in this life we understand speech in the soul. Our tongue expresses the meaning; the hearer hears it, and by hearing it reaches his soul. Thus speech reaches the soul by these means. If these means were removed so that the soul could perceive what the reasoning soul contained, a real speech on the part of the speaker could be substantiated and a real hearing on the part of the hearer, and without sound, tongue, or ear.

[1] *samʿ*. Hearing a divine message, not ordinary hearing is meant.

367 Thus are we to think that Moses heard the speech of God. Messages (*risālāt*) come through apostles (*rusul*); speech without an intermediary, but from behind a veil. The speech of God is audible with our hearing, read with our tongues, preserved in our breasts.

Al-Ashʿarī took as his authority for the possibility of the vision of God Moses' request: 'O my Lord show me! Let me look at Thee' (7. 139) and the Lord's answer 'Thou shalt not see me'. . . . Now did Moses know that God could be seen, or was he ignorant on the subject? If he was ignorant his knowledge of God ill befitted the dignity of a prophet; if he did know that it was a possibility then his knowledge agreed with the fact and his request was for the possible not for the impossible. The reply, 'Thou shalt not see me', equally points to the possibility, for God does not say 'I am not visible' but He asserts impotence or lack of vision on the part of the seer, saying 'But look at the mountain, for if it stays in its place thou shalt see me'. If the mountain in its massive strength could not support the revelation of God how could mortal vision? Thus the impediment[1] is linked to a possibility and the impediment is referred to the weak-
368 ness of the instrument not to impossibility itself. . . . Thus the vision is established as possible.

If it is objected that *lan* is to make the negative perpetual that is absurd, first because *lan* is corroborative, not perpetual, for does He not say in 18. 66 'thou wilt not (*lan*) have patience with me' a possibility; and secondly because if it marked perpetuity it would not indicate the impediment to the possibility, but the impediment to the occurrence of the possible. . . .

369 Another text on which al-Ashʿarī seized was (75. 22), 'Faces on that day shall be beautiful, looking at their Lord.'

[Shahrastānī] This question is a matter of scriptural attestation (*samʿiyya*), and thus there can be no doubt that there must be a vision of God. We have indicated the intellectual difficulties of the problem. The mind cannot rest entirely at ease as to the necessity of the vision, nor advance to a position in which intellectual difficulties are not felt.

On the whole it is best to regard the *visio Dei* as a matter of scriptural attestation, in which case the story of Moses is the *locus classicus*; but God knows best what is true.

[1] Impediment is a technical term for a condition which if it exists prevents something else occurring; but if it does not exist neither prevents nor permits its occurrence.

CHAPTER XVII

CONCERNING WHAT IS TO BE CONSIDERED HONOURABLE AND WHAT BASE, SHOWING THAT REASON MAKES NOTHING INCUMBENT ON GOD, AND THAT NOTHING WAS INCUMBENT ON MEN BEFORE THE COMING OF THE SACRED LAW 370

THE orthodox view is that reason does not determine what is base or honourable. . . . Men's actions are not intrinsically good or bad so that they earn God's reward or punishment. . . . The good is what the code approves, and the bad what it condemns. . . .

Dualists, Brahmans, Khārijites, and others, take the opposite 371
view. . . . The code gives information about good or bad actions; it does not establish them as such. . . . Reason perceives the good or the bad immediately and by discursive reasoning. . . . This is the foundation of their theory that God must do what is best, of grace, and recompense.

Al-Ashʿarī distinguished between the getting of a knowledge of God through reason, and its necessarily coming that way. All knowledge comes by reason, said he, but revelation makes it incumbent on men. Our object is to deny that the reason imposes religious obligation, not to deny its rational results.

The orthodox said: If we suppose that a man could be created with
a perfect intelligence uninfluenced by any teaching of parents or of 372
codes, and then confronted with two propositions: (*a*) two are more than one; and (*b*) a lie is evil in the sense that it deserves God's censure, it cannot be doubted that he would accept the first and hesitate over the second. He is not certain that God is injured by a lie or profited by the truth, for both propositions are in one case so far as responsibility (*taklīf*) is concerned, and he cannot give one more weight than the other by the exercise of intelligence alone.

Truth and falsehood are essentially similar. . . . Truth is a statement of what is; falsehood is a statement contrary to what is. There is no question of their being good or evil in their essential attributes. . . . Some true reports are culpable like the statement that a prophet fled from an evil person, while some false reports are commendable like a denial of the foregoing. . . . The definition of falsehood contains no mention of its being evil. . . .

Their only remaining argument is an appeal to custom. Men call the 373
injurious evil, and the profitable good, and we admit the propriety of this; but these categories change in different ages and peoples: some think right what others deem wrong, e.g. the killing of an animal. We say that it is the law which makes a thing right or wrong.

Objection.[1] If a man could attain his object by truth or falsehood equally well, it would be better that he should choose truth as his means, so were it not that falsehood was a quality to be shunned he would not have preferred the truth. This is the duty of one who has never heard of Islam or denies codes, so that there is no need of religious obligation. Thus we find that intelligent people think well of saving a drowning man, and look down on injustice and enmity.
374 Suppose that two sages were disputing before Islam, one affirming and the other denying a proposition. They would define truth and falsehood. Then one would deny the assertion of his fellow, inviting disapproval of it, and reassert his own position with a demand for its approval, until they passed from words to blows. Each would accuse his fellow of ignorance, and invite him to accept his own thesis. Now if good and evil were entirely to be avoided there could be no dispute, and assertion and denial would be impossible.[2] . . . The good in reason is the good in theology; and what is good in wisdom is necessitated by wisdom, not by religious obligation, so that nothing is incumbent on God by way of religious obligation, but He must in respect of wisdom settle and administer (all things).

If we abolish the categories of good and evil from men's works and refer them to the code, then vain are the ideas that we extract from the roots of jurisprudence. You have lost all power to compare[3]
375 words and actions, and you cannot assert the why and the wherefore, because deeds (on your own showing) have no character of their own. . . . Thus you have destroyed law altogether.

The philosophers. . . . Being embraces good and evil, and a mixture of both. Pure good is the desire of reason . . . pure evil is essentially to be shunned by reason. . . . No intelligent person doubts that knowledge . . . is good, laudable, and to be sought for, while evil is the reverse. All that the reason desires is approved by the wise: all that it shuns is disapproved by all. . . . A sound nature incites a man to attain the approved and reject the disapproved, whether law or lawgiver impel him thereto or not. Therefore the . . . moral qualities self-control, generosity, bravery, and courage are praiseworthy in deed, and their opposites are disapproved in practice.[4] Man's perception lies in the soul's effort to perfect true knowledge and good works in imitation of God and the angels.[5] . . . The only purpose of laws is to confirm what reason holds; not to present anything con-
376 trary to it. . . . Since particular intelligences are incapable of grasping

[1] The answer on p. 378 makes it plain that the Muʿtazila are speaking.

[2] Men would not fight for truth against falsehood unless they believed that it was right.

[3] *qiyās* was, of course, one of the 'roots' of the law.

[4] *v.l.*

[5] Lit. 'spiritual beings of the heavenly world'.

all intelligibles and universal good, wisdom demands . . . that there should be a law urging men to faith in the unseen in general, and guiding them to the best things in this world and the next in particular. . . . Such a law must be accompanied by signs of its heavenly origin, and must speak to men according to the capacity of their understanding; . . . cf. 16. 126. They said that the Muʿtazila were wrong in making good and evil essential properties of works. They ought to affirm that of knowledge and ignorance, because works differ with persons and times, and have no properties which permanently adhere to them. The Ashʿariyya, too, were wrong in divorcing them from knowledge which in its species is not-culpable, and from ignorance which in its species is not-laudable, seeing that eternal weal or woe are exclusively confined to them. Works help or 377
hinder accidentally, not essentially. . . .

The Ṣābians added that things in the lower world were dependent on the influence of the stars and the spiritual forces which govern the stars. . . . One man was as good as another and no man of sound intelligence needed any one to lay down what was good or evil (cf. *Sur.* 23. 24). We can infer from the nature of things whether they are good or harmful, just as we can judge whether works are good or bad. We do not need a lawgiver (*Sur.* 24. 6).

The Transmigrationists. The human race has a kind of choice in 378
its actions and . . . by reason is lifted above the animal order. If man's actions are worthy of humanity he is raised to the rank of angels or prophets. If his actions are bestial he is reduced to the rank of beasts or lower still. He is for ever working recompense or being recompensed for his works . . . so he does not need any one or any law or reason to pronounce on the character of his works. . . . Sometimes the good and evil are animal manifestations; sometimes among animals they are human acts. There is no future world of rewards and punishments.

The Brahman added: We need neither law nor lawgiver. If the prophet's words are intelligible, reason makes us independent of them: if they are unintelligible, they are not to be accepted.

Answer to the Muʿtazila. It is not necessary that a man should 379
choose truth as against falsehood as the means of gaining his object. If he does adopt truth it is because of impulse, custom, or purpose urging him thereto. . . .

As to the disputants before the days of Islam we agree, but the question is: Must God reward or punish them respectively? We cannot say, because we have no authoritative information. . . . We see that there are many things of which we disapprove but God does not disapprove, like the sufferings of the innocent, the destruction of crops,

and so on. Acts like the rescue of the drowning must be judged on
380 this basis, for drowning itself is approved by God, though we regard it as evil; and if rescuing were good drowning would necessarily be bad. There is a hidden purpose in the destruction of mortals which we cannot understand. . . .

With regard to the intellectual aspect of the disputation one man's state is knowledge, the other's is ignorance. You cannot argue that God must reward or punish them on that basis. We do not know God's judgement on the matter in question. . . . Knowledge is laudable in itself . . . and ignorance is blameworthy.

381 As to their objection that what is good in reason is good in wisdom, so wisdom is incumbent on God, not by way of religious law,[1] we reply that we mean by wisdom that an event occurs according to (fore)knowledge, apart from any advantage or aim. None incites the originator of actions to do what He does. Were there such a being he would be greater than God. . . . The wise is He who acts according to His knowledge. The ordered universe is evidence of knowledge. If any one else does something he thinks worthy of commendation without the permission of the divine King there is no philosophical reason why he should be rewarded. God is not profited thereby. So far as He is concerned action and inaction are alike.

Objection. If God does not profit the agent does. . . . Moreover,
382 gratitude, praise, and devotion are actions which reason asserts are commendable. . . .

Answer. Custom is not a safe guide. . . . Gratitude and ingratitude are alike to him who is neither hurt nor helped thereby. Gratitude does not earn the right to further bounty. . . . It is a duty incumbent on man, and God is not bound to reward it. If any one spent his whole life in giving thanks for the preservation of one limb he would fall short of his duty; for if he compared his paltry gratitude with the munificence of God how could he be counted abundantly grateful? . . .

'Necessity' in reference to God is unintelligible. It is impossible to say that man deserves anything from God, because he[2] is always being overwhelmed by God's kindness.[3] . . .

383 If gratitude is to be the ground of commendation then the gratitude should be commensurate with the kindness, but a mutual recompense between the eternal and the creature of a moment is inconceivable. What holds one way holds the other, so that man cannot claim to 'deserve' anything of God.

God's 'deserving' of his creatures is not a reasonable tenet,[4]

[1] The MSS. differ considerably among themselves, none of them agreeing with the original objection. [2] The Oxford MS. is almost certainly wrong here.
[3] The author nobly develops this theme. [4] See note 2.

because he is unaffected by man's obedience or disobedience. . . . 384
As He began by showing kindness so His omnipotence is gracious continually. How should He impose a painful service on man in this life to reward him in the next? If He were to give him free rein so that he did what he pleased and went after sinful lusts, and then lavished gifts upon him, would not that be more pleasing to men, and evil in the sight of the wise? . . .

We challenge the adversary to produce an instance (*wajh*) of (the notion of) good in the root of religious obligation. . . . Good and evil, advantage and disadvantage . . . are not to be ascribed to the Lawgiver (*mukallif*) though the ideas may be. He is able to shower his benefits upon men without a precedent law (*taklīf*). He could either lay a law upon them with positive and negative commands and reward or punish them according to their works; or give them no law and no recompense but continually favour them as he did in the beginning.

Reason is at a loss to decide such questions. . . . The divine com- 385
mand is mere subjectivity, because no attribute by which God commands can be referred to His essence. But He is a Knower, Willer, and Maker of the command as He is the maker of creation. Reason recognizes Him according to this description,[1] but cannot possibly know that He lays commands on men. All that reason can attain is a knowledge of a description which cannot include commandments, so how can it know that God wants an obedience which will be rewarded. . . . There can be no obedience when there is no command and no prophet. . . . He who denies that there is an eternal command cannot assert that an obligation rests on man or that his actions are
good or bad. This involves a denial of a revealed law which was 386
confirmed miraculously. . . . He who denies God's speech has denied (the reality) of men's works and is a Compulsionist (*Jabriyya*). . . . He who denies that men 'acquire' works has denied God's speech and is a *Qadarī*, i.e. he has (asserted)[2] that both God and man have power. . . .

To return to the case of the two disputants.[3] . . . Does the one who hits upon the truth deserve an everlasting reward? . . . An unskilled person who dives to the bottom of the sea in search of pearls at the risk of his life may be blamed by his master if he is a slave or fined by the owner if he is a partner. Approval and disapproval, denial and
affirmation, can only result in recourse to a judge whose judgement 387
is sounder than the disputants' so that he can settle the case. Thus

[1] Namely that He is a knower, willer, and maker.
[2] The argument seems to require the insertion of some such word as *athbata*.
[3] *V.s.*, p. 120 f.

good and evil cannot be settled by the usage of men but only by divine law. . . .

To deal with the accusation that we have destroyed intelligible ideas in jurisprudence. . . . Suppose a man killed another and reason were called upon to judge of different theories as to what ought to be done, viz. (1) The man ought to be killed in retaliation and as a warning to the violent. Thus the race would be preserved and anger controlled. . . . (2) It is meeting destruction with destruction and enmity with enmity and the dead is not brought to life by killing the slayer. If the race is preserved by such means in a problematical future, in the present retaliation destroys an actual life.

388 But reason will inquire whether there are other considerations than humanity. . . . Here revelation relieves its perplexity by stating from ideal principles (*maʿānī*) what is incumbent on man. . . .

If good and evil and the moral categories of actions were mental properties of individuals or of works it would be inconceivable that the law should call one thing good and another evil, and the abrogation of laws so that the forbidden became the permitted and vice
389 versa would be inconceivable. . . . The law of marriage in the code of our father Adam is in opposition to the law of marriage of our prophet Muḥammad. Often this kind of case can be explained thus: wine is forbidden, a dog is unclean, because of (a property in) itself, whereas another thing may be forbidden because of something else. Laws take the place of intellectual properties and are related legally to individual things and to works. Good and evil in truth and falsehood is like the permitted and the forbidden in fornication and marriage, and like the possible and the disallowed in buying and usury.[1] . . .

390 Al-Isfarā'inī said that thanks tired the thanker and the thanked was none the better so there was no point in giving thanks. . . .

Objection. Thanks profit the thanker and do no harm to the thanked, so they ought to be given because the advantage of them outweighs the disadvantage.

Al-Isfarā'inī replied that they might harm the thanker because he met the multitude of God's kindnesses with his puny thanks. There can be no doubt that if a man receives many benefits great and small, and chooses to offer thanks for the small, that is imputed to him as culpable folly.

Objection. The thanker does not confine his thanks to particular blessings or the least of them. He includes them all though he may mention one to cover all.

391 Al-Isfarā'inī. It is unbelief[2] to confront favours with thanks as

[1] I.e. the act itself does not determine the character of the action.

[2] Or, ingratitude. The second is the primary, the first the more common, meaning.

though they were a reward and return for favours. The innumerable benefits of God cannot be recompensed. To make the attempt is unbelief. If the idea is to profit God as the thanker is profited that too is unbelief. If the favour is beyond comparison and recompense, and the beneficent above profit and loss how can thanks be commendable? Thanks only profit the thanker if they are offered with the consent of the thanked. If his consent is only known by revelation then thanks are only commendable through the law. However, men grow up in the ways of the sacred law, perceiving that thanksgiving is approved by religious people and think that the intellect unsupported decrees its suitability.

Reply to the philosophers' contention that existence comprises good, and evil, and a mixture of both. According to you every existent thing is good, and evil is only to be predicated of the non-entity. But on this basis your argument is unsound, for if existence comprises the good then existence comprises existence! Then how can existence comprise the non-existent? . . .

Suppose the question to be about matters with which the law deals, then good and evil are intended by the noble and the base. You have helped us in the assertion that immediate and discursive knowledge cannot arrive at a judgement of the character of actions 392
because opinions differ with time and place. . . . The point at issue between us is whether knowledge, the goal of the wise, is to be rewarded by God and ignorance punished. . . .

They said that eternal happiness or misery was the lot of the wise and ignorant soul respectively just as physical well-being followed the drinking of medicine and painful sickness the drinking of poison.

Answer. In that case the soul's happiness depends upon the attaining of the faculties of knowledge and the use of it, and only after great travail does it arrive at premisses and understand how to attain its object by search. . . . Human nature is unequal to the task. The intellectual difficulty is so great that the wise man halts lest he should take the path which leads to ignorance and its miseries.[1] . . .

Reply to the Ṣābians. We will admit that the stars exert influence 393
on the noble and the base in sublunar bodies but only as created
things themselves.[2] The point at issue is the command. It cannot be 394
doubted that God has given positive and negative commandments, and men will be judged in the next life in accordance therewith.

Yet we cannot arrive at this knowledge . . . without revelation. . . . We do not agree that reason always knows what is helpful or harmful in things, for the method of scientists and physicians is experiment,

[1] Here follows the argument of the potential and the actual and the external agent which brings the change about.

[2] *min ḥaithu'l-khilqa.*

and an experiment which cannot be reproduced in every detail is useless as a guide. . . . The peculiar properties of things often contradict the results of experiment. . . . According to them these properties come from the emanation of the universal soul on the quiddities of things. . . . The complexity of things makes us posit a person with knowledge of the stars and what lies beyond them so that He sees everything as a single form. . . .

395 Reply to the Transmigrationists. . . . You say there is a reward for every work. Do the works end in pure reward, and do the rewards begin from pure work? If you say there is an infinite chain there is a vicious circle, for if there was no work except as a reward and no reward except for a work then there was no work and no reward at all! The reward's being a reward rests on a precedent work, and work being work rests on a precedent reward. . . . Therefore you must begin with a primary work which is not a reward and end with a reward which is not for a work, which is exactly our position.

They were asked: What is the highest rank of the good and the lowest of the bad? to which they replied, 'Angels and prophets, and devils and jinn'. The question was then posed: Supposing a prophet killed a snake what would his reward be, seeing that there is no rank above him? Also if a jinnī killed a prophet what would his punishment be as he is already in the lowest rank? You would have to let the noblest and the basest deeds go unrequited.

396 Transmigration is impossible, because every constitution (*mizāj*) is prepared to receive its appropriate form from the Giver of Forms. If it received that form, and the form of a soul that had been promoted joined it, there would needs be two souls in one body, and that is ridiculous.

CHAPTER XVIII

397 A Refutation of the Assertion (*a*) that the Acts of God have a Purpose or a Cause; (*b*) of Utility in God's Acts (*ṣalāḥ*), and that He must do what is best (*aṣlaḥ*) and bestow Sufficient Grace (*luṭf*) upon His Creatures. The Meaning of the Terms *taufīq* Efficient Grace;[1] *khidhlān* Abandoning; *sharḥ* Opening, and *khatm* Shutting of the Mind; *ṭab'* Sealing; *ni'ma*, Favour; *shukr* Kindness; *ajal* Fixed Term; and *rizq* Sustenance.

The orthodox view is that no final cause prompted God to create the universe, because He cannot profit or suffer harm from anything,

[1] I have followed the distinguished lead of Professor Asín in rendering *taufīq* by

nor can anything incite Him to create for the sake of the creature. His activity (*ṣanʿ*) is the cause of everything, and His activity has no cause.

The Muʿtazila argued that a wise man only does a thing for a wise purpose; and action without purpose is useless folly. . . . The wise acts for his own advantage or to profit some one else. . . . Since God is exalted above profit obviously He must act for the profit of 398
others, and all His acts must be salutary. They differed as to whether He must do what is best, some arguing that the best could be bettered *ad infinitum*.

The philosophers argued that the Necessary Existent's acts could not have a cause. Actions proceeded from the primal principles which depended on the Active Intellect. It originated the intellect through its necessary consequences and by means of it originated everything else. . . . Thus only can the existence of the Necessary Existent be conceived. . . . Profit may consist of a recompense of the same nature, e.g. money for money; or of a different nature, e.g. a reputation for liberality: but this is compensation not generosity, while the first is (customary) behaviour and not *inʿām*. Generosity and favour are the giving of what is fitting without recompense or purpose. The First (cause) conferred existence[1] on all phenomena without any necessity or need or caution[2] . . . as was fitting. . . .

The orthodox argued that if, as has been proved, the Creator is 399
absolutely independent, He needs nothing. . . . He does not sell His favours nor burden His gifts with demands for thanks. If He did anything for a motive He would be dependent, not self-sufficient. One man's meat is another man's poison, so that universal and par- 400
ticular advantage . . . are in sharp opposition. . . . We do not deny that God's acts embrace good, and work towards utility, and that He did not create the world for destruction, but the point is that it is not an expected advantage or an anticipated good which prompts Him to action; He is without a prompter. There is a difference between a good consequence following divine operation, and attributing good and utility to the disposition of those acts, just as there is a necessary difference between a perfection which necessitates a thing's existence and one which merely evokes it. The former is an excellence like an inseparable attribute; the latter an excellence like a provocative cause.

efficient grace (*la gracia eficaz*). His *gracia suficiente* corresponds to Ibn Ḥazm's *hudā*. Al-Baghdādī (d. 429) uses *hidāya* to cover both efficient and sufficient grace, explaining, however, the difference between them. Uṣūl al-Dīn, 140.

[1] *V.l.* 'generosity'.

[2] The reading is doubtful: it may be *zīnatin*, lit. 'ornament'; cf. l. 6 of the Arabic text.

The Muʿtazila argued that, it being established that God was wise and that a wise man . . . does not act without purpose, God must have a purpose and desire the good. Advantage may accrue to the agent if he needs it—and God does not—or to another. . . . He who
401 saves a drowning man does not always reap advantage or expect praise or reward. We find somewhere the words 'I have not created men to make a profit on them, but I have created them that they may make a profit on Me'. Wisdom in creation is manifest to the reason and vouched for by revelation (*samʿ*). Reason testifies that the wisdom in creation is the manifestation of signs by which God's uniqueness can be inferred, and He can be known and worshipped, and an eternal reward be granted (to men). For revelation see *Sur.* 45. 31, &c. Some savants averred that the first thing created must have been intelligent and reasoning, because to create a thing without some one to perceive its relation to God would be folly. . . . Our position is not inconsistent with God's independence of creation: it rather establishes its perfection. Perfect independence is only known through every rational being's need of it, and only the rational knows the rational's need.

The Orthodox. Granted that the wise orders and perfectly arranges
402 his work and that it is only wisely conceived if it is executed in accordance with his knowledge, and if it does so happen it is not by chance. What do you mean by saying God must have a purpose and desire the good? By 'purpose' and 'utility' you mean gaining an advantage or avoiding harm. . . . But the Omnipotent is transcendent above all this. . . . If you mean the advantage of others, what is absolute advantage and utility in the creation of the world if, as you say, it was in order that 'God's uniqueness might be inferred from the existence of the indications thereof'? If God's actions have a purpose their results cannot be partial, otherwise ignorance or impotence would be ascribable to Him. Such a purpose as you suppose in the creation of the world obviously was not achieved, whether we suppose that in the beginning the world contained few or many wise men. If (the fulfilment of) purpose depends on another's choice it is bound to be opposed and cannot be achieved unconditionally. If God had created men without the guidance of intelligence and revelation and left them to follow their own devices they would have done as they pleased and God would not have suffered loss.
403 Birds and beasts do as they please, so why should men be singled out for discipline?

The Muʿtazila replied: So that men might obey and be rewarded; for the delights of recompense will be greater than would be the delight in (divine) grace and generosity.

Retort. What wisdom and what erudition! It comes to this that God's wisdom in creating the universe is to result in man's pleasure in the reward that he gets for his work being greater than his pleasure in grace that demanded no exertion. Thus we have:

The object of creation is inductive proof (of God's existence). The object of induction is the attainment of knowledge (of God). The object of knowledge is reward. The object of reward is the attainment of a distinction between the pleasures of recompense and gift.

Therefore the ultimate object of a vast creation is not an object of an intelligent person! Could not the Creator create a pleasure by grace greater than a pleasure earned, seeing that all pleasures are His creation? . . .

The truth is that the question *Why* cannot be applied to the 404
Creator's substance or qualities or doings, so that no answer need be found. . . . 'He cannot be asked about what He does, but *they* will be asked.' *Sur.* 2. 23.

The Muʿtazila fall into two parties. Those of Baghdad said that 405
philosophically God was bound to do the best for created responsible beings in providing the greatest possible powers of mind and body. All man's afflictions of every kind . . . were the best for him—even eternal punishment was the salutary and (indeed) the best, for if men were released from Hell they would return to forbidden paths. . . . Those of Baṣra held that creation was a result of grace and favour, without any obligation on God, but if He created intelligent beings and made them responsible to Him He was bound to remove their weaknesses and do the very best for them.

The Muʿtazila maintained that both parties were right because the Creator was wise, and a wise man does not do anything which can be called in question and must be proved. . . . He confers power commensurate with obligation. True power rests in perfect capacity for action, and the purpose of the action is not fulfilled till its reward is conferred. Thus the fundamental purpose of creation and human
responsibility is the salutary . . . the highest possible degree of every- 406
thing salutary is the best. . . . Everything that is free from corruption is called salutary, namely that which makes for good in the constitution of the world in the preservation of species in this world, and that which leads to everlasting happiness in the next. The best is of two kinds, namely, that which is nearest to absolute good is 'the best', and grace is the making easy of the good which is the act that God knows a man will obediently perform. In that which is decreed by God there is no grace or act which would make infidels believe. . . .

But these definitions of the Muʿtazila have no intellectual or ecclesiastical sanction. They are but subjective deductions from this world carried over to the next. In reality these people are anthropomorphists so far as God's actions are concerned.

The Ashʿariyya replied that if there was an analogy between our
407 actions and God's actions we ought always to seek the salutary and the best, but human weakness often prevented men. Therefore the analogy broke down. They cannot say that Hell is best for some people, for if God slew them, or bereft them of reason and ended their punishment, it would be better for them. Indeed, if He pardoned and released them from Hell, seeing that He does not suffer from their wickedness, it would be better still for them. Again, if God is bound to do the best, He does not deserve praise or thanks for doing it. . . . Or is the respite given to Satan good for him or mankind? Or allowing the prophet to die? . . . Again, if God knew that premature death
408 would save a potential sinner from Hell . . . how can your thesis be upheld?

The popular idea of the meaning of *taklīf* is utility (*ṣalāḥ*)[1] and guidance (*taʿrīḍ*) to the highest degree, which can only be attained by works, so God purposed ill to those he endowed with intellect and responsibility when He knew (beforehand) that they would perish! Wisdom demands that His knowledge should restrain Him from wishing to do so. . . . No father would give his son money to engage in commerce if he knew that he would lose it; or hand him a sword to fight an enemy if he knew that he would kill himself, and the sword would go to the enemy. If he did he would be responsible for the death of his son!

It follows from Muʿtazilite teaching that if God knew that a people would be disobedient to His commands through an apostle, His knowledge would restrain Him from willing their performance. If He knew that men would disbelieve and perish, their well-being would turn Him from His wish. It is as though one let down a rope to a drowning man, knowing that he would strangle himself with it. . . .

409 It is popularly held that God can bestow grace just as easily as reward (for effort), so what is the object of guiding men to miseries? They (the Muʿtazila) replied that it is better to discharge one's obligations than to be forgiven for failure to discharge them. But this shows ignorance of God. . . . If He had created men and put them in paradise, that would have been good; or if He had created them in the world and then caused their death without a religious obligation that would have been good; or if He had made them responsible to Him and withdrawn His grace would they not have become more energetic and earned a greater reward? So why did He not do that?

[1] *V.l. istiṣlāh.*

Let us suppose that there were two infants: the first God cut off prematurely because He knew that he would become an infidel and perish eternally, so that the salutary in his case was premature death; . . . the second he allowed to reach manhood and incur the obligation of divine service and he became an infidel and said: 'Why, O Lord, did you not slay me in youth as you did my brother, so that I had not incurred obligation and eternal punishment?' Or, take two other 410
children: one the son of an infidel, one dying early, God knowing that if he lived he would believe and do right; he would say: 'Why didst thou not spare me so that I might have believed and earned an eternal reward?': the other the son of a Muslim who became an infidel.[1] . . .

In fine to say that the salutary and the best must be done (by God) would necessitate the death of the infants that God knows will grow into infidels, so that there would not be an infidel in the world; and conversely it would necessitate the preservation of those whom God knows will become believers, so that the world would contain nothing but believers! The doctrine of utility does not fit the facts. As to 'the best' it can be bettered *ad infinitum*. . . .

The Muʿtazila held views on the subject of pain contrary to al-Ashʿarī's. Nothing happens that is not decreed by God. If miseries befall men they are to be judged good, whether they happen spontaneously or by divine compulsion[2] without the assumption of antecedent deserts. . . . God does as He pleases whether the sufferer is innocent or not. . . . The problem of innocent suffering is one that we 411
all desire to have solved. . . . Nevertheless, some evils like scarification and perseverance in taking medicine have their place. . . . We often see children and lunatics suffering, and to suppose that the principle of retribution applies to them is to make matters worse.[3] But God is omnipotent in grace and recompense and knows that suffering is salutary. He does what He pleases.

As to Divine Grace we shall find the truth midway between the extreme views of the Muʿtazila and Ashʿarites.

The Muʿtazila. *Taufīq* is the manifestation of signs in God's creation which point to His Oneness. The production of intellect, hearing, and sight, the sending of apostles and revealed books is

[1] These are variants of the familiar story of al-Ashʿarī's dispute with his master al-Jubbāʾī which is said to have led to his breaking with him. See Ibn Khallikān, *Vita*, 618, and the *Mawāqif*, 150, &c.

[2] The rendering of P. (*jabran*) must be right. For *ibtidāan* in the sense given, cf. Avicenna's *Najāt*, p. 94, l. 1.

[3] This passage is difficult. If we could read *gharaḍ* for *ʿauḍ*, the meaning might well be 'to postulate a purpose in inflicting pain upon them makes matters worse'.

luṭf, (which) warns the wise against heedlessness, leads them to know God,[1] explains laws, distinguishes between forbidden and allowed. This having been done . . . man does not need renewed *taufīq* for every act: *taufīq* is universal and precedes action.

Khidhlān is inconceivable of God in the sense of leading astray and shutting the door and veiling men's minds, because divine law would thereby be made useless and punishment would be an injustice.

412 The Ashʿariyya. *Taufīq* and *khidhlān* stand in the same relation to God. *Taufīq* is the creation of special power to obey and to choose to obey. It is renewed moment by moment. Every act has a special power, and the power (will) to obey is proper to it rather than to disobedience. Thus *taufīq* is the creation of power convenient to the action and *khidhlān* is the creation of power to disobey. As to the signs (to which the Muʿtazila appeal) their relation to the 'aided' (*muwaffaq*) and the 'abandoned' is the same. Power convenient to opposites like good and evil would be *taufīq* in relation to good, and *khidhlān* in relation to evil.

The middle course. *Taufīq* is both universal and particular. It is given to all men and to particular individuals. All creatures come within the scope of God's grace, which is shown in the indications (of his uniqueness); in the power to infer the same; in the sending of apostles; and in making the path (to Him) easy so that man can have no argument against God. Particular individuals come within the scope of God's grace which is peculiar to those who know God's guidance, and that He wills uprightness. Beginning from the perfect poise of man's nature the forms that God's grace takes are innumerable. . . . There is the first prenatal impress of happiness or misery;
413 cf. the apostolic tradition, 'He who is (to be) blessed is blessed in his mother's womb'. Education and environment sometimes upset the natural poise for better or for worse. The second impress is from natural religion (*fiṭra*) and seduction. As tradition says, 'God created men with knowledge of Himself, but the devils beguiled them from it'. And, 'Every child has natural religion: his parents make him Jew, Christian, or Parsī'. Man's adult independence and mature intelligence need great support from *taufīq*. This is where men stumble and God's *taufīq* is shown in that He does not let a man rely on his own independence and unfettered will (*istibdād*). *Khidhlān* means that God does leave him to trust in himself and in his own resources: that is why the cry 'There is no might and no strength save in God' is obligatory at all times. . . . Early manhood fosters the animal
414 passions such as anger and desire; cf. *Sur*. 16. 53 and 28. 14. . . . The prophet used to say, 'O Lord leave me not to myself for the twinkling

[1] *Sc.* intimately, not *ʿilm* merely.

of an eye.'[1] The third impress rests on this state, which may be extended to life's end. . . .

He who listens to the admonitions of the law has his breast opened and receives light from his Lord. That is *sharḥ*. He who wilfully shuts his eyes to God's signs lives in darkness because he has sealed his mind.[2] That is *tabʿ* and *khatm*. But God sets his seal (*ṭabaʿa*) on the darkness because of his unbelief; cf. *Sur*. 2. 6. Sometimes the sealing and the individual nature are due to native hardness from his original *fiṭra*;[3] sometimes it is the recompense of his unbelief. . . . In fine, he who trusts in himself is in a state of *khidhlān*, while he who trusts himself to God's might is in a state of *taufīq*. . . .

Much the same may be said of 'favour' and 'sustenance'. You can 415
take a universal view and say that every blessing of man in this life and the next is a divine favour, and that 'sustenance' is everything edible, whether clean or unclean food. . . . Or you can take a particular view and say that favour is that which has a praiseworthy result and is confined to religion; cf. *Sur*. 23. 57; and 'sustenance' is really that which the law permits; cf. *Sur*. 2. 255, noting that alms may not be given from forbidden things. . . . Both views are right in their way. . . . 416
Sustenance determines the term of life. Every phenomenon has an end; the lives of animals are not peculiar in this respect. If God wills a thing to end at a certain time it does so end, and none can add to its sustenance or diminish it. . . .

Some say that two decrees are written in the preserved tablet, one absolute as to term of life (*ajal*) and 'sustenance', the other conditional so that if a man does one thing they are increased and if he does another they are diminished; but see *Sur*. 35.12 and 57. 22.

CHAPTER XIX

The Proof of Prophecy, of the Reality of Miracles, and that the Prophets must needs be Impeccable.

Brahmans and Ṣābi'ans hold that prophecy is impossible intellec- 417
tually. Muʿtazila and Shīʿa hold that a rational view of divine grace makes prophecy a necessity. Ashʿarites and Sunnīs hold that it is an intellectual possibility and an actual phenomenon. . . .

[1] Cf. Bahā' al-Dīn al-'Āmilī, *Mikhlāt*, Cairo, 1317, 129. 2, where many such prayers are collected.

[2] *Tab'* is evidently to be taken as a synonym of *khatm*; otherwise one would be tempted to see Avicenna's influence. By *Tab'* Avicenna (*Ḥudūd* 13) means specific nature—the nature of the species, not that of the individual *ṭabīʿa*.

[3] This word has already been rendered 'natural religion'. Later writers identified it with Islam. Here it means 'nature'. The philosophers use it of the untrained natural use of the intelligence.

The Brahmans and Ṣābi'ans argue that all assertions are true or false. Does the truth reside in the message itself or in some proof (*dalīl*) conjoined with it? If the prophet, of human species, could produce a miracle we could. If he could not, then it was due to God's power. So either it was an ordinary act, not peculiar to the preacher, and so no proof; or an act contrary to nature: but how could that prove his veracity? . . . Such an act must be joined to the
418 message itself and there may be other causes for such a conjunction. Therefore a miracle is no proof. . . . How can the preacher require God to perform an act, which is dependent on His will, at a given time? . . . Your own prophet says, 'Signs are the prerogative of God: but what will make you understand that if the signs come they will not believe?' (6. 109). Many a prophet when asked for a sign has failed to produce it at the time. But if the production of a sign at one time is a proof of veracity, failure to produce it at another must be proof of falsehood. . . .

Again, if the audience asks for delay on the ground that they have no intuitive knowledge of the sender much less of the apostle . . . must
419 the prophet grant them time for reflection? If he does not he wrongs them, . . . because knowledge can only come from thought (*naẓar*); and thought demands time. . . . Moreover, some people require longer than others for reflection, and if he returns to them too soon he may be told to go away again. . . .

How, too, does a prophet know that God or an angelic intermediary speaks to him? Or how does the angel know that it is God who has ordered him to speak?

420 We utterly deny your stories of the prophets such as turning a rod into a serpent, raising the dead, cleaving the moon, &c. Such things are utterly impossible. What proof is there that they happened? Again, why do you deny that some of these unusual occurrences are due to the special properties of things, e.g. minerals. A man, without any religion, can produce rain by beating stones together, and wind by certain movements. Again, sorcery, astrology, enchantment, the science of talismans, and the worship of spirits and the heavenly bodies are well-known sciences which produce miraculous wonders. How do you know that the preacher has not employed such means as these? Miracles are no proof of the truth of preaching: they merely indicate the power of the doer. Even if they accompany preaching they are no proof of its truth any more than if they accompanied any other act or assertion. You admit that miracles were performed by Him who claimed to be God. But that does not prove that His claim was true.

The Orthodox argued that it had been proved that God was the

Creator and absolute lord of all things. . . . He has the power to choose 421
a man to communicate His will to mankind so that there is no intellectual impossibility in His doing so. . . . Whether the preaching is true or false must be proved.

The Mutakallimūn argued that a miracle performed at the appropriate time by a prophet was equivalent to verbal proof of his
veracity. . . . The proof is cumulative: the miracle; its occurrence at 422
the time of preaching; and its inimitableness. . . .

Another argument of theirs is that as a miracle indicates the power of the doer, and its particular application points to his will and its planning to his knowledge, so it also points by its being an answer to the prayer of the preacher (and not an answer to the claim of the claimant) to the fact that God regards him as truthful. And if God answers a man's prayer he cannot be uttering a lie against God. . . . We do not deny that the prayer of a person may be answered and he may afterwards perish miserably; nor do we deny that a magician
sometimes works marvels. But the condition is the same. If the 423
claimant's prayer is attested by a sign at the time he asks for it so that the sign points to his veracity and standing with God, and if he can be supposed to be a liar, then the proof of veracity is turned into a proof that he is lying, which is absurd because it is self-contradictory.[1] If act indicates power it cannot indicate impotence; if plan indicates knowledge it cannot indicate ignorance. Similarly, the proof of veracity cannot indicate falsehood. This method is better than the former. . . .

Miracles are the prevention of the normal or the production of the abnormal. The first may be inhibiting the voluntary movements of the body while permitting it to retain its soundness and feeling of customary ease,[2] cf. the examples of Israel's wandering in the wilderness, Pharaoh's magicians, and Zachariah's dumbness, and it may be that we ought to add the prevention of claims to imitate the Qurān, seeing that that was within man's power. Some add the inimitableness of the Qurān but that had better be avoided. It might be thought that the preventing of people from uttering a challenge like the prophet's belongs to the sphere of miracles, for none can compete
with his claim to say nothing of miracles. . . . The prophet said: 'I am 424
the apostle of God to you and the sign that I speak the truth is that none will successfully compete with me in my claim'. . . .

I do not say that none will contradict him but that none will rival his challenge and claim. . . . We do not find that any prophet's

[1] I fail to see the application of this argument to the rain-maker, wizard, &c. But see the further discussion on p. 138.

[2] *wal-ta'atti* must be read, though there is no MS. authority for that punctuation.

challenge was answered at the time it was made. . . . The case of the lying Musailima is not apposite. For though he wrote to the prophet offering to share the land with him he did not attempt to compete with him in his claim. Had he done so he ought to have said: 'I am the slave and prophet of God. He has no associate; I am the associate of His apostle'. This is a nice point.

425 The answer to those who deny the prophets is that a contemporary miracle must either be related to the prophet's claim or to something else.

[Shahrastānī] We hold that God confirms the truth of His apostles by miraculous signs just as He shows men his divinity by signs. Sometimes He teaches by word; at others by deed (e.g. *Sur*. 2. 28). Sometimes He demonstrates a prophet's veracity by making every one impotent to imitate Him, as when He taught Adam the names of everything, or taught Muḥammad the Qurān and challenged the world to produce its like (2. 29). . . . The names and the Qurānic verses (*āyāt*) remain to attest the truth of the first and last prophets. . . .

Thus, from Adam to Muḥammad there is a continuous line of prophets who attest the truth of their predecessors while they prophesy of their successors.

God endowed His chosen messenger with beauties of diction,
426 character, and condition, which are utterly inimitable so that they are miraculous in the sight of men as men's actions are miraculous to the brute creation. . . .

The Ṣābi'ans and Brahmans . . . must agree that it is proved that God can do as He likes in laying down laws and that men's movements are governed by laws. . . . Reason asserts that the human race needs unity in peaceful society, and that unity can only be attained by mutual help and defence, and the mutual help and defence are inconceivable save through laws and those laws must be agreeable to God's laws. No living being receives these laws direct from God, nor can He make them himself: consequently reason requires that a lawgiver should promulgate a law which he receives from God by revelation for His creatures. . . .

God is not prevented from[1] making known the truth of his apostle and from designating a particular person, for that would be to charge
427 Him with impotence and imposing more than man can perform. It would be as if he had ordered His servants to know Him and then obliterated all proofs of His existence. You can only confirm by word or deed, and where word is impossible deed is the established way. . . . Such a declaration is not incumbent on God, but necessary for Him in order that He may not be charged with impotence in

[1] The reading of B. and P. 'God is not bound to' (O), presents difficulty.

furnishing proofs or with falsehood in the words of a would-be vicegerent or with not having given men warning. . . .

The fact that an apostle attributes signs to the will of God is the best proof of the truth of his words. . . . He owns his personal impotence and ascribes all power to God. Our prophet's distinctive trait was that he did not trust in himself for an instant, nor did he speak under the sway of passion nor move except with guidance, which was divine impeccability subsisting in him,[1] constituting his essence. . . .

You Ṣābi'ans acknowledge ʿĀdhīmīm and Hermes (who are Seth 428
and Idrīs) as prophets. Do you know that they are veracious because of their teaching and the report (you have heard) or by proof and thought (*naẓar*)? . . . If you say that human apostleship is impossible why do you adopt these two men as apostles? . . . If you say that they were sages, not prophets, we reply then why follow scrupulously their laws and regulations in doctrine, prayer, fasting, and alms when you are their equal in intelligence? . . .

It is remarkable that those who deny prophecy assert it in their denial, for prophecy means only a statement on God's authority that He has sent an apostle. He who denies it is really pretending that he is asserting on God's authority that He has not sent an apostle and thus claims apostleship for himself! . . .

The Ṣābi'ans admit the apostleship of spiritual beings and pay 429
homage to the seven planets, their temples; they make images (*ashkhāṣ*) after the form of the temples and venerate them. . . . Monotheists[2] admit the apostleship of mortals and pay homage to their persons (*ashkhāṣ*);[3] but they do not choose idols for gods nor believe that the prophets are divine beings (*arbāb*). They hold that they have a human and a prophetic aspect (*Sur.* 17. 95). On one side they resemble men: . . . on the other they resemble angels receiving divine sustenance from God; their eyes sleep but their heart does not; the mould may perish but the spirit within is immortal. The controversy has existed from the beginning of time (cf. *Sur.* 6. 78). See further *Al-Milal.*

As to granting an audience time for reflection . . . such as the

[1] Or, perhaps, the meaning is 'taking the place of himself'; i.e. submerging his own personality.

[2] Here Shahrastānī means Muslims, but he uses the term *Ḥanīf* as he does in the long passage in his *Milal* (pp. 202–51). The choice of this term, which in the Qurān denotes the primitive religion of Abraham in its original purity, is probably a conscious tribute to the antiquity of the religion of the Ṣābi'ans. He implicitly claims for Islam an ancestry equal to that of Ṣābi'anism.

[3] The homonym is no stranger than the somewhat similar πρόσωπον. It is interesting to find that Ibn Ṭumlus (p. 42) gives as a stock example of a homonym *insān* meaning rational animal and graven image.

430 Muʿtazila urge that is out of the question. . . . The prophet should point out that man . . . needs God his creator; cf. *Sur.* 2. 19. Why grant delay when he is commanded to preach the divine unity? . . . Delay is only justifiable when cogent proof is lacking. . . . [Here follows a series of citations from the Qurān showing that the order of preaching was first the divine unity and then the claim to prophecy, culminating in the preaching of Muḥammad in language of miraculous eloquence.]

433 The contention of the Muʿtazila that delay must be granted by a prophet would lead to the interruption of his mission . . . and a fight between him and the objector who was opposing the spread of his preaching. . . .

As to sorcery. . . . No reasonable person will deny that wonders occur through sorceries . . . but such wonders are never free from trickery wrought by actual contact; . . . a time is chosen, spells are used and preparations made. . . . In fact there are such exertions of voice and body that the observer sees that there is no question of
434 God attesting the claimant's truth. . . . But when dead and dry bones become a living person he perceives that this must be God's act manifesting his object in attesting the truth of His apostle. . . . He who has a request to make of God and whose prayer is answered knows of a certainty that He who answers him wills to answer him
435 by a special gift and grace. The possibility of the thing having happened by chance or through some other cause does not impair that knowledge. If such things can happen to ordinary persons what of him whom God chose out of all His creatures? . . .

Objections.

(1) If the abnormal is repeated it becomes the normal. How do you know that the present contains acts that will be repeated in the future and have not already taken place in the past? Do you not hold that the abnormal of the age of *taklīf* will pass away[1] at the end of time when all the laws of the universe will be broken in the cataclysmic destruction of all things. If any preacher claimed that such miracles were his doing—and they are abnormal in all conscience—they could not be regarded as humanly possible but are patently the act of God. Yet they would be no proof of the prophet's claims. Thus at the time he hears a prophet a thoughtful man may well wait to see if these signs are repeated, and the hesitation thus engendered may make him doubt whether they are signs of the prophet's truth.

436 (2) The philosophers held that just as such things may happen in

[1] O. has 'remain'. The meaning is unaffected. If the abnormal is swept away it is an argument against its being a proof of divine action. If it remains as the norm it is not abnormal!

the future they may have happened in the past, or in another part of the earth or through another agency, though they themselves could not do them, so that they are no proof of the prophet's veracity.

(3) If a miracle is a proof and removes all doubt then every one ought to be vouchsafed one. But you say that one suffices for the whole community . . . and that if a miracle persisted through the ages it would become the norm. But why should we believe in prophets of a by-gone age when we can find no proof of their truth, or why should a foreigner of the same epoch who had not witnessed the signs believe in them?

(4) If you assert that God can lead men astray how do you know that He does not work signs at the hands of a liar and not for a true prophet. He is above advantage or harm. Many a prophet has done his work without seeking a sign . . ., so why need you tie the truth of 437
prophecy to miracles in this way?

(5) If you say that mankind has no other means than miracles of ascertaining the truth of apostles you impute impotence to God. If you say that he has other means why are miracles necessary and why are they a better means of proof?

(6) You claim intuitive knowledge in the case of the evidence of miracles; you claim it for the coincidence in time of the challenge and the miracle; again for the evidence of the intention of the determinant in specifying[1] the particular act; again for it taking the place of oral confirmation; and lastly for its being beyond imitation. Why not claim intuitive knowledge for the claim itself and say that its truth is known intuitively?

You cannot say that the prophet's claim is a report which may be true or false because a similar uncertainty applies to all these aspects, so the claim to necessary intuitive knowledge is vain. . . .

The Orthodox reply: 438

(1) The normal is not a proof because it has no special connexion with the prophet's claim: the abnormal on the contrary has: either as an accompaniment like the flush of shame or the pallor of fear, or as a special connexion of the action with the claim at an appointed time, which in turn shows the purpose of the divine agent. . . . Though the miracle were repeated in the future it could not overthrow this proof, . . . for the first connexion and special relation would remain undisturbed.

Some of them say that as miracles are inimitable they can never be normal in the future. But in any case it is only a logical possibility which we have already refuted.

(2) . . . The point of the miracle is its occurrence when the prophet

[1] See Chapter I.

439 needs it. The possibility of it happening elsewhere or at another time does not annul the proof. . . . He who knows that by the law of nature the Euphrates is water and not blood, and is flowing as it always did although it is a logical possibility that God has turned it into blood . . . does not lose his intuitive knowledge because of the logical possibility of God's action. It is equally possible that pallor does not indicate fear, but if a condition and cause of fear are present it is known intuitively that it is the pallor of fear, not of sickness.

We know intuitively that the ascension, the walking on the water, &c., are contrary to human experience. So if they accompany a prophet's challenge they are a sign and a proof to men though they are not contrary to angelic order. It should be observed that a sign is a proof to him for whom it contradicts natural order. Thus if the prophet made the Jīḥūn[1] ebb and flow that would be a proof, because it is against natural order though it is usual at Baṣra; or if he said, 'A sign of my veracity is that God will make palm trees flourish in Khurāsān', that would be a miracle.

440 (3) It is right that a man should set his doubts at rest, but if men of experience are satisfied that a miracle has occurred other people ought not to cling to doubt because men of experience and insight into the nature of things and the lying ways of men are the most prone to scepticism; and if a miracle occurs contrary to their expectation they are most ready to welcome (new knowledge). . . . A prophet must not be expected to go in pursuit of every individual with a special miracle. Once his veracity is established his words bind every one either of his own time in another country when trustworthy tidings reach him, or posterity who hear the report by tradition.

(4) We do say that God leads astray[2] but only in the following conditions: (*a*) that nothing that He did not know beforehand occurs, (*b*) that the proof and the thing to be proved are not in opposition, (*c*) that no charge of impotence can be brought against Him, (*d*) that a lie cannot be imputed to Him. . . .

441 Thus (*a*) if God sent a prophet to guide people and He knew that he would furnish them with convincing proof, if he misled them with that very proof then the result would be contrary to His foreknowledge and that is an impossibility. Similarly, if He said that He would send an apostle to guide a people and he then led astray every one to whom he was sent, truth would become falsehood and that is impossible. A lie cannot be imputed to God because a lie is a state-

[1] I.e. the Oxus.

[2] It is important to bear in mind what grammarians call the 'tolerative' force of the causative conjugation. Obviously the meaning is not always 'leading astray' but 'permits the misleading'.

ment about a thing contrary to the fact, but God knows the fact. If you know a thing you have information of what is knowable about it, and information about the knowable is information of the fact. You cannot have two contradictories in one Knower. . . .

(*b*) . . . If a thing proves something it cannot prove its opposite. . . . To send an apostle, to deprive him of an indication of veracity, to produce a wonder calculated to deceive the masses, to perform a miracle through a liar in imitation of the claims of a prophet—all this is impossible. . . .

Leading astray can be ascribed to God in the sense that He creates 442
error in a person's heart, but if it points to an impossibility (as shown above) it is impossible. God does not do it because of its impossible and contradictory nature, not because it is morally wrong.

(5) Miracles are not the only means of convincing men; it is possible that intuitive knowledge of a prophet's truth could be created for them so that a miracle would be unnecessary. Other accessory indications would suffice for some people but not for others. If a trustworthy man relate something on the authority of one who
has received proof posterity are bound to believe it. Even had the 443
prophet failed to produce a single sign the innumerable proofs of his coming in Jewish and Christian scriptures would have sufficed. For this reason his miracles were given to the illiterate[1] Arabs and not to the Peoples of the scriptures.

(6) Speculative knowledge must rest on necessary knowledge; . . . sometimes the two are closely related; sometimes many processes of reason intervene. If we treat knowledge of the truth of prophecy as of the genus of knowledge which comes through contemporary conditions it is of the first class and it may be said: This claimant is either true or false. He cannot be false because miracles occur to support his claim and none can vie with him. This conjunction of ideas results in necessary knowledge of his truth, though at the beginning there was no necessary knowledge. If we treat it as of the genus of knowledge which comes through proof of his being specially designated (by the miracles) as true then the knowledge which results
thereby is like that which results from (God's) willing it—for designa- 444
tion points to will—and the special designation shows that He wills this special thing.

Prophecy and apostleship can only be postulated when it is admitted that God commands and prohibits. . . . A prophet without a sign testifying to his truth is inconceivable because the reality of prophecy is true utterance together with a supporting sign. . . . If a

[1] *ummiyyīn*. I give the meaning of the word as Shahrastānī understood it, following the lead of many of the native lexicographers.

prophet without a sign were imaginable it would be as though he had no prophecy. Sometimes the sign is specially devoted to any question which demands it: . . . sometimes it is general indicating the truth all the prophet's words. Sometimes the signs are verbal like the signs (verses) of the Book; sometimes factual like raising the dead. . . . Proof of veracity never leaves a prophet for an instant. This is what
445 is meant by impeccability. If that failed, proof would fail, and the prophet's claim would be inconsistent with itself. . . . Prophets are preserved from venial as from mortal sins for if the former are persisted in they become mortal sins. . . .

CHAPTER XX

446 PROOF OF THE PROPHETIC MISSION OF MUḤAMMAD. AN EXPLANATION OF HIS MIRACLES, AND OF THE WAY IN WHICH THE QURĀN INDICATES HIS VERACITY. SUMMARY STATEMENTS ON THE NAMES AND CATEGORIES OF REVELATION. THE NATURE OF FAITH AND UNBELIEF. OF BRANDING (OTHER MUSLIMS) AS INFIDELS. AN EXPLANATION OF THE INTERROGATION IN THE GRAVE. OF THE ASSEMBLY (*ḥashr*). OF THE RESURRECTION. OF THE SCALE. OF THE RECKONING. OF THE BASIN. OF THE INTERCESSION. OF THE BRIDGE (*ṣirāṭ*). OF PARADISE AND HELL. PROOF OF THE IMAMATE. OF THE SPECIAL GIFTS OF THE SAINTS. OF THE POSSIBILITY OF ABROGATION OF LAWS. PROOF THAT ISLAM ABROGATES ALL OTHER LAWS. THAT MUḤAMMAD IS THE SEAL OF THE PROPHETS AND THAT SCRIPTURE IS SEALED BY HIM.

447 THE Orthodox hold that the proof of the prophet's truth is the book which he brought (2. 181). This is shown by its eloquence and clearness. Man differs from beast in speech, the instrument of thought (17. 72); the Arabs excel all nations in the beauty, clearness, and ease of their language (26. 195). Equally did the prophet's words excel
448 all others in chasteness, eloquence, and aptness (16. 46). He himself said: 'I am the most eloquent of the Arabs.'. . . Compare the finest composition in Arabic with one *sura* of the Qurān, and the difference between them is greater than that between Arabic and other tongues. . . . Compare the prophet's own words with those revealed to him, and the difference is as great. . . . Thus we know of a certainty that what he said was revealed to him, and what he revealed was a proof of his truth and a miracle (wrought) for him to the confusion of the
449 poets and orators of his time. He challenged them in vain to produce anything like it (28. 49). . . . If any one wilfully blinds himself to the truth the Qurān still challenges comparison, running its course like

the procession of night and day. . . . After more than four centuries men have failed to imitate it, despite the literary genius of that age. . . . Such a proof of inimitableness should suffice us. . . . Each *sura* 450
has its own excellence: . . . sometimes there is one story which is complete in itself but is repeated in other words in another *sura*, notably the history of Moses in *suras* 7 and 20.

When the Arab orators perceived the beautiful language of the Qurān they exclaimed, 'This is nothing else than sorcery' (5. 110).

Again, the contents of the Qurān with its marvels of wisdom, such as no philosopher can equal, are proof of its inimitable character and the character of him who brought it, especially when it is remembered that he was an orphan without learning or even knowledge of letters. . . . If pure revelation did not tell him these things whence did he gain his eloquence? Whence the stories of former apostles and prophets seeing that he had never heard of them from any one nor 451
studied histories and traditions? Whence the prophecies of the future, e.g. of the downfall of the Byzantine empire?

The laws and ordinances of the Qurān, religious, social, and political, are an obvious miracle. . . . He who reads the revealed books of the Law, the Gospels, and the Psalms[1] perceives the plain difference between them and the Qurān. For all the intellectual truths and religious ordinances which they contain the Qurān enshrines in plainer language and greater particularity. . . .

In a word the Qurān, so far as the forms of the words themselves and the ideas they express are concerned, is inimitable, and its meaning is marvellous. It is a plain proof of its own true nature and the truth of him who challenged mankind to produce its like.

The foolish say: '"Qurān" means that which is read while accord- 452
ing to you that which is written is an eternal quality.' The eternal cannot be a miracle and in the sense of reading it is the act of the reader. A creature's act cannot be a miracle. If you say that God creates it at the time without the prophet acquiring it it may be replied: Then in what substrate does He create it? In his tongue? But sounds resident in the tongue are within a prophet's capacity whereas a miracle is not. In another substrate, tree, tablet, or mind of an angel? Then the miracle is that created thing, not the prophet's utterance, so we do not hear a miracle and what we do hear is not a miracle! . . .

Again you say that the inimitable nature of the Qurān is its language, its chaste expression, its arrangement, and its eloquence. Are these miraculous individually or collectively? You seem to differ as

[1] This is certainly the meaning that Shahrastānī gave to *Zubūr*, though it had a wider meaning in old Arabic.

to whether the Qurān is miraculous in resisting all attempts at imitation or in its all embracing eloquence. Again you differ as to whether the language or the expressions or the arrangement are wonderful. . . . Obviously the miraculous[1] must be plain to everybody, otherwise it is not a miracle. . . .

453 The Orthodox reply. Neither the eternal nor the thing acquired by the creature can be inimitable. There are several ways in which the Qurān is a miracle. The recitation may be said to be a miracle because (*a*) God creates its words in the tongue of the reciter without his having power over them and moving his tongue by his own power, so that it is purely God's act and he manifests its inimitability in its arrangement which is peculiar to itself. And (*b*) God creates in the prophet's soul an ordered speech to which his tongue gives expression: the movement of the tongue is in his power, but the miraculous speech is that which the inner consciousness embraces and is described as being in the breast (75. 16); and (*c*) God creates the speech in the angel's heart[2] or tongue and he conveys it to the prophet's heart, and the latter expresses it with his tongue (69. 40 and 57. 5); and (*d*) the ideas to be expressed may have been created in the preserved table

454 from which Gabriel read them to the prophet so that he heard them from him as one hears them from us. The miracle is the speech and Gabriel was the revealer, as was the prophet, and as we are when we recite it, but Gabriel's revelation was an indication of the truth of the prophet.[3] As the camel was concealed in the rock and revealed at the preaching of Ṣāliḥ, and so the revelation of the miracle was conjoined with the prophet's challenge, the revelation of the miraculous is like the creation of the miracle as a proof of veracity,[4] a nice point that should be noted.

We can learn poetry that we have heard or read until its form is impressed on our minds so that that which is heard and learnt is our

455 own but the composition is not in our power. . . . The impression in the soul is like an impression in fine dust. The form of the poetry remains however many impressions are made. The prophet's mind received revelation as dust receives a print. The print itself is not his but owes its origin to God: thus its existence is miraculous.

The word of God appeared in words, consonants, and vowels, though it is one and eternal, just as Gabriel appeared in persons, bodies, and accidents though he is in himself another reality (verity)

[1] It will have been seen that the significance of 'miracle' in the Western sense is not always present in *mu'jiza*, which means 'disabling' (*sc.* attempts at imitation). Therefore any one who thinks that the Qurān can be equalled in any aspect mentioned above would not regard it as a 'miracle'.

[2] I.e. 'mind'.

[3] Or, with P., G's revelation and our revelation were to prove', &c. The text is confused.

[4] The MSS. differ considerably here.

prior to person. It is not to be said that his reality was changed into a corporeal reality in a certain person because a change of persons is impossible. If it be argued that one reality was annihilated and another came into existence, then the latter was not Gabriel, so that it must be said that Gabriel appeared in it (the person) as the sense (*maʿnā*) appears in words (*ʿibārāt*) or a spirit appears in a person.[1] Thus as the words are the 'person' of the sense, so the form of the Arab was the 'person' of the angel. The Qurān (6. 9) illustrates this in the words 'Had we made him an angel we should have made him a man'.[2] Thus must the words of the Qurān be understood.

We will now explain the literary excellences of the Qurān and the 456
terms used thereof: a word may be used in the widest possible sense as when we say 'the body moved' (*taḥarraka*). It may refer to a mineral, plant, or animal, or the whole universe. But if a special subject is intended the movement is denoted more particularly; cf. 52. 9, 'the day when the heavens shall move (*tamūru*) and the mountains leave their place' (*tasīru*). *Maur* is a choicer word than *sair*, and both are better than *ḥaraka*. *Maur* denotes the light movement of a light body and is thus peculiarly appropriate to the heavens while the heavier word goes with the mountains. How bald the common words for moving and going would be. The passage is an example of purity (*faṣāḥa*) and chastity (*jazāla*) of diction.

Order (*naẓm*) means context and arrangement. It is of varying degrees from ordinary intercourse, correspondence, orations, to poetry 457
which demands the greatest ordering of words, and is called *naẓm* as opposed to prose. If *faṣāḥa*, *jazāla*, and *naẓm* are present the word *balāgha* can be used because the speech has reached (*balagha*) perfection.

To define the terms more nearly: *Faṣāḥa* is the expression of what the speaker desires to express in distinct and correct terms. *Jazāla* explains the meaning in the most concise way. Sometimes the two are found together; cf. 2. 175. Sometimes many ideas are contained in a few words. *Naẓm* is the arrangement of the words in relation to each other. . . . *Balāgha* unites all three if the meaning is plain,
accurate, and good. The Qurān surpasses the literature of the Arab 458
in all these aspects.[3]. . .

The Muʿtazila hold that reflection was necessary before revealed 460
religion on the ground that the reasoning man is conscious of two 461
impulses, one inviting him to think so that he may know his Maker,

[1] The influence of Christological controversies is plain.

[2] Or (Rodwell) 'as a man'.

[3] Here follows a number of examples of Qurānic eloquence which I omit. They are not necessary for an understanding of the writer's argument.

and thank Him and be rewarded; the other preventing him. Therefore he chooses the path of safety and rejects the way of fear. It was replied: If a prophet claims apostleship he may be true or false. But why is it not decided that he is true, for that would be safe because it would be dangerous to declare him false, whereas if he were false his lie would be on his own head. In demanding a miracle there is another danger, for that is treating his claim as probably false ... until a miracle decides the question. To the Muʿtazila the Qurān is a composition in Arabic and they do not believe that it is inimitable. ...

The perverse argued that the term apostleship and the claim 'I am the prophet of God' were unintelligible. Is apostleship an attribute in his (the prophet's) essence by virtue of which he can convey God's orders to men, or is it God's statement 'He is my apostle'? If the first what is the reality of the attribute? If the second it is inconceivable that God should speak to a man. A man hears the vowels and consonants of speech, but according to you God's speech is not thus.
462 ... The idea of angels in bodily form speaking to men is unintelligible and not susceptible of proof. The descent of the angel and of the Qurān is unintelligible ... and the ascent to heaven of a heavy body is impossible, so that the whole of his preaching of resurrection, balance, basin, &c., is false.[1]

The Orthodox replied that apostleship was not an attribute of the prophet himself nor a rank that any could attain by knowledge or effort ... but a mercy vouchsafed by God (14. 13, &c.).

463 [Shahrastānī] The prophet's soul and body (*mizāj*) did not lack natural perfection and moral beauty before his mission, for he became worthy of his calling thereby (3. 153). ... The prophet's person was mercy personified and his apostleship was mercy and kindness to men (21. 107). Prophets are God's kindness and proof to his creatures. They are the means by which we approach him, the doors of his mercy and the cause of his kindness. ... When they were[2] at the height of their[2] physical and mental powers at the age of forty God revealed His book to them by an angel. ... The angel did not assume
464 a body in the sense that a subtle body became gross in the way that thin air becomes a dense cloud as is popularly supposed, nor was his real nature annihilated and another brought into being, nor his nature changed to another: all this is impossible. But luminous substances (*jawāhir*) have the peculiar power of appearing in whatever person they wish (19. 17 and 6. 9). There is no parallel in this world except the relation of our souls to our bodies. ...

[1] The language of the original (which I have summarized) is surprisingly strong.

[2] The singular here suggests that only Muhammad is in the writer's mind, though he reverts to the plural again.

Do not you Ṣābi'ans believe in the revelation of the spiritual to the corporeal and assert that every spiritual being has a temple in which he appears, . . . and every temple in the upper world has a person in the lower world in which he appears? . . . You have chosen images for gods, they being the manifestations of the temples which 465 are the manifestations of the spiritual beings. . . .

[Ṣābi'ans] We, O Ḥanīfs, believe in created spiritual persons of choicest spiritual substance, related to those spiritual substances as light is to light and shade to shade.[1]

[The Orthodox] The prophet had two sides, human[2] and apostolic (17. 95). Through the first he received the revelation, through the second he transmitted his message. Revelation (*waḥy*) is the immediate transmission of one thing to another. Every intelligent form which he receives through his spiritual side from the angels whom God sends to him comes in a moment as a form appears in a mirror. This is revelation. The nearest parallel is a sleep in which one goes into a garden, feasts on its fruit, bathes in its water, and engages in conversation which would fill volumes, and all this in a moment's light sleep. The factual and verbal forms from the world of ideas coming through sleep do not demand the time and arrangement required by the wakeful state but fall into the seer's mind in a moment making an indelible impression. . . . Thus a true vision belongs to prophecy as do gentleness, patience, and moral rectitude. The office of prophet then is a whole, the essence of the parts. That whole in its complete- 466 ness belongs only to him whom God chose for his apostleship. Part of it has belonged to his righteous servants. . . . To the whole none can attain by merit (*kasb*) or obedience. . . .

The descent (*nuzūl*) of God's speech means that the angel brought it down. 'Descent' need not be taken literally, but metaphorically. . . . The 'descent' of the eternal speech means that the signs (verses) which prove it came down. [Here follows a repetition of the argument: divine king—commands—agent to announce them—credentials.]

We must believe in all traditional revelations since the truth of the 467 prophet has been established. . . . If they cannot be proved we must accept them. The impossible is plainly recognizable. We know that the true and faithful one would not assert the impossible so the right meaning of his words is to be sought for. If we have found it, it is of God's grace: if not we believe in the literal meaning and leave the inner meaning to God and His apostle.

[1] There must be some mistake here. The speakers are the Ṣābi'ans as the address to the Ḥanīfs shows. P. has *ittaba'nā* and B. *ittaba'tum*. The Muslim reply begins with the discussion of the nature of the person of Muhammad but the words *qāla ahlu'l-ḥaqq* or their equivalent have fallen out.

[2] Lit. 'carnal'. This passage has several parallels on p. 233 of the *Milal*.

The *assembling of bodies* and the *resurrection*. No religion speaks more plainly than ours on this subject. . . . The philosophical theologians believe that the spirit survives after its separation from the
468 body and since the assembling of bodies is possible essentially and is prophetically attested it must be declared true without asking how, since God can confer life a second time as he did at first, . . . as he quickens the earth after its death every spring. . . . If individual souls are separated from bodies and are not independent[1] of bodily instruments in their thoughts, they must need bodies, otherwise they would be punished, for their happiness is in their thoughts and their thoughts[2] are only (possible) through their instruments, and these only exist if they (the bodies) return with their works as they were[3] (on earth). To hold that bodies are assembled again is to pay due regard to wisdom in giving every soul its proper share of perfection according to its works. To deny it is to confine the assembly to one or two souls in every age . . . and to hold that every soul is punished. . . . The order of souls in this world remains; and when the soul leaves the body either the order ceases so that the wise and the fool are equal, or the order is confirmed. To deny a bodily resurrection is to deny rewards and punishments and leads to many contradictory theses which we have dealt with in a Letter on the Future Life.

469 The *question in the grave* is attested by sound tradition in many places. It is best to regard it as being addressed neither to a disembodied spirit nor to a body such as we see. . . . If the angels asked about belief alone, the spirit could reply; but if belief and word and deed were inquired of, the body in its proper form would have to be assembled. But the question about a man's God, religion, and prophet would require the exercise of a living man's thinking and speaking parts. If the man be unconscious like a sleeper or a drunkard it is possible that God may quicken the organs of thought and speech so that the question can be put to them. . . . But God knows best.

The scale. This is attested by *Sur.* 4. 18. Opinions differ as to what
470 it is to weigh, whether bodies, or a writing containing men's good and evil deeds. . . . However, it is best to say that everything terrestrial has a fitting scale: the scale of the ponderable is the ordinary scale of weights; the scale of dry weight is the gallon, of length the cubit, and so on; and the scale of deeds is what is suitable thereto. God knows best about what He means.

The *basin* and the *intercession* are to be taken literally. The basin is like the rivers in Paradise. He that drinks of it in the Resurrection will never thirst.

[1] Perhaps this is the reading of P. [2] Add with P.
[3] Or, perhaps, 'with their former activity'.

The Muʿtazila say that the intercession is confined to obedient believers, for according to them the unrepentant sinner is eternally damned, an object of wrath who cannot enter Paradise. . . . In a state of sin he has no right to the name of faith, because faith (*īmān*) means praiseworthy characteristics for which the believer (*mu'min*) deserves praise and credit. The sinner does not deserve praise, for he has moved the pillars of his faith by departing from obedience ; cf. 4. 471
18, &c. The Qurān speaks of no intermediate place between heaven and hell, so that they must go either to the one or to the other.

The Khārijites went further and damned a man who committed a mortal sin on the ground that Satan recognized the existence of God and obeyed Him except in his refusal to prostrate himself to Adam.

The Murjites held that faith is confession with the mouth and an undertaking though it be not supported by works. Disobedience does no harm where there is faith, and obedience does no good where there is unbelief.

The Karrāmiyya went furthest in reducing the content of faith. They said it was a bare assertion, namely a confession with the tongue, and that was all. A liar and a hypocrite could be a believer: not a believer in their sight only, but in God's sight.

The Ashʿariyya said that in ordinary language faith meant 'con- 472
fessing the truth of'; and the law had established that that was its meaning.

Al-Ashʿarī gave a different answer about *taṣdīq*. Sometimes, he said, it was knowledge of the divinity, pre-existence and attributes of the Creator, sometimes a mental speech which contained the knowledge[1] and which when uttered became confession with the tongue. Performance of the fundamental duties of religion is also a kind of *taṣdīq*. . . .

The idea subsisting in the mind is the root whence faith is to be inferred: confession and works are indications thereof. Some of his followers said that faith was knowledge that God and His apostle were true, a teaching of al-Ashʿarī. The measure of faith is the universal obligation to witness that there is no God but Allah Who reigns alone in His kingdom and has no equal in all His attributes and no partner in His works and that Muhammad is His apostle. . . . If he dies in this belief he is faithful in the sight of God and man. . . . If he belongs to a school which compels him to oppose any of these fundamentals he must not be regarded as an absolute unbeliever but 473
a victim of error and innovation. His judgement rests with God as to eternal or temporary hell-fire.

[1] *fides implicita?*

[Shahrastānī] Now we know that the prophet invited men to accept the two assertions of the *shahāda* and that he would not accept a statement with mental reservations. He called such people hypocrites and the Qurān denies them the name of believers (2. 7). . . . Al-Karrāmī asserts the contrary. It is certain from what has been said that mental acceptance is fundamental because verbal acceptance is only the expression of the state of the mind. . . . Inward attestation
474 suffices if outward attestation is impossible. . . but good works are an obligatory sequel to faith.

The Murjites divorce works from faith to the point that they say a man is none the worse if he cannot produce one act of obedience. The Waʿīdiyya, on the other hand, say that one act of disobedience involves eternal damnation. Both schools are to be rejected.

The first abrogates the commandments and would lead to the destruction of society. . . . If neither obedience nor disobedience matters there is no point in commandments at all. . . .

The second abrogates Qurān, tradition, and catholic belief and excludes divine forgiveness and leads to despair. The Qurān distin-
475 guishes between faith and works: 'Verily they that believe and do good works'. Faith and works have their own special nature. If they were identical it would follow from what the Waʿīdiyya say that an impeccable prophet would be the only believer in the world! It would also follow that no one could be called believer until he had displayed every possible virtue and thus the word (in a particular case) would have no present application but depend on works to be done in the future! These people might be called the Murjites (postponers) of faith from works while the former class are the Murjites of works from faith.

Certainly works are not so fundamentally bound up with faith that it can be said that the absence of them involves virtual excommunication in this life and hell-fire eternally in the next. Nor are they so distinct from faith that it can be said that the absence of them is blameless in this life and does not deserve punishment in the next.

To say that obedience cancels disobedience is no better than the converse. Those who say that a mortal sinner will be in Hell eternally though his punishment will be alleviated because of his confession of faith and off-setting obedience, are opposed by the Murjites, who say that he will be in heaven eternally though below the rank of the obedient because he has been obedient in other things. But if obedi-
476 ence is cancelled, how can it alleviate, and how is alleviation conceivable in eternity? And how is an eternal sentence for a temporal deed to be justified? If a man has been an unbeliever for a century why is it intellectually justifiable to send him to hell for ever? If a

man steals a hundred dinars is it right to take two hundred from him? You say it is in the belief that if he lived for ever he would for ever disbelieve. But belief that he would do is not the same as belief that he has done. . . .

Logical justice and the sacred law agree that if a man confesses God in his heart and speech and obeys Him in part and disobeys Him in part he deserves praise and blame in this life and in the world to come. Is he to be rewarded first and then punished eternally or vice versa? The first is inconsistent with grace and justice,[1] for the compassion of God is wider than men's sins and His grace inspires more confidence than our works. . . . Faith and knowledge (of Him) in justice and reason are more worthy of an eternal recompense than a temporary disobedience. . . . The prophet said: 'My intercession is for the mortal sinners of my community'. . . .

It is a mistake to give a particular application to verses of a univer- 477
sal character. To 'transgress the laws' means all the laws, and none can do that but an unbeliever. 'He that kills a believer intentionally' means 'thinking it right to kill him', because none but an unbeliever would kill a man with absolute intention. . . .

The *imāmate* does not belong to dogmatic religion but its political 478
importance demands that it should be understood.

Most traditionists of the Ashʿarites and lawyers, the Shīʿas, the Muʿtazilites, and most of the Khārijites believe in the necessity of the imāmate as a command (*farḍ*) from God. The Sunnīs said that it was a duty (*farḍ*) which all Muslims must carry out.

There must be a leader to administer their laws, protect their country, see to their armies, divide their spoil and alms, arbitrate in disputes, punish wrongdoers, appoint officials.[2] The imām must warn sinners and bring them back to the right path, and take steps to cleanse the land of error with the sword.

The institution of the imāmate is attested by catholic consent from 479
the first generation to our own day in the words: 'The earth can never be without an imām wielding authority.' When Muhammad died none contested Abū Bakr's statement that a successor must be appointed, and all know the story of ʿUmar's homage to Abū Bakr. When the latter died it never occurred to any one that an imām was not indispensable. ʿUthmān and ʿAlī were next chosen. All this 480
goes to prove that the first generation unanimously agreed that there must be an imām. The office has gone on from then till now either by

[1] It is interesting to notice how the ideas of *righteousness* and divine grace have found a footing, while the notions of abstract justice and wisdom as principles active within the Godhead have been excluded.

[2] This passage, save for a few additions, is identical with al-Baghdādī's *Uṣūl*, p. 271.

general consent of the people, or by agreement and testament, or by both. Such a consensus of opinion is decisive proof of the necessity of the office.[1]

Is the appointment of a particular imām founded on scripture or catholic consent? People differ as to whether a particular person or his (necessary) character is founded on scripture and as to whether catholic consent means every one's assent or only that of competent people.

Those who hold that *ijmāʿ* is the basis say that the scripture does not indicate a particular imām. If it did the people would be bound to obey him. There are no means of identifying him by reason, and if
481 tradition were trustworthy every Muslim would know intuitively that he must obey him as a matter of religion just as he must say the five prayers, and they would not offer to another their homage and *ijmāʿ*.

It cannot be that people would keep silence if there were a clear utterance from the prophet, especially in the days of Islam's purity. If a person were named he would be bound to lay claim to the imāmate and if he were denied his right and remained quietly at home the injustice that he was suffering would be apparent. But there is no record of any one having claimed the office by virtue of a prophetic attestation (*naṣṣ*).

The Najdite section of the Khawārij, and the Qadarites like Abū Bakr al-Aṣamm, and Hishām al-Fuwaṭī hold that the imāmate is not obligatory in law so that sin is incurred if it is not established. On the contrary it rests on the conventions of society. If men behaved
482 justly and did their duty there would be no necessity for an imām. One man is as good as another in religion, in Islām, in knowledge, and in private judgement (*ijtihād*). They are like the teeth in a comb —a hundred camels but no good mount. There is no necessity to obey a man like oneself.

If obedience to one man were necessary it must rest on the prophet's word (and you have shown that no one man was designated); or on the choice of those exercising private judgement. It is inconceivable that every one should choose the same person, and such a thing has never happened. If choice rests on private judgement and that rests on every intelligent person's resolving his hesitation we see that what is by nature a matter of dispute must still be controversial when a verdict has been given. We should expect the first caliphate to display (unanimous) agreement, the primitive age being the standard in law, and the persons most worthy of credence the Companions, and the most trustworthy of Companions the Muhājirūn, and Abū Bakr and ʿUmar the nearest to the prophet. But the facts flatly contradict this

[1] I have omitted a good deal here.

expectation. The Anṣār put up Sa'd as Amīr and had it not been for 'Umar schism would have occurred.

The dissension between the Umayyads and 'Alids and the rival 483
claims of 'Abbās all point to the absurdity of the claim of *ijmā'* in this most important of matters. Indeed it proves that *ijmā'* cannot be used as an argument in any matter.

Further, they argued that the appointment of an imām was a logical contradiction because (*a*) the chooser laid down the law in setting up an imām, so that the imām obeyed him by becoming imām; and (*b*) any independent thinker could oppose the imām when the imāmate was being established in any question. All this shows 484
that the imāmate is not binding in law. If circumstances call for a leader by general consent[1] he could be appointed on the condition that he acted justly always, and that he could be deposed for tyranny as 'Uthmān and 'Alī[2] were. 'Uthmān was deposed and killed for his refusal to abdicate and 'Alī they deposed and fought for accepting arbitration.

The Shī'as hold that the imāmate is binding in religion, logically and legally, just as the prophetic office is logically and dogmatically.

Their appeal to logic is that men need a leader whom all must obey to preserve law, order, and religion, just as they need a prophet to give them laws. The need for the preservation of law is just as great as the need for its promulgation. If the first is necessary—be it of God's grace or man's reasoning—so is the second.

Their appeal to dogma is based on *Sur*. 4. 62 'Obey God and the apostle, and those of you who bear rule', and 9. 120 'O believers . . . 485
be with the truthful'. If there were none who must be obeyed how would it be incumbent on us to 'be with them'? You can't say 'Be with so-and-so' when there is no such person. Since the world must hold an absolutely truthful person his impeccability is established. By impeccability we mean truth in all his utterances, for such a man is righteous at all times.

We are bound to respect the good faith of the Companions and to realize that the prophet knew men's need of a rallying-point against lawlessness and disorder, and that they needed some one to meet the wicked with sword and argument more than they needed instruction on how to wipe their shoes and so on. It is inconceivable that instruction on such matters should be given and nothing be said about the most important of all matters. If men could ask why a 486
prophet had not been sent to them (20. 134) they could also ask the prophet why he had left them without a properly appointed successor. Prophets were sent to deprive men of arguments against God, so why

[1] *ijtihāduhum*, the private judgement of Muslims, not *ijmā'uhum*.
[2] The scribes add mechanically 'May God be pleased with them'.

should not the prophet have designated the imām so that there should be no argument against him? If you say the prophet knew men's need and did not provide for it you disparage him: if you say he did appoint a successor but they did not follow his instructions you disparage the Companions.

But you are on the horns of a dilemma. Either you must say that the matter was left to the people at large and it was entrusted to those with independent judgement so that individual competence or otherwise might be apparent and (thus) the learned became the stewards of the law and religion; (in which case) why was not the matter subject to the independent speculation and judgement of the learned? Yet God did not send apostles to warn them in order that individual competence might be apparent. Why did not the Companions take this view, not labouring to designate an imām when the prophet had been reticent.

487 Or you must say that the matter was not left to the people at large, or for deliberation. In that case you are committed to the theory of a designated imām. But there is no text except in the case of those who claim a text. And as for those who do not claim a text how can they be designated by a text!

The difficulty arises from the Imāmites' evil view of the Companions and the forging of traditions attributed to the apostle. We cannot deal with such nonsense here. Of a similar character are the extravagant claims of the Zaidites.

The Sunnī's reply to the Najdites. The law[1] determines for us what is incumbent on us; the *ijmāʿ* of the community reveals the obligation. The dispute that you mention about the appointment of the imām is the strongest[2] argument for the imāmate itself, for if the office were not essential they would not have begun to quarrel about it.

488 As to your point that *ijmāʿ* is inconceivable in reason and impossible in fact, two people can agree in an opinion and if two why not three or four and in short everybody, so that it is a logical possibility. In the first generation *ijmāʿ* was a fact. When the Companions agreed on a matter it was because of the existence of a hidden *naṣṣ*. *Ijmāʿ* was regarded as a proof, because the Companions rebuked those who
489 acted contrary to it. . . . Your contention that the imāmate of Abū Bakr was not the will of every one is wrong, for all the Companions did him homage, though ʿAlī was busy at the time with the burial of the prophet. When he saw what had occurred he also did homage to Abū Bakr.

[1] Variant 'revealed tradition' *samʿ*.

[2] In view of the fact that Shahrastānī generally uses *ʿalā* in this context in the sense of *pro* (as does al-Ghazālī also) the true reading must be *adalla*.

It is not true to say that the vote of an individual in the election of an imām confers authority *ipso facto* on the voter, because his authority rests on an explicit or implicit word of the prophet (*naṣṣ*). He is the seat of authority and *ijmāʿ* merely makes that authority explicit.

It is true that any independent thinker may oppose his imām in certain matters, because one such cannot bind another, but such opposition must be confined to matters not governed by *ijmāʿ*. We may compare the opposite policy of Abū Bakr and ʿUmar in dealing
with the property of rebels. Many instances of conflict between ʿUmar 490
and the Companions may be adduced; but that is because they are not impeccable and may fall into error and mortal sin as well as mistakes in private judgement.

It is logically possible that a perfect people would not need an imām, but in real life men only behave properly when subject to fear and severity, and it is the imām who terrifies the wicked with the sword.

As to the Shīʿas we agree that God has commanded us to obey our rulers and to follow the truthful, but the point is whether such people have been designated by name by the prophet or designated by *ijmāʿ*. The first cannot be substantiated as there is no evidence; and it is inconceivable that people would be silent on so important a matter, especially when it is remembered that Abū Bakr produced a saying of the prophet's that the imāmate belonged to the Quraish
at the time that the Anṣār laid claim to it. If such a saying existed 491
in favour of the Hāshimites it would have been produced to allay strife, for the quarrel between Anṣār and Quraish is the same as that between the Quraish and the Hāshimites and the Hāshimites and ʿAlī.

It is remarkable that the tradition granting the imāmate to Quraish was not generally accepted (*mutawātir*); had it been so the Anṣār would not have claimed a share in power. If they followed an unauthentic tradition what must our opinion of them be? If it is objected that ʿUmar admitted the claims of non-Quraishites in his saying 'If Sālim, client of Ḥudhaifa, were alive I should have no hesitation about him', and you assert that there is no text authorizing the imāmate in spite of the tradition that 'the imāms are of Quraish': then what is your answer to one who says, If tradition appoints Quraish, why not the Hāshimite Quraish? Again you say that originally there was a latent (*thubūt*) tradition (*naṣṣ*) and you connect the decision with *ijmāʿ*: then you say that *ijmāʿ* contains a tradition[1]

[1] This is a word which it is difficult to translate. *Naṣṣ* means an explicit statement in the Qurān or in canonical tradition (*ḥadīth*). Its significance is further limited by

so that it is a legal argument and you have connected the imāmate with tradition. Why, then, do you not say that there was a tradition concerning Abū Bakr's imāmate? Why exclude tradition and posit election?

Answer. It is not apparent that 'Umar admitted the rights of non-Quraishites, because Sālim was counted as a Quraishite: that is why 'Umar had no doubt about him; moreover, the prophet had testified to his faith and works. Certainly there is an implicit tradition in
492 *ijmā'*; for if the imāmate is only established by *ijmā'*, and *ijmā'* only by *naṣṣ*, then the imāmate rests only on *naṣṣ*.[1] This implicit *naṣṣ* may be a *naṣṣ* about the imāmate, or that *ijmā'* is itself a proof. Both possibilities are open. We cannot claim a plain *naṣṣ* for Abū Bakr, but as eye-witnesses it may well be that his contemporaries became certain about that which was obscure.

Ijmā' is only a proof because those who agree in an opinion are free from sin, unbelief, and error; if that is possible of individuals then the impeccability of the community is so likewise. The judgement of the assembly is like a tradition coming from many guarantors. The cumulative force of such may be compared with drunkenness resulting from many drinks [one having no effect]. The passage you quote from 9. 125 points this way.

It cannot be said that the prophet was ignorant of the subsequent fate of the imāmate seeing that he told his companions of wars and
493 troubles and the anti-Christ. Probably God told him of those who would follow him but he did not convey the information to others because he had no command to do so. Had he been so commanded there would certainly have been a plain statement on the subject of the succession.

If it be argued that the tradition of what happened at the pool of
494 Khumm[2] is an explicit statement in 'Alī's favour you must set against that the tradition recorded by Muslim in his *Ṣaḥīḥ* in favour of Abū Bakr, 'Umar, and 'Uthmān.

495 If it be argued: The (only) wise way to appoint an imām is by an authoritative text and not election because he must have such special qualities as impeccability, knowledge, wisdom, bravery, and justice towards his subjects, and there is no scope for private judgement in such matters; and that they are only to be discovered by an oracle from the prophet which comes to him from God—for the choice of an imām for his outward graces may be to countenance secret atheism

convention to a particular meaning and no other. This is generally the sense in which the Mutakallimūn use the word. But sometimes it means a statute (based on the foregoing text or translation) or an evidence or proof. [1] See preceding note.

[2] See Goldziher, *Muhammedanische Studien*, ii, p. 116.

and denial of God and His apostle, the frustration of law, a corrupt interpretation of the Qurān, and the imputation of lies in sacred matters—we remember the crimes of the Umayyads against God and man.

Reply. Words indicate a man's intelligence, good deeds his kindli- 496
ness, skill in war his politics and bravery. Thus an imām's acts show whether he possesses the qualities you assert to be necessary. If he does not he is deposed. What you say about the Umayyads is true, save that it is not inconsistent with the imāmate according to those who hold that it is possible for the imām to do such things.

Question. Then what virtues must he possess to be worthy of the office and how many electors are necessary to form a quorum?

Answer. He must be a Muslim, a Quraishite, of active intelligence, a far-sighted administrator, a man of vigour and competence. Doctors differ as to how far more or less is required. Some hold that the homage of one just man is a valid election, some demand two or the whole of the intelligent section of the community. But these and other similar questions are outside the range of this book and must be studied in the books devoted to them. I charged myself with the task of solving difficulties in intellectual matters not with matters 497
dependent on tradition.

The *miracles of the saints* are intellectually possible and traditionally guaranteed. God's greatest miracle is to make good easy and evil hard for his servants. . . . We are bound to believe the miracles recorded of the saints, e.g. the story of Bilqīs' throne (27. 40); and of the mother of Moses and the mother of Jesus, and others beyond number. Individually these miracles might not be credible but their cumulative testimony is proof that the miracles happened at the hands of the saints.

It is important to remember that every miracle (*karāma*) wrought by a saint is an overwhelming proof (*mu'jiza*) of the prophet whom the saint follows. The *karāma* of the saint never impairs the miracles of 498
the prophet but strengthens and confirms them. . . . The prophet said that Islām would have its Abraham and its Moses (cf. 43. 57). The law and religion of Islām are the noblest (5. 5) so that a Muslim is necessarily nobler and more honourable than the adherent of any other religion, because laws and religions are the garments of souls and spirits. What greater guerdon is there than a criterion between true and false (8. 29)? What greater miracle is there than the gift of the prophet's love promised in tradition, and the promise that if we knew God as we ought we could move mountains? When it was said 499
that Jesus used to walk on the water the prophet said that if he had been more certain (of God) he would have walked on the air.

The Doctrine of *Abrogation* is akin to this subject. Islām abrogates all previous codes of which it is the perfection. Muhammad is the seal of the prophets, and with him we seal (this) book.[1]

Some of the learned say that abrogation is the withdrawal of a judgement after it has been made: others that it is its *terminus ad quem*, a sort of time limit to that which is apparently for all time.

The Jews say that it is the abolition of commandments which have been given to men and that is impossible where God is concerned, for it would imply that He changes His mind and regrets His (previous) utterances. If one of us ordered a slave to do something and then stopped him from doing it either at once or at some future time that would indicate that the matter appeared different to him, i.e. something he had not expected had occurred, or he had regretted his first order. Such propositions are impossible of Him to whom nothing in heaven or earth is obscure.

Reply. The impossible is of two kinds: (*a*) the impossible *per se*, e.g. the union of black and white in the same place at the same time; this meaning does not apply here; and (*b*) the impossible when it
500 produces the absurd, e.g. contrary to what is known. Here there is no absurdity which abrogation produces save deeming right (*badā'*) and regret. *Badā'* may be used in two senses (1) the thing appeared to Him (cf. 29. 48) and this is impossible of God who is omniscient. He does not abrogate laws because of something He did not know when He gave the laws; (2) regret at what has happened as when a man sees that something he has said or done would be better unsaid or undone. This, too, is impossible with God, for as we have explained His acts are not governed by purpose. Thus abrogation does not point to repentance and we see that abrogation is not impossible logically, and its actual occurrence in the law is the best proof of the same.

There is no doubt that Moses came after Adam, Noah, Hūd, Ṣāliḥ, Abraham and many of the prophets in time. Were they bound by the law of Moses or only by some of it? If by all of it then he did not
501 found the law; he only confirmed an existing one. If he only laid down one law other than their's the first was abrogated by his law, or we may say the time of the first expired and the new one came into being and abrogation was established. We have only to think of marriages with sisters in Adam's time; circumcision on the seventh day which was not practised till Abraham, and so on, to see that abrogation is no innovation.

The solution is that lawfulness and unlawfulness are not predications which belong to actions as if they were attributes of them, nor
502 are actions to be classed as good or evil, nor does the law-giver cause

[1] These words show that the chapter on atoms is not an integral part of this book.

them to acquire attributes which cannot be annulled or confirmed. But the predications (of right and wrong) belong to the speech of the law-giver.[1] Thus the predication is verbal, not actual; legal, not intellectual, and one can abrogate another: e.g. divorce abrogates conjugal rights. If contemporary law is subject to constant alteration to meet changing conditions why is it impossible that laws given to one people at one time should be abrogated elsewhere at another time? The law corresponds to actions; and the active changes of death and life, man's creation and annihilation, sometimes gradually, sometimes instantaneously, correspond to the legal changes of permitted and forbidden. God orders men's actions as he pleases and must not be asked what He is doing (*v.l.* saying). If we consider the formation of man from his pre-embryonic beginning to his full stature we see that 503
each progressive form abrogated its predecessor. Similarly, man progressed from code to code till the perfection of all codes was reached. Nothing lies beyond it but the Resurrection.

Muhammad, the perfect man, is the climax of man's evolution, as Islām is the climax of successive laws.[2]

I have now accomplished my purpose in composing twenty chapters to explain the present position of scholasticism. If I live long enough I shall devote twenty more to an explanation of the speculations of the philosophical divines.

[1] I.e. actions are not right or wrong in themselves, but because the legislator has declared them to be so.

[2] In O. the excursus on the atom which I have relegated to an appendix follows here. It cannot have formed part of the original work, because (1) Shahrastānī does not mention it in the heading of Chapter XX; (2) B. says *tamma'l-kitāb* here though it goes on with the section on the atom; and (3) P., the oldest and best MS., shows no trace of the excursus, and places the conclusion, common to the other copies, at this point.

It is certain from the style and argument that the excursus is Shahrastānī's own work, but it is not germane to this part of the book, and reads like an answer to objections which have been urged against the writer elsewhere. I have therefore not felt it necessary to summarize it.

www.ingramcontent.com/pod-product-compliance
Lightning Source LLC
Chambersburg PA
CBHW081439281025
34587CB00050B/1183
9789366086460